THINK
First Certificate

JON NAUNTON

Longman

Author acknowledgements

My thanks are due to:

- Richard Acklam for his help and advice throughout this project.
- Graeme Porte of the Instituto Brittanico in Granada, Spain, and Felicity O'Dell of Eurocentres, Cambridge, England, for field testing the material for this book.
- Jeremy Harmer, Sarah Walker, Diane Lyons, Tricia Watts and Vilma Gouveia De Paula for their valuable comments on the manuscript.
- Students and teachers of International House, London.
- Howard Middle (publisher), Will Capel (editor), Sally-Anne Kernahan (designer), Sandie Rolfe (art editor), Martine Parsons (production controller) and Peter Marsh (cassette producer) at Longman Group UK Ltd.

Longman Group UK Limited,
Longman House, Burnt Mill, Harlow,
Essex CM20 2JE, England
and Associated Companies throughout the world.

First published 1989

Set in Janson Roman 10/12pt by John Whittingdale Ltd, England

Produced by Longman Group (FE) Ltd

Printed in Hong Kong

ISBN 0-582-55983-9

To the student

Think First Certificate gives you a thorough preparation for the *Cambridge First Certificate in English* examination at the same time as improving your general level of English.

Think First Certificate checks and revises the language areas you should already know and introduces you to the new areas of grammar and vocabulary you need to pass the exam.

The book is called *Think First Certificate* because it places great emphasis on learner independence. You are encouraged to work out language rules for yourself. In addition, it trains you in the different skills you will need to deal with the five papers in the exam.

The Contents list on the next two pages tells you what is in the book. You will see that the units vary in their structure and composition.

The tapescripts for all the Listenings are at the back of the book except for the ones on pages 160-1 in Unit 14. These are not included as they provide a full test for *Paper 4: Listening*.

We hope you enjoy using the book. Good luck in the exam!

UNIT 1 | *English around the world*

English around the world

SPEAKING | ## Getting to know each other

1 Turn the notes into full questions and interview someone in your class. Find out as much about them as you can.

Examples: what/your/name? → *What's your name?*

where/you/from? → *Where do you come from?* or *Where are you from?*

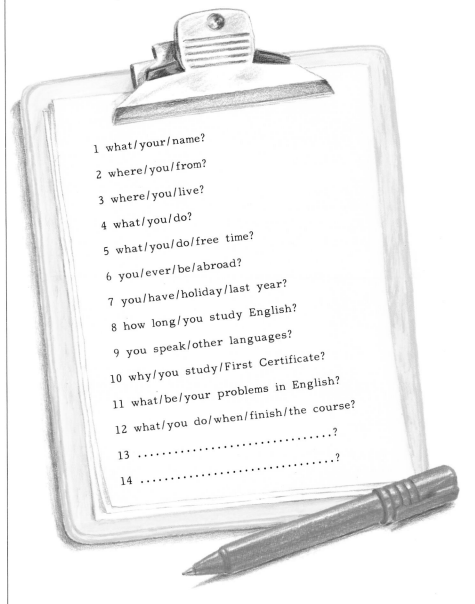

1 what/your/name?

2 where/you/from?

3 where/you/live?

4 what/you/do?

5 what/you/do/free time?

6 you/ever/be/abroad?

7 you/have/holiday/last year?

8 how long/you study English?

9 you speak/other languages?

10 why/you study/First Certificate?

11 what/be/your problems in English?

12 what/you do/when/finish/the course?

13 ....?

14 ....

2 Report back to the class and say what you have found out about each other.

READING

1 Before you read the texts, do this exercise.

Complete these sentences with a word or expression to do with language from the box below.

1 Although she was speaking English, her .... was so strong we could hardly understand what she was saying.
2 I went to a computer expert but when he started using all the technical .... , I got completely lost.
3 Young people use a lot of .... For instance, they could say *copper* instead of policeman.
4 She never studied English but she managed to .... it .... by living in America for a couple of years.
5 Even though the language is basically the same, there are several different .... In the south some of the words and structures are different from those in the north.
6 COBOL and PASCAL are two computer ....
7 English is Nick's first language. In other words, it's his ....
8 A person who speaks two languages fluently is ....

> pick up   jargon   mother tongue   slang
> dialects   bilingual   languages   accent

2 Read each text quickly and find out who:

1 uses English for work.
2 uses English as an official language.
3 enjoys studying English.
4 studies in English.
5 speaks English as a mother tongue.
6 obviously doesn't like English.

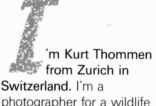

I'm Kurt Thommen from Zurich in Switzerland. I'm a photographer for a wildlife magazine. I need English because lots of handbooks are written in it and I travel a lot. Next month I'm going to visit South East Asia. I hope I'll be able to make myself understood. I've found it is often easier to speak English to other foreigners than to native speakers! One American colleague doesn't speak slowly enough for me to understand him. It is useful to know English but one thing I really don't like is the way English expressions have been incorporated into other languages.

Hi! My name's Véronique Arnaud and I come from Quebec which is in the French-speaking part of Canada. I'm an accountant in a big paper mill. I deal with foreign customers, so most of the time I have to use English. In Canada everything's supposed to be bilingual but I don't like the way English seems to be taking over. We had a real fight here, you know, to keep hold of our French past and identity.

I'm Cathy Wong and I'm from **Singapore.** I've been studying business administration in London for the past two years. I felt really homesick to begin with because I'd never been away from home. I've got fairly used to it but I still miss my parents. They brought me up to speak English and I was sent to an English-speaking school. When I got here, though, I still had a few problems with people's accents and the slang that lots of the other students used. Some of the lecturers were hard to understand at first and then there was lots of business jargon to pick up too. Living in London is expensive and I almost ran out of money but luckily I got a part-time job and now I get by.

Good day. My name's Rob **Giuliani.** I'm fifteen years old and I come from Melbourne in Australia. I'm second generation Italian. My parents came over about 20 years ago. I'm bilingual because we still speak Italian at home. Dad speaks much better English than Mum. Sometimes her mistakes are really embarrassing and her accent is so strong that some people can't understand her. I'm still studying but I always spend my spare time out on the tennis court. I've won a few local tournaments and I'd really like to turn professional.

I'm Adebayo Omere from **Nigeria** and I'm an agricultural engineer. English is the official language because there are so many different languages and dialects spoken in Nigeria. I have to travel all round the country and often English is the only way to communicate. It is a pity because it used to be the colonial language. However, if we had chosen a tribal language, it would have caused political problems. So we will just have to put up with it!

I'm Ana Gonzales from São Paulo in **Brazil.** It is eight years since I started to learn English. My biggest problem is pronunciation. I love listening to English pop music which is a great way of learning new vocabulary. My dad's a businessman and he uses English all the time. He speaks it fluently. He managed to pick it up while he was working in the States. He wants me to speak it well enough so that I can join his company. I'd rather work in advertising.

3

3 Decide whether the following statements are **true** or **false**. Find evidence from the texts on pages 2 and 3 to support your answer.

1 Rob's parents were born in Australia.
2 Rob's mother doesn't speak English as well as his father.
3 Cathy still feels very homesick.
4 Cathy's problems with English weren't too serious.
5 Kurt likes everything about English.
6 Véronique is ashamed of her French origins.
7 Ana hasn't decided about her future career.
8 Adebayo accepts that English was probably the best choice for his country.

4 Write a paragraph about yourself. Say:

● where you come from.
● what you do.
● why you are studying English.
● what your biggest problems are with the language.
● how you feel about English.
● what your ambitions are.

LANGUAGE STUDY

Identifying basic constructions

Knowing the names of the basic tenses and constructions will help you to understand the grammar you need for the examination.
Match the constructions with sentences taken from the texts.

A **I've been studying** business administration in London for the past two years.
B He managed to pick it up while **he was working** in the States.
C ... **if we had chosen** a tribal language, **it would have caused** political problems.
D **I'm still studying** but I ...
E ... **he uses** English all the time.
F My parents **came over** about 20 years ago.
G I **love listening** to English pop music ...
H He **managed to pick it up** ...
I **I've won** a few local tournaments.
J My **biggest problem** is pronunciation.
K I hope **I'll be able** to make myself understood.
L Dad speaks **much better English than** Mum.
M **I'd never been** away from home before.
N ... **I was sent** to an English-speaking school.
O Next month **I'm going to** visit South East Asia.

1 present simple	6 present perfect	11 verb+infinitive
2 past perfect	7 third conditional	12 comparative
3 past simple	8 passive	13 *going to* future
4 verb+gerund	9 superlative	14 present perfect continuous
5 future simple	10 past continuous	15 present continuous

VOCABULARY

Identifying phrasal verbs

1 Study these two sentences.

*They **brought** the wine **up** from the cellar.*
*They **brought** me **up** to speak English.*

The meaning of the first sentence is clear. **Bring** is an independent verb followed by a preposition **up.** In the second sentence, **bring** and **up** belong together and act as a single verb which means **to raise** or **educate.** Here, **bring up** is being used in a non-literal way. In this book, verbs which operate in this non-literal way are called **phrasal verbs.**

2 Look at these sentences and decide when phrasal verbs are being used.

1 She picked up the pen from the floor.
2 Cathy was brought up in Singapore.
3 Can you move your bicycle so we can get by?
4 We changed hotel because we couldn't put up with the noise.
5 We have run out of cigarettes.
6 Can you bring the report up to my office please?
7 Véronique picked up Spanish by visiting South America.
8 The girl ran out of the room.
9 They put the picture up with a nail.
10 I don't know how she gets by on such a small pension.

3 Which phrasal verbs mean:

1 to raise/educate?
2 to endure/tolerate?
3 to learn?
4 to finish?
5 to manage?

4 Complete the following sentences with one of the **five** phrasal verbs. Remember to choose the right tense.

1 I don't know how they .... They have six children and he doesn't earn very much.
2 She is very clever. She .... how to use the computer without any training.
3 We had to come back early from holiday because we .... money.
4 Passengers are having to .... long waits at airports because of a strike.
5 They .... that child very badly. She is so spoilt!

3 USE OF ENGLISH
Sentence transformations

Question 2 of **Paper 3: Use of English** tests your understanding of the relationship between different constructions.

Look at this example of what you have to do.

It isn't necessary to translate every word.

You *don't have to translate every word.*

The second sentence means exactly the same as the first sentence even though the constructions are different.

Finish the following sentences in the same manner as the example above.

1 We still speak Italian at home so I'm bilingual.
   I'm bilingual ....

2 Mum doesn't speak English as well as Dad.
   Dad speaks ....

3 She speaks with such a strong accent some people can't understand her.
   Her accent ....

4 I came to study business administration in London two years ago.
   I have ....

5 My parents sent me to an English-speaking school.
   I ....

6 Knowing English is useful.
   It is ....

7 He speaks too quickly for me to understand.
   He doesn't speak ....

8 I don't have a bigger problem than pronunciation.
   My ....

9 I started to learn English eight years ago.
   It is ....

10 We didn't choose a tribal language so we didn't have any political problems.
   If we had ....

● Now look back at the texts on page 3 to find the answers to the exercise. All the answers are in the texts.

 PRONUNCIATION
Using a dictionary

A good dictionary not only gives you the meanings of words but it also helps you with their pronunciation. To use the dictionary effectively in this respect, you need to understand the symbols for the sounds (*phonemes*) of English and the system which is used for marking stress.

1 **The sounds (*phonemes*) of English**
Study the pronunciation table and think of one more keyword which will help you to remember the pronunciation of each of the sounds.

CONSONANTS		VOWELS	
Symbol	Keyword	Symbol	Keyword
These symbols are used for both the British and American pronunciations			
p	pack	e	bed
b	back	æ	bad
t	tie	iː	sheep
d	die	ɪ	ship
k	class	ɑː	calm
g	glass	ɒ	pot
tʃ	church	ɔː	caught, horse
dʒ	judge	ʊ	put
		uː	boot
f	few	ʌ	cut
v	view	ɜː	bird
θ	throw	ə	better
ð	though		
s	soon	eɪ	make
z	zoo	əʊ	boat
ʃ	shoe	aɪ	bit
ʒ	measure	aʊ	now
		ɔɪ	boy
m	sum	ɪə	here
n	sun	eə	hair
ŋ	sung	ʊə	poor
h	hot	eɪə	player
l	lot	əʊə	lower
r	rod	ɔɪə	employer
j	yet	aɪə	tire
w	wet	aʊə	flower
These symbols are used for the American pronunciations			
		ɑ	hot, father
		ɔ	horse, long
		ɜ	bird
		o	hoarse, court

from the *Longman Active Study Dictionary of English*

● Now check your chosen words in a dictionary.

2 Word stress

Word stress is important for two main reasons. First of all, if you stress an English word in the wrong place, you may not be understood. Secondly, in **Paper 5: Interview** you are marked on stress! Study this dictionary entry for the word **policeman**.

This symbol shows where the main stress lies.

> **po·lice·man** /pəˈliːsmən/ also **police officer**
> /·ˈ ·,···/ –n **-men** /mən/ a male member of a police
> force

Look at the following words and decide where the main stress lies.

Example: **advertise** has three syllables
→ **ad·ver·tise** /ˈædvətaɪz/.

1 **ad·ver·tise·ment** /ædvɜːtɪzmənt/
2 **ad·ver·ti·sing** /ædvətaɪzɪŋ/
3 **in·dus·tri·al** /ɪndʌstrɪəl/
4 **in·dus·try** /ɪndəstrɪ/
5 **ag·ri·cul·ture** /ægrɪkʌltʃə/
6 **pho·to·graph** /fəʊtəgrɑːf/
7 **pho·tog·ra·phy** /fətɒgrəfi/
8 **pho·to·graph·ic** /fəʊtəgræfik/
9 **pho·tog·ra·pher** /fəˈtɒgrəfə/
10 **co·mmu·ni·cate** /kəmjuːnɪkeɪt/
11 **co·mmu·ni·ca·tion** /kəmjuːnɪkeɪʃən/
12 **pro·nounce** /prənauns/
13 **pro·nun·ci·a·tion** /prənʌnsɪeɪʃən/

• Now check your answers in the dictionary.

3 Use the phoneme chart and the stress markings to help you work out what these common English words are.

1 /fɜːst/
2 /səˈtɪfɪkət/
3 /ɪgzæmɪˈneɪʃən/
4 /ˈkwestʃən/
5 /ˈɑːnsə/
6 /ˈlæŋgwɪdʒ/
7 /ˈdɪkʃənərɪ/
8 /əˈfɪʃəl/
9 /ˈɑːftəwədz/
10 /ˈtʃɒklɪt/
11 /ˈjuːʒʊəlɪ/
12 /ˈɪŋglɪʃ/
13 /ɪmˈpɔːtənt/
14 /θɪŋk/
15 /piːz/

4 Use your dictionary to check how you say the following words.

1 thorough
2 colleague
3 baggage
4 produce (*verb*)
5 whole
6 clothes
7 aisle
8 record (*noun*)
9 argue
10 vegetable
11 comfortable
12 cough

 LANGUAGE STUDY

Adverbs of frequency

Rob Giuliani said *I always spend my spare time out on the tennis court.* **Always** is an adverb of frequency which tells us how often someone does something.

1 Place these adverbs of frequency on the scale.

> often seldom occasionally
> sometimes rarely usually

◄— *never* _____ *always* —►

2 It can be difficult to know where to put the adverb in a sentence. You can put some adverbs at the beginning, the middle or the end of a sentence; others can only be put in one place.

With a partner, look at the following sentences and decide if they are **right** or **wrong**.

1 **Seldom** she uses a monolingual dictionary.
2 **Occasionally,** we read English magazines.
3 He **seldom** watches films in English.
4 **Always** she comes to class late.
5 He **sometimes** is late.
6 He checks his spelling **never.**
7 He gives us **often** homework.
8 We **rarely** write in English.
9 We study **usually** English in the evening.
10 They go **always** to the cinema on Fridays.
11 Do you speak **often** English?
12 They are **never** on time.
13 We **always** should help.
14 They can **sometimes** watch English films.

3 Decide:

1 where the **safest** place to put these adverbs is.
2 where you put the adverb with the verb **to be**.
3 where you put the adverb with modals like **can**, **will** and **should**.

4 Find out from your partner how often he/she:

- speaks English outside the classroom.
- uses a monolingual English dictionary. (*English — English*)
- listens to English on the radio or watches films in English.
- reads English outside the classroom.
- writes in English.

USE OF ENGLISH

In **Paper 3: Use of English** you have to fill in the gaps which are left in a passage. This is one of the most difficult parts of the whole examination so there will be lots more opportunities to practise this throughout the course.

In this passage you are given either the beginning or the end of a word to complete.

400 years ago, there were only about six million speakers of English in the world. Recent estimates (1) *sug*..................... that there are now over 300 million who use it as their mother tongue. This is, of course, largely due to its (2) ....*read* use in the USA. However, globally native speakers are in the (3) *min*..................... as perhaps as many as a billion more people use it as a foreign language.

In some countries such as Nigeria and Ghana it has the status of an (4) ....*cial* language. It was chosen so that none of the

Chinese learning English in a park in Shanghai

many different languages (5) *be*..................... to different ethnic groups would be placed above the others. In India, English is an official language alongside Hindi and no fewer than 3,000 English newspapers are (6) *pub*..................... throughout the country.

All round the world people are trying to learn English. In China 25 years ago everybody used to carry a copy of *The Thoughts of Chairman Mao*. (7) *Now*..................... it's an English course. In 1983 more than 100 million people watched a course on Chinese TV made by the BBC to teach the language at (8) ....*tary* level.

People are motivated to learn because it has become the main language of communication in (9) .... *macy*, business, (10) *tour*..................... and sea-faring. It is also the official language of air-traffic control and airports. Three quarters of the world's mail is (11) *writ*..................... in it as well as 80% of all information stored in (12) *com*..................... . Two thirds of all scientists write in English. A Japanese company wishing to (13) ....*iate* with an Arab client would conduct its (14) *nego*..................... in English. A Columbian doctor reports that he spends as much time improving his English as he does (15) ....*ing* medicine.

READING

Paper 1: Reading comprehension

1 Paper 1 is divided into two parts. **Section A** tests vocabulary while **Section B** tests your understanding of texts.

In this unit we shall look at **Section A** where you are given 25 multiple choice vocabulary questions. Both the meaning and the grammar of vocabulary are very important. Look at these five examples.

1 The doctor .... him to smoke a few cigarettes each day.
  A let **B** made **C** stopped (**D**) allowed

Choice D is right because it is the only verb that is grammatically correct in this sentence.
You make/let someone smoke. (infinitive without **to**)
*You stop someone **from** doing something.*

2 After some years, the curtains .... in the sunlight.
  A melted (**B**) faded **C** dissolved **D** disappeared

Choice B is correct because it is the only verb whose meaning makes sense.
Snow melts in the sun. An aspirin dissolves in water.
Disappeared is clearly wrong in the context.

3 We are tired .... hearing your excuses.
  A from **B** at **C** off (**D**) of

Choice D is correct because the preposition **of** is the only one which can go with the adjective **tired**. In English, lots of adjectives and verbs are followed by particular prepositions.

4 I've been trying to ring him all evening but I can't ....
  A get over **B** get across (**C**) get through **D** get by

Choice C is correct. All the choices are phrasal verbs but C is the only one that makes sense in this sentence.
To get over means **to recover**. **To get across** means **to communicate** and **to get by** means **to manage**.

5 I feel tired; I think I'll have a .... sleep before dinner.
  A rapid **B** speedy (**C**) quick **D** fast

Choice C is correct. Although all the choices have the idea of speed, we can only talk about a **quick sleep** in English. It is a kind of idiom which means **to have a short sleep**.

A quick sleep

9

2 In pairs, do this exercise and be ready to explain **why** only one choice is correct.

1 Don't .... to bring a hairdryer. I'll lend you mine.
   A mind   **B** bother   **C** forget   **D** worry
2 The building was badly .... in the fire.
   A hurt   **B** wounded   **C** damaged   **D** injured
3 Their parents do not .... very well.
   A get over   **B** get off   **C** get on   **D** get away
4 Paul was so .... with his examination results that he did not smile all week.
   A disappointed   **B** delighted   **C** proud   **D** satisfying
5 Even though she hated the food, her father .... her to eat it.
   A let   **B** made   **C** allowed   **D** forced
6 She did not listen to her mother's .... and ran across the road.
   A announcement   **B** warning   **C** news   **D** notice
7 Lots of people .... yoga to relax.
   A give up   **B** take up   **C** practice   **D** make
8 Every Sunday we .... go walking.
   A seldom   **B** usually   **C** rarely   **D** never
9 This necklace is .... It's made of glass!
   A priceless   **B** invalid   **C** worthless   **D** valuable
10 This wine is much too dry. Could we have a .... one, please?
   A wet   **B** sweet   **C** soft   **D** cold
11 He is an extremely .... child. He cries very easily.
   A sensitive   **B** nonsense   **C** sensible   **D** senseless
12 Mother smiled .... at the joke.
   A quietly   **B** loudly   **C** strongly   **D** widely

WRITING

In **Paper 2: Composition,** there are **five** questions of which you have to answer **two. Question 1** usually asks you to write an informal or semi-formal letter. In this unit we are going to look at writing an informal letter. We will study writing a semi-formal letter in Unit 5.

1 Read the letter on the next page from Caroline Edwards, an English girl, to a Spanish girl, Marisol Rodriguez, who is coming to London.
Answer the following questions.

1 What are the meeting arrangements?
2 What advice does Caroline give Marisol?
3 What are Caroline's ambitions?
4 Where will Marisol sleep?
5 What favour does Caroline ask?

23 Clarence Road,
London NW2 5EW

11th October

Dear Marisol,

Thanks very much for your lovely letter. I'm really looking forward to meeting you. My dad will drive me to the airport to pick you up when you land. We'll be waiting for you when you come through customs and immigration. If we're not there, don't worry. Just wait at the <u>meeting point.</u>

You asked me what you should bring. The most important thing is the right clothes. You'll need a warm coat and strong boots too. It starts to get very cold at this time of year. Don't bother to pack a hairdryer or a radio because you can borrow mine. Don't forget your camera though because we are going to have lots of fun sightseeing.

Thanks for the photograph and for telling me all about your life. Now I'll tell you something about myself. I'm 17 years old and I'm still at school. I'm studying languages: Spanish, French and Italian. Afterwards, I hope to get a job which will allow me to travel. I think I'd like to become an interpreter or work for an international company.

We live in the suburbs about half an hour away from the centre of London by underground. I've enclosed a picture of me taken recently. We'll be sharing a room. I hope that you don't mind. My parents own a small grocer's which sells food and vegetables and things like that. I've got a younger brother, Derek, who's nine. The only other member of the family is our dog, Jasper!

Anyway, that's all for now. I'll see you on the 25th! Have a good flight and we'll be there to meet you.

Best wishes,
Caroline

P.S. Could you buy me some duty-free cigarettes? Winchesters preferably. It's my dad's birthday next month and cigarettes are so expensive here! I'll pay you back as soon as you get here.

Thanks and introduction	▼
Arrange to meet.	▼
Say what to bring and what not to bring.	▼
Give personal details.	▼
Say where you live.	▼
Talk about your family.	▼
Say goodbye.	▼
Extra points — things you have forgotten	

2 Now imagine that a British friend is coming to stay with you. Write him or her a letter like the one from Caroline. Remember to keep it informal!

LISTENING

In **Paper 4: Listening Comprehension** you have to do three or four different listening tasks, for example, answer true or false questions, fill in missing information or choose the right picture.

1 Marisol Rodriguez is checking in at the Air Magnesia desk. Decide whether the following statements are **true** or **false**.

1 Marisol is given a window seat.
2 She wants to sit in the non-smoking area.
3 Her seat number is B3.

4 Her luggage weighs 22 kilos.
5 She has to pay nothing extra.

2 Marisol is now on the plane and is listening to the captain's announcement. Complete the sentences.

1 Takeoff was delayed because of ....
2 The plane will arrive in London at ....
3 It will be flying at .... feet.

3 An air hostess is helping Marisol with duty-free goods. Tick the boxes to show what she buys.

PERFUME	SIZE small	medium	large
Seduction			
Blue Lady			
Jennifer			

CIGARETTES	
Marylebone	
Winchester	
Churchill	

4 Marisol is describing her luggage, which has been lost, to an official at Heathrow Airport, London. Choose the two items which most closely resemble the luggage she describes.

VOCABULARY

The language of airports

Complete this summary of Marisol's trip. Fill each gap with a word or expression to do with airports and travelling by air from the box below.

Last autumn, Marisol went to England for a holiday. She took a .... (1) flight rather than a .... (2) one because it was much cheaper. She arrived at the airport and went straight to the .... (3) desk where the ground steward gave her a .... (4) with her seat number on it. She had too much luggage and she was almost charged for .... (5). Unfortunately, she was too late for a window seat and had to sit by the .... (6). Afterwards, she went to the .... (7) and waited for her flight to be called. Eventually, after a short delay, she was told to go to .... (8) number 19 and boarded the plane. The captain welcomed the .... (9) aboard on behalf of himself and the rest of the .... (10). The plane .... (11) from the .... (12) and the flight went smoothly. After she had had a meal, the air .... (13) came round offering .... (14) goods. Marisol bought some perfume and cigarettes. As soon as the plane had .... (15) at London Airport, she went to the .... (16) area to pick up her luggage. At first, she thought she had lost it and gave a description to a clerk. Fortunately, just as she was about to leave the airport, the luggage turned up. Half an hour later, she passed through .... (17) and .... (18) and met her friend and her parents who had been waiting for her.

duty-free	took off	immigration	departure lounge	gate	runway
stewardess	check-in	passengers	excess baggage	landed	customs
scheduled	charter	boarding card	baggage claim	crew	aisle

LANGUAGE STUDY

Question tags and the way you say them 📇

1 In the **Listening,** Marisol Rodriguez spoke to an airport official about the loss of her luggage. He said to her

*You kept the receipts, **didn't you?***

His intonation falls through the question tag because he is sure about the answer and is just checking. He expects the answer to be *yes.*

Later on Marisol said

*You will find them, **won't you?***

This time, there is a rising intonation through the question tag because it is a real question. She does not know what the answer will be.

2 Listen to these five sentences and decide if the speaker is just checking or asking a real question.

1 You're married, aren't you?
2 It's cold, isn't it?
3 You'll have some cake, won't you?
4 You'd like to go, wouldn't you?
5 She's got three brothers, hasn't she?

● Now listen to the sentences again and imitate the speaker. Copy the intonation that is used, and also think about the pronunciation of **aren't you?** and **won't you?**

3 Here is how to make the question tag.

Take the original sentence.	→ *She comes from Spain.*
Make it negative.	→ *She doesn't come from Spain.*
Invert the subject and the auxiliary.	→ *doesn't she?*
Add it to the original sentence.	→ *She comes from Spain, doesn't she?*

Now make tags of your own.

1 It's freezing, ... ?
2 We need some milk, ... ?
3 She bought one, ... ?
4 You've grown, ... ?
5 We'd better take a taxi, ... ?
6 She always plays tennis on Sundays, ... ?
7 Do be careful, ... ?
8 I'm so stupid, ... ?
9 Let's go out, ... ?
10 He never smiles, ... ?

● When you have finished, practise saying these sentences with a falling intonation.
● Look round the classroom for someone you do not know very well. Make some guesses about them: whether they are married, what they do for a living, and so on. Decide whether you are sure or unsure and then ask your questions. Practise both intonation patterns.

UNIT 2 | *Time Out*

How do you feel about these different kinds of entertainment? Complete the questionnaire and then compare your opinions with a partner.

	CAN'T STAND	NOT KEEN ON	DON'T MIND	FOND OF	REALLY LOVE
BOXING					
DISCOS					
POP MUSIC					
OPERA					
HORSE RIDING					
HORROR FILMS					
FOOTBALL					
READING					
EATING OUT					

15

 LISTENING

1 Jeff and Emma are flatmates. Emma is ringing the local cinema to see what's on. Listen to the recorded message and fill in the missing information.

SCREEN 1	NAME OF FILM	**RAW DEAL**
	KIND OF FILM	
	TIMES	
	SMOKING	
SCREEN 2	NAME OF FILM	*Crocodile Dundee II*
	KIND OF FILM	
	TIMES	
	SMOKING	
SCREEN 3	NAME OF FILM	*A Room with a View*
	KIND OF FILM	
	TIMES	
	SMOKING	
	PRICES: Adult	Children

2 Emma and Jeff are discussing what to do this evening. Listen to them and choose the correct answers.

1 Jeff and Emma live
  A in the suburbs of London.
  B in the centre of London.

2 Jeff and Emma
  A have already seen *Raw Deal*.
  B don't like violent films.

3 Which statement is true?
  A Jeff saw *A Room With A View* more recently than Emma.
  B Jeff doesn't want to see *A Room With A View* again.

4 Which statement is false?
  A Emma didn't like *Crocodile Dundee 1*.
  B Jeff liked *Crocodile Dundee 1* more than Emma.

5 They are having their conversation at about
  A 7.10 pm.
  B 7.30 pm.

 LANGUAGE STUDY

It's time .../I'd rather ...

1 Look at these two sentences from the **Listening**.

JEFF: *Then it's time we left.*
EMMA: *I'd rather we went to that than any of the others.*

● Which tenses are used?
● Are they talking about the past/now/the future?

● Study these two groups of sentences and decide which ones are correct.
  1 **A** It's time to leave for the airport.
    B It's time for us to go to the airport.
    C It's time that we go to the airport.
    D It's time we went to the airport.
  2 **A** I'd rather go to the theatre.
    B I'd rather that we go to the theatre.
    C I'd rather we went to the theatre.

● In pairs work out a rule for **I'd rather** ... and **It's time** ... .

2 What would you say in the following situations?

1 You feel tired. You think you need a holiday.
2 A friend suggests going to a party. You would like to go to a disco.
3 You're looking after a small child. It's 11 o'clock. You think he ought to go to bed.
4 It's raining. Your friend suggests walking home. You want to take a taxi.
5 Your favourite pop singer is coming to your town. Your friend thinks there will be lots of tickets left. You think you should buy them now.
6 You've been to a party with Bill and Simon. Bill has had a lot to drink. What would you say if he offered to drive?
7 You and your friend are both hungry. Your friend suggests a Chinese meal. You prefer Thai food.
8 This exercise is getting boring!

Short replies

JEFF: *I've seen it.*
EMMA: *So have I.*

1 Match the statements and replies.

A Carol really liked the film.   1 She can't either.
B She'll love the party.   2 I would too.
C I won't eat there again.   3 Neither do we.
D We can't stand discos.   4 So did Julian.
E I'd rather go to the cinema.   5 They didn't either.
F She doesn't mind opera.   6 So am I.
G We didn't enjoy the play.   7 Daisy will too.
H Anita is fond of Chinese   8 Neither shall I.
  food.

2 When do we use **so**, **too**, **neither** and **either**?
In pairs, work out a rule. Then move around the
class and find someone who shares your opinions in
the questionnaire on page 15.

 SPEAKING

An evening out

In **Paper 5: Interview**, you may have to do an
activity like this.

Work in groups of three or four. Your group has
decided to go out for the evening together. You can
each spend £15. Look at the options available and
decide on an evening's entertainment which everyone
will enjoy. You must all agree about what you will
do.

USEFUL LANGUAGE

What would you like to do?
Why don't **we go** to the disco?
Let's **have** a hamburger instead.
We could always stay at home.
How about eat**ing** out?
Do you fancy go**ing** to the cinema?

THE WHITE RHINOCEROS
Disco night club
All the latest sounds
at your favourite rendezvous.
From 8 p.m. till 3 a.m.
Entrance: £5 (includes one drink).
Drinks £1 before 10 p.m.

ODEON CINEMA

SCREEN 1	SCREEN 2
ROCKY XVI	*Last Snows of Spring* *A dying girl finds eternal love*
PERFORMANCES AT 7.10, 9.15.	PERFORMANCES AT 6.45, 8.50.

ENJOY THE LATEST POP VIDEOS AT THE VIDEO CAFÉ
MEALS FROM £3 – ENTRANCE £2.50

MACBURGERS
SPECIAL OFFER
Giant Burger with fries and small cola
for just **£1.50**
See you soon !

KINGSWAY ROLLER-RINK
TONIGHT!! **ROLLER DISCO**
Skating to all the rock and roll classics.
Entrance £3 Ladies free before 7.30 p.m.
Skate hire £2.50 (£5.00 returnable deposit)

NORTHWOOD COMMUNITY HALL
The Northwood Amateur Players
present
South Pacific
the musical for all the family.
Performance 7 p.m. Tickets £3
ALL PROCEEDS TO CHARITY

CHUNGS CHINESE RESTAURANT
*Spend a delightful evening in
tasteful surroundings.*
*Traditional Chinese Cuisine
4 course set dinner £8.50*

READING

Fiction to capture the imagination

1 Before you read the book descriptions, working in small groups, find out:

- how often people read books.
- whether they have a favourite book or author.
- what type of book they prefer.

2 Quickly read the descriptions of the four books and decide which one is:

1 a thriller.   **A B C D**   3 quite serious.   **A B C D**
2 light reading.   **A B C D**   4 science fiction.   **A B C D**

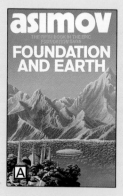

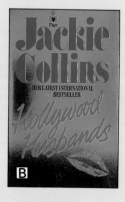

FOUNDATION AND EARTH
Isaac Asimov

The fifth in the bestselling *Foundation* series of science fiction novels, *Foundation and Earth* continues Golan Trevize's search for the mystical origins of humanity and charts his quest through time, space and beyond.

HOLLYWOOD HUSBANDS
Jackie Collins

Sizzling on from where *Hollywood Wives* left off, Jackie Collins changes up a gear with her raciest and most daring novel yet. It's about sex and success — getting it, having it, keeping it.

FAMILY AND FRIENDS
Anita Brookner

Anita Brookner probes deeply behind the veneer to observe the highs and lows of family relationships and friendships.

LONDON MATCH
Len Deighton

The story should have been over when the KGB major defected, but now some of his revelations threaten to rock the foundations of British intelligence. The final part of Len Deighton's spy trilogy, which is also available in a gift set.

3 Assuming that you could buy these books in translation, which one would you give your:
- mother? • brother? • boy/girlfriend? • teacher?
- father? • sister? • best friend?

• Which book would **you** most/least like to get as a present?

4 Choose the word which you think is the closest in meaning to the words in the text. Check the context. See what comes before and after the words in the text. If in doubt, use your dictionary.

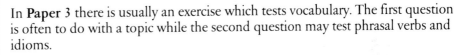

1 **charts** (A)   **a** examines   **b** discovers   **c** records
2 **quest** (A)   **a** travel   **b** search   **c** discovery
3 **sizzling** (B)   **a** speeding   **b** moving   **c** continuing
4 **raciest** (B)   **a** beautiful   **b** exciting   **c** interesting
5 **probes** (C)   **a** wonders   **b** digs   **c** looks
6 **veneer** (C)   **a** lies   **b** back   **c** surface
7 **defected** (D)   **a** died   **b** returned   **c** left
8 **rock** (D)   **a** shake   **b** dance   **c** improve

USE OF ENGLISH 3

In **Paper** 3 there is usually an exercise which tests vocabulary. The first question is often to do with a topic while the second question may test phrasal verbs and idioms.

1 Complete the following sentences with a word to do with **books**. Here the first letter is given to you. This isn't done in the exam!

1 Len Deighton is an *a*..................... I admire a great deal.
2 He forgot to return the books to the *l*..................... so he had to pay a fine.
3 I prefer fact to *f*..................... .
4 She looked on the top *s*..................... for her dictionary but she couldn't find it there.
5 A *b*..................... tells the story of somebody's life.

2 Complete these sentences with a word or expression using **look**.

1 You should .... the word in the dictionary if you don't know how to spell it.
2 I can't wait to read that new thriller. I'm really .... to it.
3 This is an interesting .... book. Can I borrow it?
4 I'll lend it to you provided you .... it properly.
5 Would you mind .... this book if you go to a bookshop?

"Don't worry about Moses. He can look after himself."

LANGUAGE STUDY
Past simple or present perfect?

1 You are going to read a short biography of the author, Len Deighton, who wrote *London Match.* He is one of the most famous living authors of spy fiction.
Quickly read the text and find out how many occupations Len Deighton has had.

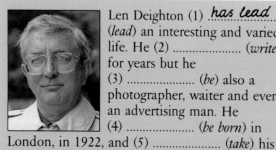 Len Deighton (1) *has lead* (*lead*) an interesting and varied life. He (2) .... (*write*) for years but he (3) .... (*be*) also a photographer, waiter and even an advertising man. He (4) .... (*be born*) in London, in 1922, and (5) .... (*take*) his first job as a railway clerk. He (6) .... (*do*) his National Service as a photographer in the R.A.F., and (7) .... (*be*) stationed in Germany. It was during his time in Berlin that he first (8) .... (*come*) into contact with the shady world of espionage. Afterwards, he (9) .... (*go*) on to become an art student at St. Martin's School of Art in London. He (10) .... (*work*) part-time as a waiter in order to make money. While he (11) .... (*work*) as a waiter, he (12) .... (*become*) deeply interested in cookery and (13) .... (*produce*) a regular comic strip on the subject for *The Observer* newspaper. (14) .... (*follow*) on from this, he worked in New York (15) .... (*return*) to England to take over as the art director of an advertising firm. At the beginning of the sixties he (16) .... (*go*) to settle in France where he (17) .... (*live*) ever since. In 1962, his first book, *The Ipcress File*, (18) .... (*be*) published. Since then, he (19) .... (*write*) over 25 books. Not only (20) .... (*write*) his famous spy novels but he (21) .... (*write*) also a history of the R.A.F.

2 Working in pairs, complete the text by changing the verbs in brackets into an appropriate form or tense.

When we use the present perfect

1 Past simple or present perfect?
In pairs, discuss why we can say:

He has been a photographer.
but not *He has been a photographer five years ago.*

What did he do when he was in Berlin?
but not *What has he done when he was in Berlin?*

Try and work out a rule.

We use the present perfect to ....

2 Different uses of the present perfect
The same tense can be used in very different ways.

A She has known him for seven years.
B She's been to India.
C Oh! You've had a haircut.
D I've written three letters this morning.

Which of the four sentences, **A**, **B**, **C** and **D** describes something:

1 that happened in the past where you can still see the result now?
2 that started in the past but which is still going on now?
3 that has happened in a period not yet finished?
4 that happened in the past but we do not know when?

3 Present perfect simple or continuous?
We use the **present perfect simple** when an action is finished and we want to talk about the **result** of the action.

Len Deighton has written more than 25 books. ✓
Len Deighton has been writing 25 books. ✗

We use the **present perfect continuous** when we are talking about an activity which started in the past and is still going on. We are more interested in the **activity** than the result, for example, *He has been writing for 30 years.*

● Look through the biography of Len Deighton once more and explain the different uses of the present perfect.

4 Adverbs and word order

Put the following sentences into the right order.

Example: they/arrived/already/have?
→ *Have they already arrived?*

1 for/not/she/spoken/him/to/years/has/ten

....

2 had/house/decorated/have/just/their/they

....

3 never/meal/wonderful/a/I/before/have/such/had

....

4 that/you/have/seen/yet/movie?

....

5 never/she/musical/been/to/a/has

....

6 are/they/have/waiting/left/or/they/still/already

....

7 food/this/kind/before/ever/she/eaten/of/has?

....

8 not/ever/the/he/seen/film/has?

....

 PRONUNCIATION 📼

Sentence stress

1 Every word in a telegram or telex is expensive so we limit the number of words to those that carry the main meaning.
For example: *I'm coming on Friday. Can you meet me at the airport?* becomes COMING FRIDAY MEET ME AIRPORT STOP

We do a similar thing when we speak. Of course, we don't leave words out. We just stress the words that carry the most meaning. Sentence stress and meaning are closely connected.
The words in **bold** letters are strongly stressed. Match the sentences with the speaker's **message**.

1 **What** have you done with the keys?
2 What have **you** done with the keys?
3 What have you done with the **keys?**

MESSAGE
A I didn't have them last.
B ... not the cheese!
C Surely you didn't do something so stupid!

● In pairs, practise saying this sentence in different ways: *You might have killed him.* How can you change the meaning through changing the stress?

2 Grammar words that are not stressed can become weak. Let's hear how this works with some sentences in the present perfect.

1 Listen to the sentences and decide which words are **strong** and **weak.** Put a line under the strong syllables and a circle around the weak ones.

Example: Len Deighton's been a photographer.

A He's been living in France.
B He's been writing books for ages.
C What have you done to my car?
D How long have you been a dancer?
E How long have you been learning English?
F It's late. Where have you been?
G I've been trying to phone.

2 Listen to the sentences again and try to copy the speaker's pronunciation as closely as you can.

 SPEAKING

Role play

You are going to take part in an interview with a famous ballet dancer. Before you begin, practise saying these two sentences. Use the correct sentence stress and weak forms.

*How **long** have you been a **dancer?***
*I've been a dancer for **twenty years.***

Student B: You are the ballet dancer. Go to page 28 for your information.

Student A

You are the interviewer. You are a reporter from *Hi!* magazine. Find out about Lydia/Leonid, why she/he left the Soviet Union, when she/he started dancing, her/his family and so on. Remember that you want an interesting story with as much gossip as possible! So ask her/him lots of questions about her/his private life!

READING

1 Before you read about the pop singer, Michael Jackson, make a list of a) the things you know about him and b) the things you would like to know about him. Then read the text to see if it answers your questions.

2 Read the text again and choose the best answers to these questions.

1 Michael's father
   A worked in the construction industry.
   B did not work in an office.

2 His childhood home
   A was too small.
   B contained a large family.

3 Which statement is **not** true?
   A He made $15 million for an advertisement.
   B *Thriller* has had the biggest sale of any album.

4 Michael takes care of himself by
   A breathing fresh air.
   B being careful about what he eats.

5 His appearance since childhood
   A has not changed naturally.
   B is quite different.

3 Discussion points

1 Imagine that you wanted to interview Michael Jackson. What questions would you ask him?
2 Would you like to be famous? What are the advantages and disadvantages of fame?
3 Performers like Michael Jackson and Madonna earn millions of dollars each year. In the Republic of China a singer who sells millions of records gets paid the state wage. She still lives with her mother and only recently got a refrigerator.

In the USSR famous pop groups have an *open door policy* which means that fans can call in at any time and discuss music with performers. In the West performers are rarely seen outside concert halls and are protected by security men.

What do these differences tell you about social attitudes?

Michael Jackson is one of the biggest success stories of entertainment history. He has been performing since the age of seven and is still one of the most successful singers and entertainers in the world over 20 years later. He has survived in an incredibly competitive world.

Michael was born on 28th August, 1958, in a small town in Indiana in the USA. His father was a crane operator and his mother a deeply religious Jehovah's Witness. Michael was the seventh of nine children and their small house must have been really crowded. His parents, Joe and Katherine Jackson, were both musical and their children all took after them. Through their encouragement, the children learned to sing and play musical instruments. Their father organized the boys into the Jackson Five and in 1965 they won their first talent contest.

Even though Michael was only seven years old, he had such talent that it was natural for him to become the band's lead singer. The star quality he has always had was obvious from a very early age. He could take off other performers and copy their style after only hearing them once. He was still only 11 when a Jackson Five single sold over two million copies.

In 1972, he started his solo career. He sold millions of albums, made videos and even turned his talents to acting. He is said to have received five million dollars for making a Pepsi Cola advertisement. His *Thriller* album has sold around 40 million copies, more than any other album in history. He is a very generous person and has shared his wealth with charities.

Michael has certainly changed from the little boy of his talent contest days. A price of fame is that his private life is always under the microscope and he is the source of rumours and gossip. He lives in a castle in Encino, California, which he hardly ever leaves. The star is also supposed to be very health-conscious and wants to live until he is 150. One of the ways he hopes to do this is by sleeping in a box which has pure pressurized air pumped into it. This special chamber cost a quarter of a million dollars. He eats very little but takes large numbers of vitamin pills. When he goes to restaurants, he takes his own chef

STAR QUALITY

who prepares Michael's diet of vegetarian food. The pop star also loves animals and has his own private zoo which houses snakes, deer, llamas, chimpanzees and spiders.

Controversy surrounds the way in which his appearance has changed. It is hard to believe that the changes in his facial appearance and skin colour have occurred naturally. It looks as though he has had several operations on his nose and changed the appearance of his chin, eyes and cheekbones. One expert believes that his skin has become lighter through the use of acid. One explanation for all of this is that he wants to widen his appeal with white audiences.

Whatever people may think about his private life, the fact remains that Michael Jackson is an enormously talented individual who will continue to surprise us with his mixture of music and star appeal. He is still a young man and has many more years of fame and fortune to look forward to.

3 USE OF ENGLISH
Changing verbs to nouns

You may have to do a task like this in **Paper 3**. Change the verb in CAPITAL LETTERS into an appropriate noun to complete the sentence. There is a more detailed look at this kind of exercise in Unit 8.

Example: *She is one of the greatest .....performers....... to appear in this theatre.* PERFORM

1 The .... she gave last night was marvellous. PERFORM
2 She received a lot of .... from her mother. ENCOURAGE
3 Does this .... suit you?. ARRANGE
4 Conversation is one of the most enjoyable forms of .... ENTERTAIN
5 .... is such a competitive profession. ADVERTISE
6 Have you seen the latest .... for Pepsi? ADVERTISE
7 There's a lot of .... in show business. COMPETE
8 There were 50 .... in the talent contest. COMPETE
9 .... is an extremely popular hobby. PHOTOGRAPH
10 She is a .... of theatre programmes. COLLECT
11 She has one of the biggest .... in Britain. COLLECT

VOCABULARY

Phrasal verbs with **take**

1 In this unit there are a number of phrasal verbs using **take**. Match the definition on the right with the phrasal verb on the left.

A take on   1 gain control/responsibility
B take after   2 start a new activity/hobby
C take off   3 like
D take over   4 have the same looks or character as an older relative
E take to   5 copy/imitate somebody

2 Complete these sentences with one of the phrasal verbs using **take**.

1 He was punished for taking his teacher ....
2 She has just been taken .... at the bank.
3 I am afraid that I don't take .... my new boss. He is an extremely unpleasant person.
4 Can you take .... while I go to lunch?
5 You really take .... your grandfather. You're both bad-tempered!

WRITING

In Unit 1 we looked at writing an informal letter. Here is some more practice for this part of **Part 2: Composition.**

1 Celia Walker has just moved to a new flat. She is writing to her brother, Andy, to bring him up to date with all her news. Put the letter into the right order. The beginning and end have been done for you.

Dear Andy,
  Thanks a lot for the lovely letter. It was great news about your promotion. Well done.

1. Do let me know as I'll have to get tickets.
2. Would you like to come too? You can stay at my place.
3. What's more, I have just started a new job.
4. I've been taken on as a shop assistant in a bookshop.
5. You'll be sad to hear that Mr. Green, our old teacher, passed away last month.
6. I am really sorry for not having written earlier but life has been busy since moving here.
7. The other staff are nice and friendly, and it's quite well paid.
8. Guess what! She has just moved here, too.
9. Poor Mr. Green. Still, life goes on.
10. Incidentally, I've arranged to go to the theatre to see 'Cats' with Anna in a couple of weeks time.
11. She told me some awful news, though.
12. By the way, the other day I bumped into Anna Granger in the bookshop.

  Anyway, I must sign off as I want to catch the post.

  Hope to see you soon.

         Lots of love,
         Celia

2 Understanding the organization of the letter

Which words and expressions are used to:

1 introduce bad news?	4 say **and**?
2 move to another subject?	5 make an invitation?
3 apologize?	6 introduce a surprise?

3 Changing the subject study note

Anyway, by the way, and **incidentally** are all ways of showing that you are going to change the subject. We use them a lot, particularly in informal letters and conversation.

Anyway means that you are going to talk about something totally different. **By the way** and **incidentally** show that you are going to move onto something which is less important or that you've just remembered.

4 In pairs, plan and write letters based on the following situations.

1 Write to your friends, Paul and Suzanne, congratulating them on the arrival of their new baby. Give a reason why you won't be able to go to the christening.
2 Write to your friends, Sarah and Patrick. Congratulate Patrick on finally passing his driving test. Invite them to stay for the weekend. Tell them what you have been doing recently.

- Imagine that you are writing to an English friend. Tell him or her all your good and bad news.

USE OF ENGLISH

Transformation exercise

Continue the second sentence so that it means exactly the same as the one above. In Unit 1 we introduced you to this kind of exam task.

1 We ought to turn on the TV now.
   It's time ....
2 I like westerns more than thrillers.
   I prefer ....
3 It's better if we cook instead of eating out.
   I'd rather ....
4 His record player is still for sale.
   Nobody ....
5 She hasn't appeared live for years.
   It's years since ....
6 We have not seen this quiz show for two months.
   The last time ....
7 The aerial is still broken.
   The aerial hasn't ....
8 Michael learned how to sing when he was small.
   Michael has ....
9 That soap opera has been on TV for 15 years.
   It's 15 years ....
10 I haven't seen her at this disco before.
   It's ....

USE OF ENGLISH

1 Complete the passage using the words in the box to make a speech.

PARA

A Good morning girls and boys. I have come (1) .... today to tell you something about my hobby, stamp collecting. I have been a collector ever since I was (2) .... your age, which means I have been (3) .... up my collection for over 50 years.

B I took it (4) .... when when I was very sick and (5) .... to be off school for a couple of months. I was (6) .... fed up (7) .... my grandfather brought me (8) .... stamp album and a big packet of stamps (9) .... get me going. I took to it (10) .... I was fascinated by the beautiful colours and designs and the (11) .... names of faraway places.

C When I grew up, I decided to (12) .... and I have now got (13) .... of the largest collections of French stamps in the country. It really is a marvellous hobby and has given me thousands of hours of (14) .... People think it (15) .... be very lonely but it isn't at all. You can go to fairs and exhibitions and get to meet other people who (16) .... the same interest. It needn't be expensive (17) ....

D Anyway, I have brought along a (18) .... of my albums, so if you'd like to (19) .... up to the tables then you can all have a look. (20) .... one thing, you can look at them but you must promise not to touch!

> must so either come mysterious really just
> share along a number building immediately
> up one enjoyment specialize about had to

2 Read the text again and underline the words and expressions that would be useful if you were writing a speech about one of your hobbies. What is the topic of each of the four paragraphs?

3 Writing

Imagine that you have been asked to talk to a group of people about a hobby or pastime. You may have to do something like this in **Paper 2: Composition.**

- Make notes planning what you will say. Let your teacher check your plan.
- When you are ready, write the speech.

USE OF ENGLISH

In **Paper 3** you have to show how well you can read and process information. Usually you are given a text and then have to do a written task based on it.

Study the information and then read the example answer after it. Can you improve on this answer? Is it clear and logical? Is it fair to all the family?

The Smith family is going to have an evening at home watching television. Study this evening's programmes and the information you have about the family. Then plan an evening's viewing that will be fair to everyone. Write a paragraph of about 120 words describing your plan for their viewing.

BBC 1

7.00 What's in the garden? Gardening weekly.
8.00 The Family — latest in the US soap opera.
9.00 The News
9.30 Vista Documentary on animal experiments.
10.30 Checkmate Cold war spy thriller starring Dolly Frick.
12.00 Closedown

ITV LONDON

7.20 Guess the Price Quiz show with fabulous prizes.
7.50 Pop World Oscar Jones sings his latest hit-single.
8.20 Oliver Twist First episode of six part dramatization of Charles Dickens classic.
9.00 Variety Song and Dance spectacular hosted by Bruce Monkhouse.
10.00 Match of the Week Football highlights.
11.40 Invaders from Space Science fiction horror movie. Will aliens take over the world?
1.15 Closedown

James Smith — He is keen on gardening. His favourite programme is *Match of the Week*. He can't stand quiz programmes.

Eileen Smith — Her favourite programme is *The Family*. Tonight she would like to watch *Vista* as she is an animal lover.

Granny Smith — Her favourite programmes are *Guess the Price* and *Variety*.

The family — Everybody quite likes films with Dolly Frick in them.

Jason Smith (Aged 11) — His favourite singer is on *Pop World* tonight. He loves science fiction films. His teacher wants the class to watch *Oliver Twist* as it is a set book for the school examinations. He has to be in bed by 12.00 at the latest.

First they can watch 'Guess the Price' as Granny likes this. Afterwards they can see 'Pop World' because Jason's favourite singer is on it. At eight o'clock they should change to BBC1 so Eileen Smith can watch 'The Family'. At nine they can watch half an hour of 'Variety' on ITV and turn over to see 'Vista' at 9.30. At 10.30 they can watch the film 'Checkmate'. Afterwards Jason must go to bed because the science fiction film is too late for him.

Here is the letter on page 24 in the right order.

Dear Andy,

Thanks a lot for the lovely letter. It was great news about your promotion. Well done. I am really sorry for not having written earlier but life has been busy since moving here. What's more, I have just started a new job.

I've been taken on as a shop assistant in a bookshop. The other staff are nice and friendly, and it's quite well paid.

By the way, the other day I bumped into Anna Granger in the bookshop. Guess what! She has just moved here too. She told me some awful news, though. You'll be sad to hear that Mr. Green, our old teacher, passed away last month. Poor Mr. Green. Still, life goes on.

Incidentally, I've arranged to go to the theatre to see 'Cats' with Anna in a couple of weeks time. Would you like to come too? You can stay at my place. Do let me know as I'll have to get tickets.

Anyway, I must sign off as I want to catch the post.

Hope to see you soon.

Lots of love,
Celia

Here is an improved version of the example on page 27.

Everybody must be reasonable. James can watch the first half of the gardening programme. Then they can turn over to let Granny watch the rest of the quiz. James can take a walk! Afterwards, Jason can watch the first ten minutes of 'Pop World' and might catch his favourite singer. Eileen can see the first twenty minutes of 'The Family', but then they must turn over for 'Oliver Twist' as this is important for Jason's school. Between 9.00 and 9.30 Granny can watch 'Variety', then Eileen can watch the first part of 'Vista'. Afterwards, James can watch part of 'Match of the Week'. At 10.30 everyone can watch 'Checkmate' but Jason must promise to go to bed as soon as it finishes. The science fiction film is far too late.

Student B

| You are Lydia/Leonid. Answer A's questions. Use this information. Age: 26. Born in Moscow. Started dancing when you were six. Mother doctor. Father dancer too. Studied music and ballet at conservatory. Like classical music and jazz. | Danced with Bolshoi when 17. Travelled to England and France. Four years ago met Italian ballet dancer. Defected to West. Love not politics the reason. Married dancer. One child. You miss parents and sister. Love Russia. Hope to return one day. |

UNIT 3 | *Survival*

1 Yesterday, four teams of mountaineers set out in a race to conquer an unclimbed peak in the Himalayas. The Canadian party chose a long but safe route while the American, Chinese and Russian teams chose a steep and dangerous route up the mountain.

When night fell, the teams made camp on the mountainside. Then disaster struck. The early morning sun caused a terrible avalanche and members of the American, Chinese and Russian teams were swept away and killed. The Canadians are unaware of what has happened.

It is an hour after the disaster and there is no hope of finding any survivors. The leaders of the teams meet to discuss what supplies and equipment they have left.

	USA	USSR	CHINESE
MEMBERS	3	2	2
ICE-AXES	3	×	×
TENTS	1 two-man	×	1 four-man
SLEEPING BAGS	3	2	2
ROPE	25 metres	150 metres	×
FOOD	3 people for 2 days	2 people for 6 days	2 people for 1 day
MEDICINE	×	×	all equipment
COOKING EQUIPMENT	×	saucepan	nearly all

Complete the following sentences using one of these words:

most none all little few no much many lot both every any

1 The Americans have got a .... metres of rope left but the Chinese have ....

2 .... of the rope belongs to the Russians.

3 .... the Americans and the Russians lost their medical supplies.

4 .... the ice-axes belong to the Americans. The other teams don't have ....

5 The Americans have a .... food but the Chinese have hardly ....

6 The food will only last a .... days.

7 How .... medicine have the Chinese got?

8 The Chinese have .... ice-axes but .... the medicine.

9 How .... climbers were killed in the avalanche?

10 .... member has got a sleeping bag.

2 Working in small groups, find a way to conquer the mountain. Decide who the members of a new climbing team should be. Which country should put its flag on the peak if the climb is successful?

EXTRA POINTS TO CONSIDER

- The Canadians will certainly conquer the mountain first if the remaining members of the other teams do not agree to work together.
- One of the Americans is badly injured and needs constant medical attention.
- The last two hundred metres of the climb are on ice like glass.
- One of the Chinese team is a doctor.
- The best climber is a Russian.
- Unhurt members can return to base camp in half a day.
- It will take two days for one climber to accompany the injured American to Base Camp.
- It will take two days to climb the remaining distance to the peak and a further day and a half to climb down to Base Camp.

 READING

1 Read the text quickly and answer these questions.

1 Where exactly did the Littles make their home?
2 What do you think their life was like in the jungle?
3 What caused their sickness?
4 Why was Jan forced to leave their hut for the first time?
5 How did she overcome her problems?
6 Why is her survival extraordinary?

The remarkable story of
Jan Little

There can be few stories of survival stranger and more terrifying than that of Jan Little. Jan was born and brought up in rural California. As a child, she suffered from poor vision and hearing. In 1952, when she was 21, she went to San Francisco. After a few years and with an unsuccessful marriage behind her, she decided to give up city life and become a farmer.

With her three-year-old daughter, Rebecca, she went to Mexico, where she met and married an American called Harry Little. He was a strong-willed and charismatic character who came to dominate Jan. After 15 years as homesteaders, they finally moved to the jungle on the border between Brazil and Venezuela. With very little money, they started a farm on a hill overlooking a river. Their nearest neighbours were a five-day canoe trip away.

They built huts and cleared land in the jungle and started growing crops. There were many hardships and Jan gradually became blind. Rebecca was fit and strong and could do the work of a man.

Life was hard but they managed to survive. They continued like this until 30th December 1979 when disaster struck. The family went down with an awful disease which resembled malaria. Jan couldn't move from her bed and was terribly weak. Cruelly, it was her daughter, Rebecca, who was the first to die. Jan was not able to walk so she had to crawl out of the hut to drag Rebecca's body away. For days Jan and Harry stayed in their hut too weak to do anything. They lived off a little flour mixed with water and a few tins of food. Harry was completely helpless.

They became dangerously short of water so Jan had to make her way down the steep path to the river with a bucket. Somehow, she managed to get back to the hut with a little water left. By this time, they had almost run out of supplies and Jan realized that survival depended on her being able to reach the store hut, which was situated at the top of the hill.

Over several days, by carefully using rope and pieces of cloth so that she could mark her trail, she gradually made her way towards the hill-top hut. She was terrified of the snakes and the wild animals which surrounded her so she carried a stick in case she met any.

Finally, six weeks after Rebecca's death, Harry died leaving Jan on her own with only the company of her pet monkey, Maggie. The poor woman even lost her hearing-aid. Even when the situation looked hopeless, Jan's refusal to give up meant she lived. She succeeded in reaching the store hut where she found matches. This allowed her to prepare her first hot food for months. Her pet monkey disappeared, depriving her of the companionship of another living creature. Yet, the will to survive did not desert her. By now, almost completely deaf and blind, she chopped wood, made fires and successfully moved up and down the dangerous paths in order to get water and other supplies.

On the last day of May, four and a half months after her daughter's death, she felt a hand on her shoulder. Help had arrived.

2 Read the text carefully and choose the best answers to these questions.

1 Jan's sight
   A used to be OK.
   B had never been good.
   C improved.

2 Their farm
   A could only be reached by canoe.
   B was by a river.
   C was expensive.

3 The disease
   A struck just before Christmas.
   B was a kind of malaria.
   C was mysterious.

4 Their hut
   A was on top of a hill.
   B was between the river and the store.
   C had running water.

5 Jan's trail
   A led to the store hut.
   B was made of pieces of cloth.
   C was fairly safe.

6 Jan was without human company for
   A 12 weeks.
   B 16 weeks.
   C 18 weeks.

3 Find the words in the first four paragraphs of text that mean:

1 raised/educated
2 of the country
3 sight
4 to stop doing something
5 a kind of farmer
6 frontier
7 things a farmer grows
8 difficulties
9 to fall sick with something
10 to move on your hands and knees
11 to pull something along without lifting
12 to survive on
13 unable to do anything
14 to finish the supply of something
15 at a large angle

VOCABULARY
Phrasal verbs using give

Look at these two sentences from the text about Jan Little.

1 *She decided to give up city life and become a farmer.*
2 *Jan's refusal to give up meant she lived.*

Give up is being used in two different ways. Look at the dictionary entry for **give up** to see which meaning is represented in each case. Note the number of each meaning.

> **give** sbdy./sthg.↔ **away** *v adv [T]* **1** to make someone a present or prize of (something): *She gave away all her money to the poor.*|*(fig.) Our team just gave the match away by playing so badly.* **2** to deliver or formally hand over (a woman) to the husband at the wedding: *Mary was given away by her father.* **3** to make known (a secret) intentionally or unintentionally: *He tried to pretend that he wasn't worried, but his shaking hands gave him away*/**gave the game away.** (=showed his real feelings) –see also GIVE-AWAY
>
> **give** sbdy. **back** sthg. *v adv [T]* to return (something) to the owner or original possessor: *Give me back my pen.*|*Give me my pen back.* –see Study Notes on page 429
>
> **give in** *v adv* **1** [I *to*] to yield: *The boys fought until one gave in.*|*Don't give in to him.* **2** [T] (**give** sthg.↔ **in**) to deliver; hand in: *Give your examination papers in (to the teacher) when you've finished.*
>
> **give off** sthg. *v adv [T]* to send out (esp. a liquid, gas, or smell): *to give off steam*
>
> **give out** *v adv* **1** [T] (**give** sthg.↔ **out**) to give to each of several people: *Give out the examination papers.*/*Give the money out to the children.* **2** [I] also **run out**– *infml* to come to an end: *His strength gave out.*
>
> **give over** *v adv* [I;T (=**give over** sthg.) + *v-ing*; often *in commands*] *BrE infml* to stop
>
> **give up** *v adv* **1** [T + *v-ing*] (**give up** sthg.) to stop having or doing: *The doctor told me to give up smoking.*|*I gave that idea up a long time ago.* **2** [I;T (=**give** sthg.↔ **up**)] to stop working at or trying to do (something): *to give up one's studies*|*He tried to swim the English Channel, but had to give up halfway.* **3** [T] (**give** sbdy. **up**) to stop believing that (someone) can be saved, esp. from death: *The boy was **given up for lost/for dead.*** **4** [T *to*] (**give** sbdy. **up**) to offer (someone or oneself) as a prisoner: *He gave himself up (to the police).* –compare SURRENDER **5** [T *to*] (**give** sthg.↔ **up**) to deliver or allow to pass (to someone else): *Give your seat up to the old lady.*

Using the phrasal verb entries for **give,** substitute the words **in bold** with a suitable phrasal verb. Write down the number of the meaning which is expressed.

Example: *The explorer's food ~~finished~~ in the middle of the desert.* gave out 2

1 Can you **distribute** the books to the class, Claudia?
2 Before she died, she **left** all her money to the dogs' home.
3 When the plastic caught fire, it **produced** a terrible smell.
4 Joanna **offered** her seat to the man with the walking stick.
5 They had to **stop** the climb when it started snowing.
6 Stop! Stop! **You win.** Don't hurt me any more!
7 She talked in her sleep and **said** where the money was hidden.
8 If I were you, I'd **stop** drinking whisky.
9 He never **returns** the books he borrows.

LANGUAGE STUDY
in case and so that

1 in case
*Jan Little carried a stick **in case** she met any wild animals.*

↓   ↓

precaution she took in advance   *something unpleasant or unwelcome that might happen*

In other words, we use **in case** to talk about things we do in advance to help us if there is a problem later.

We can use **in case** + the simple present tense to talk about the future, e.g. *Take an umbrella **in case** it rains.*

We can use **in case** + the simple past tense to talk about any time in the past.
*She took an umbrella **in case** it rained.* This means the same as *She took an umbrella **so (that)** she wouldn't get wet.*

2 so that

*Jan used rope and pieces of cloth to mark her way **so that** she could find her way.*

We use **so that** to show a first action is performed to prepare for and help achieve a second action. However, we could change this sentence to *Jan used rope and pieces of cloth to mark her way **in case** she got lost.*

3 Join the following sentences using either **in case** or **so that**. Make any changes that are necessary.

1 You should insure your house. You may have a fire.
2 The film star wore dark glasses. He didn't want anyone to recognize him.
3 She packed the glasses carefully. She didn't want them to get broken in the post.
4 You should always have a jack and carry a spare tyre. You may have a puncture.
5 Take this serum with you. There are snakes in the forest and you might get bitten.
6 The thief wore gloves. He didn't want to leave any fingerprints.
7 The notices in the hotel are in seven languages. The manager wants everyone to understand them.
8 You had better take traveller's cheques. If they get stolen, you can get some new ones.

4 Imagine some friends are going on a camping holiday in the middle of a forest. What advice would you give them?

LISTENING

1 It is two o'clock in the morning. You and a friend are driving along a lonely Canadian mountain road. It has been snowing heavily for the past two hours and you realize there is no possibility of continuing any further because the snow is too deep. You know that last winter two travellers died in similar conditions. You each have a winter coat and a pair of gloves with you. You think that there might be a petrol station in another kilometre or so. What would you do? In pairs, discuss your survival plan.

2 Listen to the radio programme on surviving in cold weather and decide if you would have survived!

3 Listen to the interview again and complete these notes.

Your most important piece of survival equipment is .... (1).
Rule number one is .... (2).
You should make sure you have the following things in the car: blankets, ... (3), ... (4), ... (5).
You should make sure that your window is open .... (6) on the .... (7) from the wind.
Car fumes can kill you in .... (8).
You should run your car engine for a maximum of .... (9) every hour.
Before you leave on your journey, you should .... (10).

USE OF ENGLISH

Here is some more practice in completing sentences with words from one root.

1 Complete the following sentences with a word based on **live**.

Example: *What do you do for a* ....*living*.... ?

1 They managed to find three miners who were still .... three days after the underground explosion.
2 She was sent to prison for .... for murdering her husband.
3 The rock concert isn't going to be recorded. Instead, it is going to be broadcast .... on television.
4 Young children are often very .... They have so much energy they can't sit still for a moment.
5 She was married six times in her ....
6 Cats are supposed to have nine ....

2 Complete the following sentences with a word based on **die**.

1 'Look after your mother,' were his .... words.
2 This bottle contains a .... poison.
3 The snake and the alligator fought to the ....
4 I can't get through; the phone seems to be ....
5 There was a .... silence when he mentioned his ex-wife's name.

3 Complete the following sentences with an expression based on **live** and **die**.

1 I'm .... a drink. I'm so thirsty.
2 Jan had to .... the little food she had in the hut.
3 Whales are .... because people keep on hunting them.
4 It took him 20 years to .... the scandal.
5 Come quickly, doctor. It's a matter of .... or ....

PRONUNCIATION

Voicing word endings

1 Some nationalities find it difficult to voice the endings of words where necessary. Say these two sentences paying particular attention to the pronunciation of the last words.

She was sent to prison for life.   no vibration = voiceless
The concert is going to be live.   vibration = voiced

2 Look at the words in the box. Put the voiced ones in column A and the unvoiced ones in column B.

dead rise heart debt
rice knees niece safe
mend save hard meant

A	B
voiced	voiceless
live	life

SPEAKING

Discussing a photograph

In **Paper 5: Interview** you will be shown a photograph and asked to describe what you see and talk generally around the topic of the photograph. There is a more detailed look at this part of the exam in Unit 8.

Discuss where the man is and why, and how the picture makes you feel.

USE OF ENGLISH

Fill the gaps using the words in the box. Use each word **once** only.

Austin's luck finally ran out on day 92 when a cobra bit him on the arm. He had wanted to .... (1) the world record for .... (2) in a glass cage with poisonous snakes. It was .... (3) part of a publicity stunt to .... (4) visitors to a snake and animal park in South Africa.

His companions had been no .... (5) than 36 deadly snakes. They included 20 cobras and, ... (6) dangerous of all, six black mambas .... (7) bite can kill in under a minute. He hadn't been able to relax for a moment as .... (8) movement which was made excited his 'room mates'. He fed .... (9) on live mice but had to make sure .... (10) he didn't touch them in case he was mistaken for food too!

By day 92 he had .... (11) been bitten twice, but on .... (12) occasions, ... (13) a miracle, no venom entered his bloodstream. One day he .... (14) fell on top of a black mamba. Fortunately for him, ... (15) of striking the mamba shot across to the other side of the cage.

When he was bitten for the third time, Austin .... (16) have left the cage but decided to wait for the antidote to arrive. Even though he was .... (17) terrible pain, he thought he .... (18) as well die trying to break the record. .... (19) it was, he managed to survive and .... (20) a further two weeks in the cage to set a new record of 107 days.

might	them	instead	most	both	spent	in	by	break	whose
as	attract	all	any	could	that	living	already	even	fewer

WRITING

In **Paper 2: Composition** you may be asked to imagine that you are demonstrating how to do something.

1 Read the talk on how to treat snake bites and put the paragraphs in the right order.

PARA

A Right, thanks a lot, Fatima. So, that's how you do it. Who would like to have a go?

B Now, just a few words before I start. First of all, do all you can to calm the victim down. You may have to treat them for shock too. Then do your best to clean the wound. Let's pretend that Fatima has been bitten on the ankle, shall we?

C As I was saying, the secret of the technique is to make the bandage tight enough without being too tight. How does that feel? One last thing, don't try to suck the poison out. This can be extremely dangerous.

D So, the object of the exercise is to prevent the poison from spreading through the body. As I said earlier, make the victim relax, making sure that the heart is higher than the bitten area.

E Right everyone, can I have your attention, please? I'm going to show you what to do when someone is bitten by a poisonous snake. Now, I'm going to need a volunteer. Thank you, Fatima. OK, can everyone gather round, please?

F This means we'll have Fatima sitting up, not lying down. Then you need to take a bandage and start bandaging above the cut — like so — working your way down. Don't start over the cut itself. Also, whatever you do, don't tie it too tight like a tourniquet in the westerns.

---

2 Analysis

1 Which words or phrases helped you to put it in the right order?
2 How does the demonstrator:
   A get everybody to listen?
   B ask people to come near?
   C give instructions?
   D ask for people to try and do the treatment?
3 Are there any other useful words or expressions that you could use in a talk like this?

3 Imagine you have to tell a group of people how to perform the Kiss of Life. Use the diagrams and notes to help you to write a short speech.

1 Act quickly.
  Check for danger.
● Make sure it is safe to approach.
● Do not move casualty more than necessary.

2 Check breathing.
  Clear mouth of any debris.
● Lie casualty on back and check breathing.
● Clear mouth and stretch neck to clear airway.

3 Start mouth-to-mouth respiration.
● Continue artificial respiration to restart natural breathing.
● If natural breathing cannot be restarted, check for blockage in airway.

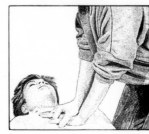

4 Apply chest compression.
● If casualty is still not breathing, check pulse, begin chest compression.
● Send for medical aid.

USE OF ENGLISH

1 In **Paper** 3 you may have to complete a dialogue. Study this example and read the comments the teacher has made.

INTERVIEWER: *I want to ask you some questions.* *Fairly logical but not very appropriate because the question isn't polite enough. Not accurate - the answer is 'Not at all.' So the question must begin 'Do you mind...?'*

EXPERT: Not at all. Go ahead. I'll try my best to answer them.

INTERVIEWER: *Are many people bitten by snakes?* *Good. Appropriate and logical.*

EXPERT: To be honest, the risks are extremely low in Britain.

INTERVIEWER: *What happens to people?* *Fairly logical and accurate but not enough.*

EXPERT: Well, in Britain only one or two people dies each year although quite a few are bitten.

INTERVIEWER: *What must we do?* *Again, this is fairly logical but not complete enough.*

EXPERT: First of all, make the victim relax and examine the wound.

INTERVIEWER: *What should we do next?* *This is illogical - the answer is 'no' - and incomplete.*

EXPERT: No. Whatever you do, don't use a tourniquet. A tight bandage is much safer.

INTERVIEWER: *Anything else?* *Two words are not enough - sounds impolite.*

EXPERT: Yes. Never suck the poison from the wound or cut it.

INTERVIEWER: *Do you know Westerns?* *Completely illogical!*

EXPERT: I know but Westerns are pure imagination.

INTERVIEWER: *How can we avoid getting bitten?* *The answer begins with a 'yes' so it must be a 'yes/no' question.*

EXPERT: Yes. Prevention is always better than cure. Avoid walking through grass, particularly in hot weather and always wear strong walking boots. Snakes normally go for the feet.

---

2 What can we learn from this example?

1 It is important to be logical. If what you write does not make sense, you will not score any marks at all. Make sure that you read the sentence **before** the gap and the sentence **after** the gap.

2 Make sure that you write enough.

3 Make sure that the style of what you write is appropriate. In other words, if the situation is formal, the language should be formal. If two friends are talking, don't use any language which is too formal.

4 Try to be accurate. Check for silly mistakes.

3 Working with a partner, decide where the problems are with this answer. Try and identify if they are problems of logic, accuracy, range or even naturalness. Then try and improve it.

Carlo is studying English at a language school in England. He wants to change his accommodation and is talking to Barbara Granger, the accommodation officer.

BARBARA: Hello, Carlo. what seems to be the problem?

CARLO: *My roomate is a horrible boy. He smokes always.*

BARBARA: So he smokes in the room, does he? Have you spoken to him about the problem?

CARLO: *He said bad things to me.*

BARBARA: Well. That wasn't very nice! So, you'd like to change, would you?

CARLO: *Yes, I would like to change.*

BARBARA: I can understand that you've had enough of sharing. I've got a single room at £65 a week.

CARLO: *That's too expensive.*

BARBARA: Well, there's another one, just outside town, at £45.

CARLO: *O.K.*

BARBARA: About three miles, but there's a bus.

CARLO: *It is too far.*

BARBARA: I'll phone the landlady and try to fix a time for you to see the room. Will this afternoon be OK?

CARLO: *I prefer later on.*

BARBARA: All right. I'll arrange it for tonight.

4 Now complete this dialogue. Remember to be logical, appropriate and correct.

Sally has just seen some boots in a shop window. She is talking to a shop assistant.

SALLY: I'd like to try on a pair of those boots you have in the window.
S.A.: (1) .... ?
SALLY: No, sorry. I mean the dark brown ones next to them.
S.A.: (2) .... ?
SALLY: I think I'm size six.
S.A.: (3) .... ?
SALLY: Well, actually they're a bit tight. Can I try the next size?
S.A.: (4) .... ?
SALLY: What a pity! If only I'd come earlier.
S.A.: (5) .... ?
SALLY: Not really. I had my heart set on that style.
S.A.: (6) ....
SALLY: I didn't know there was a branch in Castle Street. That's a good idea. Thank you very much.

SPEAKING

Discussing texts

In **Paper 5: Interview** you are given a text which you have to read and discuss with the examiner. Read these texts and, with a partner, discuss: **1** what the situation is; **2** who is speaking; **3** where and when you would come across the text.

A When the plane crashed, all the lights went out. Everybody panicked except Blond. He could control his fear. The terrorists stood up and fought for the exit, their screams turning to coughing and silence. Blond was able to get out because he remembered his army training. 'Crawl along the floor where the air is purest.' He got to the door, his lungs bursting and, with a mighty kick, managed to force it open. As he fell to the ground, the plane exploded above him.

B Royal Navy helicopters are continuing their search for members of the capsized fishing boat. They are being assisted by lifeboat services from Sidmouth. They have succeeded in rescuing nine of the crew but another two, including the captain, are unaccounted for. Hope is fading fast but the search is continuing. We will now go over to the fishing village of Sidmouth for a live report from the centre of rescue operations.

C Joe: Come on! Damn you Billy. Don't give up now, boy! The sheriff and his posse ain't that far behind.
Billy: I can't go on, Joe. I'm hurt bad. I must have some water.
Joe: There ain't no water here but you'll be able to have all the water you can drink when we get somewhere safe. Come on, when you was a kid you could walk for miles. You can do it. We'll be at the hideout soon.

LANGUAGE STUDY

Ability

1 *Everyone panicked except Blond. He **could** control his fear.*

1 Read the texts you have just discussed and underline all the other words and expressions that are used to talk about **ability**.
2 In Text A why does it say *Blond **was able to** get out*, and not *Blond **could** get out*?
3 What are the differences in structure between **manage** and **succeed**?

2 Complete these sentences. In some cases **both** answers may be correct.

1 When he was a child, he .... swim like a fish.
   A was able to   **B** could
2 We drove into town but we .... find anywhere to park.
   A couldn't   **B** weren't able to
3 They have finally .... in selling their old car.
   A managed   **B** succeeded
4 They .... escape by climbing through the window.
   A were able to   **B** managed
5 She .... to sing beautifully as a little girl.
   A was able   **B** could
6 Good news! I .... buy the last tickets.
   A could   **B** was able to
7 Did you .... to open the tin?
   A succeed   **B** manage

Survival Games

1 It's Monday morning and three friends are talking about what they did at the weekend.

1 The object of the game is to
   A kill the enemy.
   B attack the enemy's camp.
   C take something.

2 If you get hit with ink,
   A you can carry on playing that game.
   B you can challenge the decision.
   C you are dead.

3 Survival games are so good because
   A there are lots of centres.
   B people are warlike.
   C they are outdoor fun.

4 The two men
   A basically disapprove of the game.
   B change their minds about the game.
   C would rather play rugby.

5 Most players are
   A country lovers.
   B older office workers.
   C young.

2 Discussion points
1 Would you like to play this kind of game?
2 Do you have anything like it in your country?
3 What effect could it have on people who play it?
4 Should there be a minimum age for playing it?

Here is a model answer to the dialogue completion task on page 37.

INTERVIEWER: Do you mind if I ask you some questions?

EXPERT: Not at all. Go ahead. I'll try my best to answer them.

INTERVIEWER: What are the chances of being bitten by a snake?

EXPERT: To be honest, the risks are extremely low in Britain.

INTERVIEWER: How many people are bitten and what happens to them?

EXPERT: Well, in Britain only one or two people die each year although quite a few are bitten.

INTERVIEWER: I see. What should we do if someone is bitten?

EXPERT: First of all, make the victim relax and examine the wound.

INTERVIEWER: What about using a tourniquet?

EXPERT: No. Whatever you do, don't use a tourniquet. A tight bandage is much safer.

INTERVIEWER: Is there anything else that we mustn't do?

EXPERT: Yes. Never suck the poison from the wound or cut it.

INTERVIEWER: But they do this in Westerns.

EXPERT: I know but Westerns are pure imagination.

INTERVIEWER: Have you got any advice about prevention?

EXPERT: Yes. Prevention is always better than cure. Avoid walking through grass, particularly in hot weather and always wear strong walking boots. Snakes normally go for the feet.

UNIT 4 *Storytelling*

SPEAKING

All around the world small children are told stories at bedtime.
What stories were you told? What were your favourites?

LANGUAGE STUDY

Past tenses

1 Read the beginning of *The tale of Little Red Riding Hood* and find examples of these past tenses in the text:

1 the past simple tense, e.g. *She went … .*
2 the past continuous tense, e.g. *She was going … .*
3 the past perfect tense, e.g. *She had gone … .*

NCE UPON A TIME there was a girl called Little Red Riding Hood who lived with her mother. Little Red Riding Hood's grandmother had invited her to her cottage, so one fine day she set off to visit her. The little girl got ready, waved goodbye to her mother and promised to be careful. On her arm she carried a basket which contained a cake her mother had baked specially. It was a lovely spring morning, the sun was shining and the birds were singing, happy that the winter was over.

Even though Little Red Riding Hood's mother had told her to follow the path through the fields, the naughty child decided to take a short cut through a wood. As she went deeper and deeper into it, the cold and darkness frightened her. She was making her way along the narrow path when she heard a noise. All of a sudden a big, fierce-looking wolf jumped out from behind a bush and came towards her …

2 We can use these three past tenses in different ways. Study each of the example sentences and the description of their use.

Past simple
Once upon a time there was a little girl called Little Red Riding Hood who lived with her mother.
Here the past simple is being used to describe simple facts and states.

The little girl got ready, waved goodbye to her mother and promised to be careful.
Here the past simple is used on its own because the events follow each other in a chronological sequence.

Past continuous
The sun was shining and the birds were singing.
Here the past continuous is being used to set the scene.

*She **was making** her way along the narrow path when she heard a noise.*
Here the past continuous is being used together with the past simple to show that one action was going on when it was interrupted by a sudden action.

Past perfect
*... which contained a cake her mother **had baked** specially.*
Here the past perfect is used to show that the cake was baked earlier. In other words, it is like the **past in the past.**

3 Put the verbs in this continuation of the story of Little Red Riding Hood into the most suitable past tense.

... licking his lips in anticipation of a tasty meal. He (1) .... (*ask*) her where she (2) .... (*go*). The girl, who never (3) .... (*see*) a wolf before, (4) .... (*tell*) him all about her grandmother and where she (5) .... (*live*). Just as he (6) .... (*be*) about to attack, he (7) .... (*hear*) two woodcutters approaching and (8) .... (*hurry*) off saying he (9) .... (*forget*) an important meeting on the other side of the forest. While the little girl slowly (10) .... (*make*) her way along the path, the wolf (11) .... (*rush*) through the forest towards the old lady's cottage.
The cottage door (12) .... (*be*) locked so the wolf (13) .... (*pretend*) to be Little Red Riding Hood by copying her voice. Granny (14) .... (*open*) the door to let her in and ...

4 Working in pairs or small groups, write the rest of the Little Red Riding Hood story. Pay special attention to your use of past tenses.

PRONUNCIATION
Past tenses

1 Regular verbs in the past
Listen to these regular verbs and put them in the correct column.

stayed	asked	waited	invited	promised
carried	contained	decided	frightened	

/d/	/t/	/id/
stayed	*asked*	*waited*

2 was and were
In *The Tale of Little Red Riding Hood* it says *It was a lovely spring morning, the sun was shining and the birds were singing ... .*

1 Which words are stressed in this sentence?
2 How does this affect the pronunciation of **was** and **were**?
3 Listen to this short dialogue which contains **was** and **were**. When are **was** and **were** strong and when are they weak?
   A: Where were you last night?
   B: I was at the office.
   A: Were you?
   B: Yes, I was. I was working late.
   A: You were with Paul!
   B: No, I wasn't.
   A: Yes, you were.
4 Practise reading the dialogue in pairs, paying attention to the strong and weak forms.

3 USE OF ENGLISH

Complete the sentences with a word or expression based on **sleep**.

1 Do you know the story of .... *Beauty*?
2 I feel .... It's bedtime.
3 The driver fell .... as he was driving along.
4 The doctor gave her some .... to help her sleep.
5 She is a light .... The slightest noise wakes her up.
6 Take a .... if you go camping.
7 Since the baby was born, they have had a lot of .... nights.

LISTENING
An alternative Cinderella

1 Listen to this modern version of the Cinderella tale and answer these questions.

1 What was Cinderella's great ambition?
2 Why did the king organize a ball?
3 Why did Cinderella go to it?
4 What happened at midnight?
5 How did she help the Royal Family with its problems?

2 Work in groups and either tell a traditional story from your own country or invent a modern version of the same tale.

WRITING

1 Read the story and give it a title.

This story is set in Wales in the Middle Ages. There was a prince whose name was Llewellyn. He lived in a valley. He had a baby son. He also had a dog called Gelert. One day the prince went hunting. He left the dog to look after the baby. Some wolves came from out of a wood. They ran towards the cottage. The dog saw the wolves and hid the baby. The dog ran outside and fought the wolves. He killed two but was wounded. He was tired and lay down to sleep. The prince returned. He saw the dog covered in blood. He saw that his son's cot was empty. He took his sword and killed the dog while it slept. Then he heard the baby cry and found him. Through the window he saw the two dead wolves. Then he understood. He carried the dog to the top of a hill and buried it. He collected a pile of stones to mark the grave. You can still see it today.

2 The tale is told in a basic way. Expand it to make it more interesting. Also, put it into paragraphs and vary the use of past tenses.

Answer these questions in your version.

1 What did the prince/the dog/the wolves/his house/ the valley look like?
2 What was the time of day and what was the weather like at each point in the story?
3 How did the prince feel at different times?

● Try to use the following useful words and expressions:

afterwards   just then   one day   that afternoon
many years ago   when   while   as   so   before

USE OF ENGLISH

Complete the story using just **one** word for each gap. Here are ten of the words. Supply the other ten.

needless   accordingly   popular   up
on   bright   been   from   it   so

A lot of people are familiar with the story of *Brave Gelert*, the dog that faithfully defended the prince's baby son, but which was then killed through a .... (1) misunderstanding. However, only a .... (2) people know that the story is really a pack of lies. Let me explain.

About a hundred or .... (3) years ago there was a hotel owner in Wales who was fed .... (4) with business being so bad. His hotel was stuck in the middle of nowhere and .... (5) anyone came to stay. Then, one day, he had a .... (6) idea. A famous prince called Llewellyn .... (7) lived in the area during the Middle Ages and he had been fond of dogs. This is hardly .... (8) as hunting was extremely .... (9) at that time. So .... (10) he did was to invent the story of the brave and faithful Gelert and how he had .... (11) killed by his ungrateful master.

Of course, people .... (12) be far more likely to believe the story if there was .... (13) something they could see. .... (14), one day, the hotel keeper went to the top of a high hill and built a sort of monument from the stones he found lying around. A friend of .... (15), who was, incidentally, an accountant, helped him to construct .... (16).

The 'legend' soon caught .... (17) and developed a life of its own. People came .... (18) far and wide to see the spot where .... (19) hound was buried. .... (20) to say, business became very good for the hotel owner!

VOCABULARY

Phrasal verbs in this unit

1 Match the phrasal verbs with their definitions.

A	put up with	**1**	find by chance
B	take in	**2**	stop/discourage from doing something
C	find out	**3**	criticize
D	look after	**4**	discover information/facts
E	set off	**5**	have relationship with someone
F	turn down	**6**	give hospitality/shelter
G	tell off	**7**	endure/tolerate
H	fall for	**8**	take care of
I	come across	**9**	refuse/reject
J	get on with	**10**	love/be attracted to someone
K	turn up	**11**	leave on a journey
L	put off	**12**	arrive

2 Complete the following sentences using one of the phrasal verbs above.

 1 They went to the bus station to .... the time of the next bus to Edinburgh.
 2 When they were cleaning out the attic, they .... their grandmother's old school books.
 3 The teacher .... the children .... for not doing their homework.
 4 A farmer .... the travellers .... during the snow storm and gave them a bed for the night.
 5 She did not .... her new boss so she got another job.
 6 Please could you make less noise. It's .... me .... my work.
 7 While she was studying in England, she .... her landlady's son and they later got married.
 8 I can't .... your childish behaviour any longer. I'm leaving.
 9 He was .... for the job because of his dirty appearance and long hair.
10 A babysitter .... the kids while they went to the cinema.
11 They finally .... at the party at twelve o'clock just as everybody else was leaving.
12 After she had finished loading the car, she .... on her holiday.

3 Choose the four phrasal verbs that you find the most difficult and write a sentence for each that clearly shows the meaning of the verb. Use a dictionary to help you if you like.

LANGUAGE STUDY

The grammar of phrasal verbs

1 Transitive and intransitive verbs

Our intuition often tells us all we need to know about the grammar of phrasal verbs. However, it can be useful to know the difference between transitive and intransitive verbs to understand better how phrasal verbs operate.

1 Transitive verbs

We can say   *Anne likes John.*   or   *She saw him.*

SUBJECT VERB OBJECT   SUBJECT VERB OBJECT
                                 PRONOUN   PRONOUN

But we can't say   *Anne likes.*

Like is a transitive verb. In other words, it must be followed by an object. Without an object it does not make sense. In the *Longman Active Study Dictionary* transitive verbs are shown like this: [T].

2 Intransitive verbs

We can say   *The sun rose.*
SUBJECT VERB

We can't say   *The sun rose the sky.*
This is because **rise** does not take an object. It is intransitive. In the *Longman Active Study Dictionary* intransitive verbs are shown like this: [I].

3 Using your dictionary, find out if these verbs are transitive, intransitive or both: *rise, raise, thank, understand, go, see, open, laugh. arrive.*

2 Exploring the grammar of phrasal verbs

1 With a partner, look at these groups of sentences and quickly decide if they are correct. Use your intuition about English!

A turn up (meaning **arrive**)   i) She turned up.   ii) She turned up him.
                                   iii) She turns up late for everything.

B tell off   i) She told off.   ii) She told off Dick.   iii) She told Dick off.
                iv) She told off him.   v) She told him off.

C look after   i) She looked after.   ii) She looked after him.
                  iii) She looked him after.   iv) She looked after Bill.
                  v) She looked Bill after.

D get on with   i) She gets on with.   ii) She gets on her with.
                   iii) She gets on with her.   iv) She gets on with Ann.

2 In pairs or small groups, work out the four types of phrasal verbs. Decide:
A whether each phrasal verb is transitive or intransitive.
B where we can put the object if it is transitive.
C what happens to the object if it is a pronoun.

3 Look at the dictionary entry for **turn up.**
How many different meanings does it give? Is the grammar of **turn up** always the same?

> **turn up** *v adv* **1** [T] (**turn** sthg.↔**up**) to find: *to turn up new information* **2** [I] to be found: *The missing bag turned up, completely empty, in the river.* **3** [T] (**turn** sthg.↔**up**) to shorten (a garment) – compare TURN-UP **4** [I] to arrive: *She turns up late for everything.*|*Don't worry, something will turn up.* (=happen) **5** [T] (**turn** sthg.↔**up**) to increase the force, strength, loudness, etc., of (a radio, heating system, etc.) by using controls

Note   The most important thing you have to discover when you meet a new phrasal verb is whether it is possible to separate the verb and the particle.

VOCABULARY

Time expressions

Complete the sentences using one of the time expressions or words in the box.

1 The phone rang .... he was in the bath.
2 Mary had a stomach-ache .... the night.
3 Everybody got up and left .... of the film.
4 We queued for the tickets .... two hours.
5 She told us she had .... lived in Paris.
6 The bus .... arrived half an hour late.
7 .... I decide to play tennis it always seems to rain.
8 The plane's arriving in an hour. .... , let's have a cup of tea.
9 She insisted on staying .... the film ended even though it was awful.
10 Why don't we go to the park? .... we can visit Lucy.
11 We couldn't get a taxi and we had decided to walk but .... someone gave us a lift.
12 Just .... leaving work, an important customer arrived.

| whenever before while until during |
| afterwards at the end for eventually |
| in the meantime in the end previously |

READING

1 Quickly read the story of Dick Whittington and put the pictures in the right order. Compare your answer with a partner.

2 Complete the story using one of the words or expressions in the box.

| however once unfortunately following |
| one day each time nevertheless finally |
| once upon a time eventually on so as |
| afterwards meanwhile whenever when |

3 Are there any words in the story which you do not know the meaning of? See if you can work out their meaning from the **context** they are in.

(1) .... there was a poor orphan called Dick Whittington. The boy had heard stories about the great city of London where the streets were paved with gold. Although London was a long way away from his tiny village, he wasn't put off from making a bundle of his few possessions and setting off to seek his fortune.

(2) .... Dick had arrived, he soon realized that work and money were no easier to come by than in the country. At every shop and market stall he came across, he asked for work but the answer was always no.

(3) .... he was turned down, his bundle seemed to grow a little heavier. (4) .... night fell, he grew tired and hungry. While he was walking through the streets, he came across the doorway of a fine house which looked like a good place to sleep. Having nowhere else to go, he lay down using his precious bundle as a pillow. The house belonged to a rich merchant called Mr Fitzwarren who, being a kind gentleman, took pity on the boy. He took him in and fed him. (5) .... hearing Dick's story, Mr Fitzwarren told him that he would give him a job.

The boy was given a place to sleep in the attic but was greatly disturbed by the rats and mice that lived there too. (6) ...., with his last penny, Dick bought a cat which soon chased the rats and mice away. It became his greatest friend.

48

Dick was extremely grateful to Mr Fitzwarren and fell for his lovely daughter, Alice. Dick got on well with everybody. (7) ...., his life was made a misery by the cook, who always told him off (8) .... he did anything wrong.

(9) ...., his master called all the servants together to tell them that he was going to send a ship off on a long trading voyage. He then asked whether anyone had anything they wished to send on the voyage which could be sold or bartered. Young Dick thought about this a lot and (10) ...., after much heart searching, decided to send his beloved cat.

(11) .... , he felt sad and lonely and the cook's treatment of him became more and more cruel. (12) .... he couldn't put up with it any longer and decided to run away. (13) ...., as he reached the edge of the city, he heard the bells of a nearby church which seemed to be telling him to turn back from his journey. What is more, the bells told him that he would become Lord Mayor of London, not just once but three times. He decided to obey the message and returned home before anyone had noticed that he was missing.

(14) ...., Mr Fitzwarren's ship had arrived in port where no European had ever been before. The captain was invited to the palace of the king of this strange country for a feast in his honour. When he got there, he was taken to a dining room where there was a magnificent meal waiting. The moment they sat down to eat, hundreds of rats rushed in and ate the food in front of their eyes. The king was embarrassed and apologized to his guest who told him that what he needed was a cat. The monarch had no idea what a cat was, so the sailor ordered Dick's cat to be sent ashore. It was the first time anyone had ever seen one and the king himself was even a little afraid of the creature. However, (15) .... he saw how it dealt with the rats, he was delighted. Within a couple of days, the entire palace had been cleared of them. The king was so pleased that he gave the captain gold and silver in return for the cat.

(16) ...., on the ship's return to England, the captain handed over the money and jewels he had got and Dick became extremely rich (17) .... the sale of his pet. He continued to work for Mr Fitzwarren and he eventually married Alice. His fortune grew and, as the bells had promised, he became Lord Mayor of London. He never forgot what it had been like to be poor and he became famous for the good work he did to help the poor and orphans.

WRITING

Understanding style

1 Let's have another look at one of the paragraphs from the Dick Whittington story and see how it is constructed.

1 Look at the text and work out what the words in **bold** refer to.

> ... strange country for a feast in **his** honour. When **he** got **there,** he was taken to a dining room **where** there was a magnificent meal waiting. The moment **they** sat down to eat, hundreds of rats rushed in and ate the food in front of **their** eyes. The king was embarrassed and apologized to his **guest who** told **him** that what he needed was a cat. The **monarch** had no idea what a cat was, so the **sailor** ordered Dick's cat to be sent ashore. It was the first time anyone had ever seen **one** and the king himself was even a little afraid of the **creature.**

2 How does the writer manage to avoid repeating the words **captain, cat, king** and **palace** too often?

2 Read the following story and rewrite so that you don't repeat the words **princess, pond, frog** and **witch** too often.

THE PRINCESS SAW A FROG. The frog was in a pond. The pond was near a castle. The frog spoke to the princess. The princess was surprised. The princess went to the pond every day to talk to the frog. The princess fell in love with the frog. One day the frog asked the princess for a kiss. The princess gave the frog a kiss. The frog turned into a handsome young prince. A witch had cast a spell on the prince. The witch had taken the prince's castle. The witch lived in the castle. The prince went to the castle. The prince killed the witch. The princess married the prince. The princess and the prince lived happily ever after.

LISTENING

An expert on folk and fairy tales is being interviewed about Cinderella and Dick Whittington.

1 Listen to the part of the interview about Cinderella and decide if these statements are **true** or **false**.

1 There are about 315 versions of the tale.
2 In the German version the sisters are pretty.
3 In the Italian version Cinderella doesn't wear rags.
4 In the Indian version there isn't a fairy godmother.
5 The story is popular because it has a prince in it.
6 The English version may be a poor translation.

2 Listen to the part about Dick Whittington and answer these questions.

1 Why isn't Dick Whittington really a fairy story?
2 Who was the real Dick Whittington?
3 What part does a cat play in the story?

READING

1 Read the summary of the film *Dirty Harry* and answer the questions

THIS IS A THRILLER SET IN SAN FRANCISCO AND STARS CLINT EASTWOOD AS INSPECTOR HARRY CALLAHAN. He is known as Dirty Harry because he gets all the tough cases and uses his own special methods. The film opens with a young woman swimming in a pool on the top of a tall building. A gunman shoots and kills her from the top of a nearby skyscraper. Dirty Harry is given the case and finds a note from the killer, demanding $100,000. The killer, who calls himself Scorpio, threatens to kill again unless he receives the money.

The mayor wants to pay the money but Callahan disagrees. As the money is not paid, Scorpio kills a young black boy. He escapes a trap set by Callahan and kidnaps a little girl. This time he asks for $200,000. Callahan almost manages to trap Scorpio and wounds him with a knife. Later on, he tracks him to a football stadium and forces Scorpio to tell him where the girl is. The girl is found but she is dead. However, Scorpio is released because of the way Callahan got his confession.

Even though the case is closed, Callahan tracks Scorpio waiting for his next move. Scorpio then hijacks a school bus full of young children. After an exciting battle, the inspector kills the criminal. It is an exciting and sometimes brutal film.

Are these statements **true** or **false?** If they are false, say why.

1 Callahan's nickname is Dirty Harry.
2 The killer was above the woman in the pool.
3 The killer's real name is Scorpio.
4 Scorpio plays a lot of sport.
5 Scorpio kills four people.
6 Scorpio and Callahan meet twice.
7 Callahan always follows the law.

2 Write a description of a film or play you have seen. Remember to use the present simple tense.

LISTENING

A tall story

1 Working in pairs or small groups, try to make the connection between a dead cat, a department store and a thief! Then listen to the story and see if it is similar to the one you invented.

2 Listen to the story once again and answer these questions.

1 From what Arthur says, we understand
  A Carol seldom tells stories.
  B Carol has a reputation as a storyteller.
  C Carol knows a lot of jokes.

2 The cat
  A was in the street.
  B was asleep under the car.
  C was near the garage.

3 Why doesn't Carol put the cat in the dustbin?
  A The children could find it.
  B She wants to bury it properly.
  C It's against the law.

4 Carol takes the bag to the department store because
  A she thinks her friend can help.
  B she picked it up by mistake.
  C she intends to leave it there.

5 The middle-aged woman
  A was a customer.
  B had a horrible shock.
  C was trying to escape from the store.

WRITING

The narrative composition

1 Question 3 of **Paper 2: Composition** nearly always asks you to tell a story in the past. To answer this question well, you should;

1 be relevant, i.e. answer the question!
2 show a good command of past tenses.
3 show that you can link sentences and ideas well.
4 use a good range of vocabulary.
5 write in a well organized and logical fashion.
6 keep within the word limits set by the exam.
7 be accurate.

Always remember that:
1 First Certificate is an English examination *not* a philosophy exam! Keep your ideas simple and don't be too ambitious.
2 Accuracy is very important in the examination. If you know what you are writing may contain mistakes, then change it and write something else. Many mistakes are avoidable.

2 Here is an example answer to the exam task *Write a story ending with the words 'We never saw him again'*.

1 Study it and decide what is good about it in terms of:
  ● range of structure.
  ● range of vocabulary.
  ● organization.

(1)

When we arrived in London, we were two hours late because our train had been held up by the bad weather. Outside the station it was snowing hard and there was a long queue of people waiting for taxis. As we were about to join it, a young man pulled up in his car and asked us where we wanted to go. Although it was not an official taxi, the car was new and shiny and the young man looked clean and respectable; so we decided to accept his offer. When we told him that we did not have a hotel, he said he could take us to one which was clean and cheap.

(2)

He put our luggage in the boot and we drove off to the hotel. On the way, we chatted and he pointed out any interesting sights. We could hardly believe our luck and thought of all the people we had left queuing in the freezing cold. When we got to the hotel, he told us that he would wait while we checked in. After we had found out that the hotel was full, we went down the steps only to find that our driver and our luggage had disappeared. Needless to say, we never saw him again.

2 Look at the first paragraph again. Why does the writer use so many different past tenses?
3 You were having a meal in a restaurant when suddenly somebody shouted 'Fire'. Describe what happened next in between 120 and 180 words.

UNIT 5 *A Sense of Adventure*

SPEAKING

Choosing a holiday

People often base their choice of holiday on the activities shown in the picture. Which of these activities are important to you? Which are the least important? Work in small groups and share your opinions. Tell each other about your last holiday and why you chose it.

VOCABULARY

Complete the following sentences with **one** word to do with the topic of holidays and travel.

1 We sent off to the tour operators for a
b..................... giving details of their holidays
in Thailand.
2 Last year we went on a p.....................
t..................... . Everything was organized for us:
the flight, the hotels and all the entertainments.
It was all included in the price.
3 They're going on s..................... in Kenya. They'll
be able to see lots of wildlife.
4 We brought back some local handicrafts as
s..................... . Each time we look at them, we
remember what a great time we had.
5 I wouldn't get a scheduled flight, if I were you.
A c..................... flight would be much cheaper.
6 A holiday r..................... is a town which
welcomes and entertains tourists.
7 Bed and breakfast is £15 a night. If you want
b..................... b..................... , it costs an extra £6
which includes either lunch or dinner.
8 We really enjoy s..................... –c.....................
holidays where you rent a house and look after
yourselves.

USE OF ENGLISH

In Unit 2 we did some work on reading and processing information. Here is another activity to prepare you for this part of the exam.

1 Read the details of different types of holidays and decide which one would be most suitable for the people described below the ads.

2 Continue each paragraph giving and explaining your choice for the people. Each paragraph should be about 60 words in length.

If I were Peter Donaldson, ...

Albert and Vera Rogers should ....

If Warren and Diana Harris went ....

Welcome to Bontlins!

Bontlins Holiday Camps can be found in the best of British resorts. Fun and good value for all the family. Rain or shine, there are indoor and outdoor activities for the kids organized by our friendly Greencoats. Evening baby sitting facilities mean that mums and dads can take a break too! Great value and all from as little as £70 a week for adults with half price deals for kids.

CLUB 20-30

Make friends and enjoy yourself at one of our villa parties from a choice of over 15 continental resorts. Try Club 20-30 for action-packed holidays.

Sun-soaked days on the beach and fun evenings at parties and discos. *Not for old folk over 30.*

Plain sailing

Spend a lazy two weeks exploring Yugoslavia's lovely Dalmatian coast and little visited islands on a lovely wooden sailing boat. Friendly and relaxed local crew. Maximum 15 guests per boat. Guaranteed mix of couples and single people. Prices include full board and wine. Book now! Last few places left.

PEACE AND QUIET

Peace and quiet in one of our self-catering bungalows on the Norfolk coast three hours' drive from London. Nice beaches and lovely country walks. Nine hole golf course nearby.

Peter Donaldson. Aged 23. A little lonely since moving to London for his job. Enjoys night life.
Albert and Vera Rogers. Both in their late sixties. Albert hates hotels and foreign food. Vera is a keen golfer. Their dog, Sandy, needs long walks.
Warren and Diana Harris. Aged 34 and 33. Two children: Mandy, aged seven and Chris, two. They have a limited budget.

READING

A holiday with a difference

1 Find out from your partner about the most interesting or exciting holiday they have ever had. Then read the text and:

1 mark the route the tour takes on the map.
2 find out how many different types of transport are used.
3 note the best places for buying souvenirs.

2 Choose the most suitable answers to the following questions and then study closely the explanations on page 65.

1 The buildings in Dakar are
 A fairly new.
 B good to photograph.
 C boring.
 D a contrast.

2 The isle of Goree
 A imported slaves.
 B used to be important.
 C is a centre for slaves.
 D is cut off from the land.

3 The journey from Dakar to Bamako
 A moves from rainy to dry country.
 B takes three nights.
 C is not by bus.
 D passes through hills.

4 The town of Mopti is
 A just like Venice.
 B a market.
 C not cosmopolitan.
 D west of Bamako.

5 Visitors are .... on the River Niger.
 A required to go
 B discouraged from going
 C are recommended to go
 D are obliged to go.

3 Imagine that you have to organize a tour of a region in your country.
Write a brief description of the route the tour will take and the places of interest which will be visited.

THE IVORY COAST TRAIN

Two weeks by rail and local taxis in West Africa visiting Senegal, Mali, Burkina Faso and Ivory Coast.

This escorted tour lets you experience two of West Africa's most important railways, the lifelines from the coastal countries of Senegal and Ivory Coast to landlocked Mali and Burkina Faso. We use hotels and sleeper trains throughout the tour.

We spend time in the busy modern coastal capitals of Dakar and Abidjan. We also explore the remote region of the Niger river around Mopti where ancient kingdoms once held power in this fascinating area of West Africa.

Our journey starts in Dakar, the capital of Senegal, which is situated on the Cape Verde peninsula. The modern buildings contrast with the lively African markets, which are a photographer's delight and a source of fine souvenirs such as tie-dyed cloth and exquisite jewellery.

We shall take a boat ride to the Isle of Goree which was once an important slave trading centre. Slaves were brought here from the interior and shipped to the New World until the abolition of this shameful trade. Goree's museum and the terrible House of Slaves show visitors what life must have been like. We board the train in Dakar for a two-day journey through an ever-changing landscape. The train takes us across the dry region of Sahel to the lushness of Bamako, the capital of Mali. Bamako is a modern city dependent on the river Niger which supports this arid area of West Africa. There are busy, colourful markets and many interesting areas for us to see and explore.

The next stage of our journey will be by local taxi from Bamako to Mopti with a night stop at Segou on the way. Mopti, an important market town, is often called the Venice of Africa, because it lies in the middle of islands and waterways where the Bani and Niger rivers join. Mopti is an exotic and fascinating city. It is extremely cosmopolitan. Here you will see members of many different African tribes who come to Mopti to trade. A boat trip on the river Niger is a must. There is a wide variety of river transport ranging from marvellous old river steamers to narrow canoes called *Pirogues,* the type we are going to use. There is a constant flow of river traffic carrying all forms of goods to and from the major ports with magical names like Gao and Timbuctoo.

Leaving Mopti, we travel by local taxi to Bobo-Dioulasso in Burkina Faso. The next day we will take the train to Abidjan, capital of Ivory Coast. The train journey will take approximately 15 hours and goes from arid, landlocked Burkina Faso to the rich green lands of the Gulf of Guinee.

Abidjan is built in an area of lakes, forests and beaches. The city has clean, modern buildings but its market offers all the excitement of West Africa, with exciting spicy foods, colourful traders and African music. We will have a guided tour of the city and visit the excellent museum. Local craftsmen, who are famous for their wood-carvings, will give us the opportunity to buy souvenirs.

Our tour ends in Abidjan and in just two weeks you will have experienced many of the different faces of West Africa, travelling with the local people as they go about their everyday lives on West African railways.

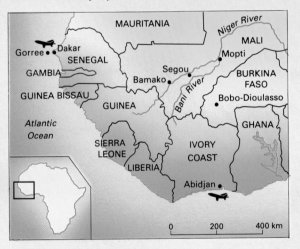

Far left *Mopti*
Left *Goree*

LISTENING

1 Listen to Julie talking to a friend about her planned holiday in the Lake District and put a tick by all the objects in the photo she says she is going to take with her this year.

2 Listen to Julie again and note down the ways in which she talks about her future plans, e.g. *We're going to the Lake District.*

PRONUNCIATION

Listen to the difference between the pronunciation of l in these two words: **hotel, hostel.**
In **hotel** the sound is made towards the front of the mouth.
In **hostel** the back of the tongue is raised.

Now listen to these words from the **Listening** and decide if they are like **hotel** or **hostel.**

	HOTEL	HOSTEL
1 holiday		
2 tell		
3 able		
4 lake		
5 kettle		
6 This'll		
7 Well		
8 We'll		
9 lot		

LANGUAGE STUDY
Ways of talking about the future

1 Working in pairs, match the sentences A–G with the most appropriate description from 1–7.

A **She will be** 30 in June.
B Travel agent: There aren't any flights left.
Customer: In that case, **I'll go** by train.
C **The bus leaves** at eight o'clock on Mondays.
D **I'm flying** to Paris tonight.
E **We're going to visit** Tunisia this summer. We've already booked the tickets.
F Look at those clouds. **It's going to rain.**
G **You will live** until you are 100.

1 A future personal arrangement
2 A future prediction
3 A future prediction based on present evidence
4 A decision taken at the moment of speaking
5 An event which happens regularly
6 Something in the future which will definitely happen
7 Something that the speaker has intended to do in the future for some time

2 Decide what you would say in the following situations. Use an appropriate future form.

1 You feel tired and have decided to stay at home this evening. A friend rings you up to invite you out to a party. How do you refuse?
2 A child you are looking after has just dropped his ice cream and starts to cry. What do you say to comfort the child?
3 Tonight you're responsible for preparing the family's meal. How do you tell a friend that you can't go out with him/her.
4 A cousin is coming to stay for a few days. You promise to meet him/her at the station at seven o'clock. What do you say?
5 You friend Samira is pregnant. Tell the news to your mother.
6 A friend is going to visit your hometown. Predict what they will like/dislike about it.
7 Your friend smokes far too much. Warn him/her about future health problems.

3 USE OF ENGLISH
Dialogue completion

Patrick wants to spend five days in Paris. He is at a travel agency trying to book a flight. Complete the conversation.

T.A.: Good morning, sir. Can I help you?
P: Yes, I'd like to book a return flight to Paris.
      (1) What ....?
T.A.: The cheapest flight? Let me look.
      (2) How ....?
P: I'd like to stay for five days.
T.A.: (3) Will ....?
P: Yes. I'll be there for the weekend. I'd like to leave this Friday and come back on Tuesday.
T.A.: That's good. If you spend the weekend there, you can get a discount return flight.
      (4) It .... How ....?
P: £70. That sounds very reasonable.
      (5) What ....?
T.A.: Morning flights leave London Heathrow every hour from 6.30, Mondays to Fridays.
P: (6) Could ....?
T.A. The 7.30 flight for this Friday. Certainly, sir. I'll just check availability on the computer.

SPEAKING

Role play

You are going to take part in a conversation between two friends and make plans for the weekend.
Student B: Go to page 65 for your information.

Student A:

> Your parents live in the country. You are planning to visit them this weekend. Your parents have told you that you can invite a friend.
> There are two trains on Friday evening. One is at five o'clock and one is at six. You think that the five o'clock train would be better because there will be more seats. They both leave from Charing Cross Station in London. Your brother will meet whichever train you take. It is possible to go for long walks near your parents' house. Horse-riding and tennis are also possible.

 USE OF ENGLISH

Question 1 Gap-filling

In Unit 1 we had a look at the gap-filling question. Now we will have a close look at this part of the exam.

1 Study this example to see the **type** of word that is often left out. Note that nouns are not usually omitted.

1 noun
2 adverb (*modifying an adjective*)
3 preposition
4 comparative adverb
5 determiner (*possessive adjective*)
6 present participle
7 verb in the simple past
8 adjective
9 adverb used with negative expressions
10 determiner
11 verb part of a phrasal verb (*came across*)
12 reflexive pronoun
13 conjunction used in comparatives
14 preposition
15 verb
16 definite article (*determiner*)
17 determiner used for countable nouns
18 auxiliary for past perfect
19 preposition
20 adverb of manner

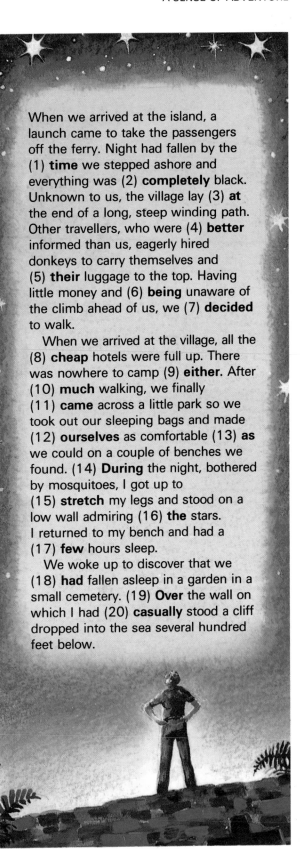

When we arrived at the island, a launch came to take the passengers off the ferry. Night had fallen by the (1) **time** we stepped ashore and everything was (2) **completely** black. Unknown to us, the village lay (3) **at** the end of a long, steep winding path. Other travellers, who were (4) **better** informed than us, eagerly hired donkeys to carry themselves and (5) **their** luggage to the top. Having little money and (6) **being** unaware of the climb ahead of us, we (7) **decided** to walk.

When we arrived at the village, all the (8) **cheap** hotels were full up. There was nowhere to camp (9) **either**. After (10) **much** walking, we finally (11) **came** across a little park so we took out our sleeping bags and made (12) **ourselves** as comfortable (13) **as** we could on a couple of benches we found. (14) **During** the night, bothered by mosquitoes, I got up to (15) **stretch** my legs and stood on a low wall admiring (16) **the** stars. I returned to my bench and had a (17) **few** hours sleep.

We woke up to discover that we (18) **had** fallen asleep in a garden in a small cemetery. (19) **Over** the wall on which I had (20) **casually** stood a cliff dropped into the sea several hundred feet below.

2 The following three exercises concentrate on words which are often blanked out. Complete each exercise using the words in the boxes only **once**.

1 A .... it was cold, they swam.
  B .... he locked the car door he remembered the keys were inside.
  C They left early .... they wanted to get to the airport on time.
  D We'll play tennis .... it doesn't rain.
  E It was foggy .... the ferry didn't sail.
  F .... Helen nor Peter can drive.
  G She married him in .... of his age.
  H .... you keep quiet or I'll have to ask you to leave.
  I She was exhausted; .... , she did her homework.
  J The food was awful, ... , the wine was good.
  K I'll clean the house .... you're cooking dinner.
  L He was wounded .... the war.

| spite so however nevertheless during as |
| because while neither if either although |

2 A There isn't .... food for four.
  B That restaurant was .... rather expensive.
  C We were upset as .... anyone came to the party.
  D She is usually miserable but .... she enjoyed herself.
  E There were .... a few people at the boxing match.
  F We .... missed the train but managed to jump on it as it was leaving.
  G She was .... annoyed at their rudeness.
  H He asked if there was anything .... we needed.
  I He knows he smokes far .... much, but he won't stop.
  J I do apologize. It was .... my fault.

| hardly else entirely only quite |
| almost too really even enough |

3 A Do you want .... one or that one?
  B She was hiding in the room .... the time.
  C There are just a .... tickets left.
  D We had very .... money left by the time we came back from holiday.
  E .... he and his father are extremely bad-tempered.
  F Can you tell me .... the matter is?
  G .... one would you like? The green one or the orange one?
  H It was one of .... moments I shall never forget.

| both those few what little all which this |

3 Complete this passage using just **one** of the **two** words that you are given.

Marco Polo was born in Venice in (1) **maybe/about** 1254. Both his father and uncle were leading merchants who had (2) **already /still** met the Mogul emperor, Kublai Khan. When he was 17, Marco set off with them on an adventure (3) **who/that** would last over 20 years. His father had been given letters to give to the emperor. From Palestine they (4) **passed/drove** through Turkey into northern Iran. In Afghanistan they stopped for a year, probably (5) **recovering/getting** over malaria. They continued overland (6) **through/along** the Great Silk Road and across the Gobi desert.

(7) **So/Eventually**, in 1275 they reached the summer capital (8) **when/where** they met the emperor (9) **that/who** was quite taken (10) **over/by** young Marco. The young man was sent on missions to report back on his master's vast empire. (11) **Although/However** the travellers wanted to return home, the (12) **possibility/opportunity** only came 17 years later. They were given permission to leave (13) **whether/provided** they accompanied a Mogul princess who was to be married in Persia.

They took what, in those days, (14) **should/must** have been a dangerous sea voyage (15) **by/down** the east coast of China and modern Vietnam. They crossed open sea to Ceylon and passed up (16) **a/the** west coast of India. Finally, their party reached Persia. On the last (17) **stage/trip** of their journey home the family was robbed of most of what it has acquired. At last, in 1275 they arrived back in Venice where (18) **few/little** people, if any, believed them to still be alive. Amazingly, this great story would have gone unrecorded if Marco had not been (19) **arrested/captured** in a sea battle. (20) **In/During** his captivity he dictated his story to a fellow prisoner.

4 Complete the passage using only **one** word for each gap.

For a fortnight each summer, we .... (1) to rent the same house by the sea. The house, ... (2) owner worked with my uncle, was on a cliff top overlooking .... (3) channel. .... (4) it was only a couple of hours' drive away .... (5) our house, our preparations .... (6) have done justice to a polar expedition. Suitcases were .... (7) down from the attic and filled with clothes for .... (8) kinds of weather. .... (9), all these things would find .... (10) pushed into the boot. .... (11) extra was placed .... (12) the seats. .... (13) everyone had climbed into the car, there was just a .... (14) space for me between my mother and grandmother. On the way, three .... (15) always happened: we would stop at a pub to please my grandfather, we would eat an .... (16) picnic, and I would .... (17) car sick. .... (18) experiences probably help .... (19) explain why I always insist .... (20) travelling light, preferably by train.

SPEAKING

Discussing texts

In Unit 3 we looked at this part of **Paper 5: Interview.** Here is some more practice on it. Read the texts and, with a partner, discuss:

1 what the situation is.
2 who is speaking.
3 where and when you might come across the texts.

> **A** Oh, we had an absolutely wonderful time. The weather was fantastic. I needn't have taken half my clothes. It was nice going out of season because there were hardly any other tourists there and it was much cheaper. We didn't even need to book, we just turned up and took our pick of places to stay. The only problem was that someone pinched my camera with an exposed film in it. That reminds me — I really must send the form off to the insurance people.
>
> **B** Here are a couple of tips for readers planning a trip to India. You should take some warm clothing, particularly if you are planning a trip to one of the hill stations where it can get chilly at night. To be on the safe side, you should also take anti-malaria pills with you. You have to start them two weeks before you leave to build up your resistance. One last thing — you really must avoid drinking the water. Don't even rinse your mouth out or brush your teeth with it. Watch out for ice cubes too.
>
> **C** We'll be coming in to land shortly, sir. Have you filled out an immigration form? Oh no, that's right, you don't have to if you're an EC citizen. You'll fasten your safety belt now, won't you?
>
> **D** Visitors have to submit their currency declarations before proceeding with immigration formalities. May we remind you that it is strictly forbidden to export local currency when you leave the country.

LANGUAGE STUDY

Obligation and necessity

1 In the four texts there are a number of ways of talking about **obligation** and **necessity**. Match the sentences and definitions.

1 I needn't have taken half my clothes.
2 We didn't even need to book ...
3 I really must send the form off to the insurance people.
4 You should take some warm clothing ...
5 You have to start them two weeks before you leave ...
6 You really must avoid drinking the water.
7 ... you don't have to if you're an EC citizen.
8 Visitors have to submit their currency declarations ...

A Giving simple advice
B Saying that something is not necessary
C Stating a strong internal obligation
D Saying that something is a duty or requirement
E Saying something was not necessary so you did not do it
F Making a strong recommendation
G Saying you did something that was not necessary
H Giving an order/an external obligation

2 In pairs, discuss suitable responses for the following mini-situations.

1 You saw a wonderful exhibition of African art a couple of weeks ago. Tomorrow is its last day. Strongly recommend that your friend goes to see it.

2 A hotel receptionist is explaining what his/her job involves to a visitor. What would he/she say? What would he/she say about things that were not his/her responsibility?

3 You are writing some rules for a student hostel. What would you say about washing-up, noise and guests?

4 You were going to call a taxi but your friend gave you a lift home instead. What would you tell your parents about the taxi?

5 You have had a telephone bill which you have not paid. If you do not pay it tomorrow, your phone will be cut off. What do you say to yourself?

6 A friend is going to study in England. You think it is a good idea if she takes some warm clothes. What would you say to her?

7 You went on a coach trip and took lots of sandwiches with you. You did not eat them because lunch was provided by the tour company. What would you say when you get back home?

8 You went to a friend's house for the weekend. They told you not to bring any food.

LISTENING

Anita is talking to a friend at work about her holiday. Choose the most suitable answers to the following questions.

1 Anita mentions the names of
  A one person.
  B two people.
  C three people.
  D four people.

2 There were about .... on the boat.
  A six
  B ten
  C fifteen
  D twenty

3 The passengers were mostly aged between
  A 20 and 30.
  B 25 and 35.
  C 35 and 45.
  D 45 and 55.

4 The cabins were
  A cramped.
  B airy.
  C big.
  D dirty.

5 Anita liked
  A everybody.
  B nearly everyone.
  C everyone except Ronald.
  D hardly anyone.

WRITING

A letter of complaint

1 In Units1 and 2 we looked at writing an informal letter. Now we will look at writing a semi-formal one. Peter Carr went on a Club 20-30 holiday but did not enjoy himself very much. He wrote a letter of complaint to the travel company.

1 Read his letter and note how many complaints he has to make. Which complaint do you think is the most serious?
2 Underline any words and expressions you think are particularly useful for a letter of complaint.
3 What is different about the layout and the language of this letter that makes it formal?

```
                                                        43 Railway Cuttings
The Managing Director                                   Birmingham
Club 20-30 Holidays
26 Spratt Street
LONDON
W3

1st July 1989

Dear Sir

I am writing to complain about a Club 20-30 holiday I went on at the
resort of Karamelli between 14th and 28th June.

According to your brochure, accommodation was supposed to be in a small
villa. However, when I got to Karamelli, I was taken to a modern hotel a
mile from the sea. Even though it had just been built, there were cracks
everywhere and it looked as if it was going to fall down. The walls were
paper thin and you could hear everything from the neighbouring rooms.

To make matters worse, there were only two other young people in the
hotel and they were both men. The hotel had been taken over by a
package tour of old age pensioners who insisted on playing bingo in the
discotheque every evening. Where was the 'nightlife' I had been promised?

On top of everything, when I mentioned my complaints to your company
representative, she was extremely rude to me. She only reappeared at
the end of my stay and became abusive when I refused to give her a tip.

You can imagine how upset I am at having spent a considerable amount of
money on this holiday. In fact, I expect a full refund plus compensation
for the inconvenience and discomfort I suffered. I trust you will give this
matter your immediate attention.

I look forward to receiving a satisfactory reply by return of post. If I
do not receive satisfaction, I am going to write to the TV Programme
'Value for Money' and expose your operation.

Yours faithfully

Peter Carr

PETER CARR
```

2 Imagine that you are the Managing Director of 20-30 Holidays. You get a lot of complaints but make it a company policy never to refund money. Write a suitable reply to Peter.

3 Write a letter of complaint to the manager of a restaurant where you had a particularly awful evening.

THE IVORY COAST TRAIN

Answers to the multiple choice questions

1 The buildings in Dakar are
   A fairly new. CORRECT
   B good to photograph. WRONG (*The market is good to photograph.*)
   C boring. WRONG (*It does not say this anywhere.*)
   D a contrast. WRONG (*This sentence is incomplete because it does not say what the buildings are a contrast with.*)

2 The Isle of Goree
   A imported slaves. WRONG (*It exported them.*)
   B used to be important. WRONG (*It is **still** important.*)
   C is a centre for slaves. WRONG (*It used to be.*)
   D is cut off from the land. CORRECT (*It is an island*).

3 The journey from Dakar to Bamako
   A moves from rainy to dry country. WRONG (*Although we know that Sahel is dry, we are not told if Dakar is rainy.*)
   B takes three nights. WRONG (*The journey takes two days. We are not told whether this means two or three nights.*)
   C is not by bus. CORRECT (*The journey is by train.*)
   D passes through hills. WRONG (*We do not know this from the text. The landscape changes but it says nothing about hills*).

4 The town of Mopti is
   A just like Venice. WRONG (*It is called the Venice of Africa but this does not mean it is **just** like Venice.*)
   B a market. WRONG (*It is a market **town**.*)
   C cosmopolitan. CORRECT (*We are told that people from different tribes and nationalities mix together, i.e. it is **cosmopolitan.**)
   D west of Bamako. WRONG (*It is east of Bamako.*)

5 The correct answer is C, i.e. *Visitors are **recommended** to go on the River Niger.* Choices A, B and D suggest that there is some sort of obligation.

Conclusions

1 The reading comprehension paper has a lot of tricks and traps. You must approach it with a great deal of respect!
2 This means that you have to study the questions carefully and check every word in them.
3 You can work out the correct answer by eliminating the other possibilities that are wrong.
4 Do not make your choice without thinking very carefully. Answers that appear obvious are often traps!

Examination advice

Try following this pattern when dealing with the reading comprehension paper.

1 Quickly read the text to get a general idea of what it is about.
2 Carefully read the questions so you have a clear idea of why you are going to read the texts.
3 Read the text extremely carefully, identifying those parts of the text that carry answers to the questions.
4 Choose your answer by logically eliminating all the other choices. Don't rush.
5 If in doubt, guess from the most likely answers.

Student B

You are free this weekend. Your friend is going to invite you to his/her parents' house in the country. You love the countryside. You finish work at five o'clock at an office near Charing Cross station in London. Make arrangements to meet and ask what clothes you need to bring.

U N I T 6 *Changes*

LISTENING

1 Rosie York was asked to think of the most important people in her life now and five years ago. Then she had to arrange them in two circles according to how close she was to them.

Study Rosie's *social circles* and try and guess what changes have taken place in her life.

2 Listen to Rosie talking about her life and see if your guesses were correct.

3 Listen again to Rosie and note down the words or expressions to do with relationships which she uses, e.g. *go out with*.

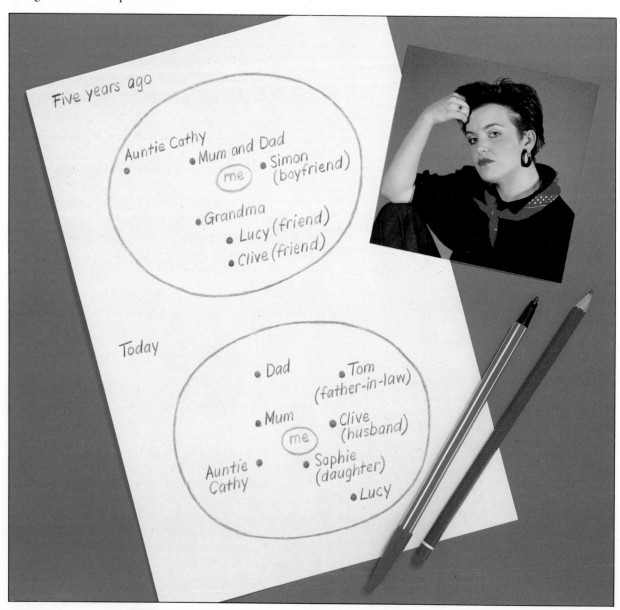

Five years ago

- Auntie Cathy
- Mum and Dad
- me
- Simon (boyfriend)
- Grandma
- Lucy (friend)
- Clive (friend)

Today

- Dad
- Tom (father-in-law)
- Mum
- Clive (husband)
- me
- Auntie Cathy
- Sophie (daughter)
- Lucy

VOCABULARY

In Unit 1 we looked at **Section A** of **Paper 1: Reading comprehension.** Here is some more practice. Remember the grammar of the vocabulary is as important as the meaning. Note that all 25 items here are related to one topic which is not the case in the exam!

1 They took the baby to church to be ....
   A named   B christening   C christened
   D baptism

2 Babies have to learn how to .... before they can walk.
   A creep   B crawl   C stride   D stroll

3 She was unhappy .... her childhood.
   A during   B for   C while   D as

4 The twins look so .... their father.
   A likely   B likeness   C alike   D like

5 Katie really .... her mother. She has got the same character.
   A takes after   B takes up   C takes in
   D takes on

6 That child is really .... by its grandparents.
   A stained   B polluted   C spoilt   D naughty

7 All the children have gone .... mumps.
   A along with   B down with   C out with
   D through with

8 His parents were so .... that he ran away from home.
   A struck   B striped   C severe   D strict

9 It took him ages to .... living in the new town.
   A used to   B accustomed   C get used to
   D use to

10 Don't worry, it's just a difficult stage. She'll .... it.
   A get on with   B get through to   C get up to
   D grow out of

11 Her parents never .... her to go out after eight.
   A made   B let   C agreed   D allowed

12 He .... his best friend over a girl they both liked.
   A fell over   B fell down   C fell out with
   D fell off

13 It is time he .... a wife.
   A seeks   B find   C found   D discovered

14 Are you married or ....?
   A alone   B solitary   C single   D bachelor

15 They are .... to be married next year.
   A promised   B engaging   C engaged
   D intended

16 When they got married, Peter was ....
   A best man   B witness   C groom
   D stepfather

17 Robert and Anna have .... after only two years of marriage.
   A divorce   B broken down   C departed
   D split up

18 They .... the wedding because they no longer loved each other.
   A broke off   B called up   C called off
   D broke up

19 They .... on her new baby.
   A mentioned   B congratulated   C praised
   D commented

20 Godparents .... them when their parents died.
   A took in   B looked for   C took after
   D looked after

21 People often put on weight in ....
   A middle ages   B middle aged   C middle age
   D pension

22 She is so .... even though she is over 90.
   A alive   B lively   C living   D vivid

23 Her aunt's .... was a sad occasion.
   A cemetery   B internment   C coffin
   D funeral

24 They were left a lot of money in their aunt's ....
   A testament   B inheritance   C heritage
   D will

25 They were surprised to come.................... such a large sum.
   A up to   B over   C into   D through

READING

1 Read the description by Maeve Binchy, the Irish writer, of her childhood and answer these questions.

1 How does Maeve feel about her childhood?
2 What was her relationship with her parents like?

I have a very clear earliest memory. I, the first born, was three and a half and my mother was expecting another child. I was constantly asking God to send me a new brother or sister. The 'me' was important because I loved receiving presents. I was furious when the baby arrived, because all the attention moved from me to this small red-faced thing in a cot. It was a great disappointment to me. I had been praying for this moment and now here was a 'thing' which kept on crying with everybody saying how beautiful it was. 'Honestly', I said, 'I would have preferred a rabbit!'

I got very used to walking as a child. I was the eldest of four so there was always somebody in a pram to be wheeled out for a walk.

My mother had this view that if she made our home a centre for lots of our friends to come to then she would know where we all were and she would not have to worry about us. So our house became a meeting point for children of all ages. My mother didn't have much of a home life when she was young: her parents had died when she was a child and she had been brought up by relations. I think that she tried to make up for this by ensuring that her own family would be a very definite and important entity. I know that there is always the danger that you look back too sympathetically — rose coloured spectacles and all that — but my childhood was a great joy.

My Childhood

My father always encouraged us to read. We had a lot of books at home and I was very lucky to grow up in such a house of books. Of course, as a teenager I always felt that when my father advised you to do something you should resist as much as possible, so, when my father used to tell me to read the English classics, I resisted. It was only when I reached my late teens that I started to read them and I began to think that they were good.

My mother was terrific at explaining the facts of life to us. I had known from a very early age how children were born because we had rabbits so there was no great mystery in birth, but I wanted to know how babies were conceived. She told me and I flatly refused to believe it. I thanked her

very much and decided that this was absolutely impossible. Wasn't it terribly sad that my mother was going mad? I discussed the subject with my father.

'I'm very sorry to tell you, Daddy, that Mummy is going insane,' I said.

'Why?' he enquired.

'I could not tell you the things that she has said,' I replied tactfully, 'but she has a very peculiar explanation of how children are conceived.' I gave him a broad outline of her description. 'Don't you think that we should get her a doctor?' I asked with great concern.

'Ah, no,' he said, 'I think she had a point. I think a lot of that could be right.'

I thought to myself, isn't he a wonderfully loyal man!

I went to my first dance when I was 17. I thought that I looked so gorgeous that I could hardly keep my eyes off myself. I wore a blue dress that my cousin had lent me, with a big blue velvet band set down the middle of the dress to let it out. I wore earrings which had made sores in my ears when I was 'rehearsing' for the dance, so I had put sticking plaster on my ears and painted it blue to match the dress. I must have looked absolutely horrific.

Nobody — not one single person — danced with me that night. That was a black time. There weren't many dark passages in my childhood but that most definitely was one.

2 Now read the text more carefully and choose the best answers to these questions.

1 When the baby arrived, Maeve was
   A excited at getting a new present.
   B was disappointed with her mother.
   C was jealous.
   D was fascinated by the new arrival.

2 Friends were always welcome at Maeve's house because her mother
   A liked having children around the house.
   B wanted to keep an eye on her children.
   C had been brought up by relations.
   D had been an orphan.

3 When her father told Maeve to read, she
   A eventually followed his advice.
   B felt lucky to be surrounded by books.
   C naturally obeyed him.
   D never listened.

4 When Maeve was told how babies were conceived, she
   A was not surprised as she had rabbits.
   B believed every word.
   C was deeply shocked.
   D checked with her father.

5 When Maeve went to the dance, she
   A had a good time.
   B dressed up.
   C wore fancy dress.
   D thought she looked awful.

LANGUAGE STUDY
Different forms of **used to**

1 Look at these three sentences and decide what their difference is in meaning.

1 *When my father **used to tell** me to read the English classics, I resisted.*
2 *I **got used to walking** as a child.*
3 *She is **used to sleeping** late on Saturday mornings.*

Used to and its different meanings can be confusing. Study this presentation.

1 *When Arthur was younger, he played tennis every weekend. Two years ago he hurt his back, so he stopped playing tennis. Now he swims instead.*
→ *He **used to play** tennis.*
   used to + INFINITIVE (WITHOUT **to**)

2 *Six months ago Janet left home to go to college. She missed her parents and her hometown, and felt very lonely.*
→ *She **was not used to living** away from home.*
   be used to + VERB + **ing**

3 *Things improved for Janet. Slowly she made friends and started to enjoy herself. After a few months, she no longer missed her family quite so much.*
→ *She **got used to living** away from home.*
   get used to + VERB + **ing**

Notice the pronunciation of **used to**.

Practise saying the following sentences.

1 She used to smoke.
   /ˈjuːstə/

2 I didn't use to live in London.
3 Did you use to play football?

Note He used a pen. /juːzd/

2 Answer these questions using one of these forms:

• used to + infinitive (without *to*).
• be used to + gerund.
• get used to + gerund.

1 Is Bangladesh still part of Pakistan?
2 Do Chinese people find it difficult to eat with chopsticks?
3 Do politicians mind always being criticized in the newspapers?
4 Do your parents still wash you?
5 Why should British and Japanese people be careful when they first drive abroad?
6 Do contact lenses always stay uncomfortable?
7 Do Eskimos complain about the cold?
8 Do parents mind being woken up at night by their babies?

USE OF ENGLISH

1 Fill each of the numbered gaps in the passage using **one** word only in each space.
Here are five of the words to help you.

| except | which | did | about | her |

I have always found it difficult to say .... (1) certain what my memories from my .... (2) childhood are. Are .... (3) memories learnt at a later age from overhearing our parents tell of our exploits? .... (4), there is a particular incident that I would love to claim as a genuine memory.
When I was .... (5) three years old, I went to the post office with my mother .... (6) she was going to buy some stamps. While she was .... (7) served, I happened to notice a small stocking .... (8) was hanging from the counter. It was there .... (9) collect contributions for a charity for .... (10) blind. While .... (11) back was turned, I took the stocking and emptied .... (12) contents into my coat pocket. Of course, I was .... (13) young to know any better. When it was realized what I .... (14) done, everybody roared with laughter .... (15), that is, for my mother who was a little embarrassed. She .... (16) emptied the money back into the stocking .... (17), incidentally, a few pennies of my .... (18). One of the clerks was something of an amateur cartoonist and he .... (19) a drawing of me robbing an old lady. This cartoon .... (20) displayed in the post office for the next couple of years.

2 Change the words in capital letters to fit the context of the sentences.

1 He claimed that his .... had caused him to become a criminal. BRING UP
2 He was given a light sentence because of his .... YOUNG
3 I am tired of your .... behaviour. When are you going to grow up? CHILD
4 .... is a time that is supposed to be free of worries. CHILD
5 It was a difficult .... and she almost lost the baby. PREGNANT

6 .... is traditionally a time when parents and children don't get on very well with each other. ADOLESCENT
7 She was shocked to find out she had been .... ADOPT
8 They were sent to an .... run by nuns. ORPHAN
9 He is thinking of taking early .... next year. RETIRE
10 You would hardly think she has two .... girls. She just looks so young! TEEN

 LISTENING

Listen to Harriet Williams talking about her childhood and some of the major changes that took place during that time. Answer these questions.

1 Harriet's father
   A was a builder.
   B had a responsible job.
   C worked at home a lot.
   D was Indian.

2 How many children were in her family?
   A one
   B two
   C three
   D more than three

3 The worst thing about returning to England was
   A the change in her father.
   B living in a small house.
   C being poorer.
   D not having her clothes made.

4 When Harriet returned to England, she
   A still felt special.
   B enjoyed her new freedom.
   C quickly got used to her new life.
   D eventually helped in the home.

5 Nowadays Harriet
   A regrets the past.
   B is a different person.
   C appreciates what happened.
   D thinks life was unfair to her.

PRONUNCIATION
Long and short vowels

In the **Listening** there are many words which sound almost the same, e.g. **live** and **leave**. The difference is that **live** has a short vowel / ɪ / while **leave** / iː / has a long vowel.

1 Listen to six words and decide which one you hear.

LONG VOWEL	SHORT VOWEL
1 reach	rich
2 feel	fill
3 pool	pull
4 fool	full
5 short	shot
6 caught	cot

2 Decide what the speaker is saying.

1 When did she | leave? / live?
2 Was she | shot? / short?
3 Can you | feel / fill | it?
4 He's a little | fool. / full.
5 What a pretty | pot! / port!

LANGUAGE STUDY
Causative have

1 What is the difference?

1 *Harriet had her clothes made.*
2 *Harriet made her own clothes.*

We use the **have something done** form when we want to say that instead of doing something ourselves someone else does it for us. We usually use the form to talk about some kind of service we receive. In sentence 1 someone made her clothes for her. In sentence 2 she made them herself.
Look at the form of this construction.

*Harriet **had** her clothes **made**.*

2 Transform these sentences using the **causative have.**

1 A local firm redecorated our kitchen.
We ....
2 It's time for me to have a haircut.
It's time I ....
3 A doctor took out her tonsils when she was six.
She ....
4 A tailor altered his suit for the wedding.
He ....
5 She took her photographs to be developed.
She ....
6 A doctor is taking the woman's temperature.
The woman ....
7 A plumber came to fix our central heating.
We ....
8 You look different. Has someone done your hair?
Have you ....

• Can you think of any other things we have done for us?

LANGUAGE STUDY
make or do in fixed combinations

*Harriet's mother **did her best** but at first she **made a mess** of everything.*
Put the words in the box into columns according to whether they combine with **make** or **do**

the bed   money   nothing   an appointment
one's duty   a fuss   a noise   a fool of oneself
someone good   the work   the washing-up

make	do
a mess	*one's best*

WRITING | A biography

1 Read this biography of Charlie Chaplin and find out:

1 how old he was when he first performed in America.
2 when he invented *The Tramp*.
3 how many of his films are mentioned.
4 how many countries he lived in.
5 how many times he was married.

The person I am going to write about is Charlie Chaplin. He has always been one of my favourite actors and I really admire his films.

Charlie was born in London in 1889. Both his parents were music hall performers. His father was a drunkard and his mother later went mad. Life was hard and Charlie and his half-brother, Sidney, were sent to an orphanage for a time.

He first appeared on the stage when he was seven and by the time he was ten was a regular performer. When he was 17, he went on a tour of the USA where he was spotted and given a part in a Hollywood film.

His early films were not particularly successful but in 1915 he made his masterpiece, "The Tramp", in which he first appeared in the baggy trousers and with the hat and cane. Soon he had had his own studio built and was making his own films which included "The Gold Rush", "Modern Times" and "The Great Dictator".

In the 1940s his reputation in the USA started to decline. Silent films were no longer so popular. Chaplin went to Europe but was not allowed to return to the USA because he was suspected of being a communist. The authorities finally let him back in 1972 and he was awarded an Oscar, but by this time he had made Switzerland his home.

Chaplin did not have a very happy personal life and was married four times. He only found happiness with his fourth marriage in 1943. When he died on Christmas Day 1977, the world had lost one of the greatest ever comedians.

2 Read the biography again and decide how happy and successful you think he was at different times of his life on a scale of 1 to 5.

5 = very happy/successful   1 = very unhappy/unsuccessful

	CHILDHOOD	YOUTH	MIDDLE AGE	OLD AGE
happy				
successful				

When you have finished, discuss your opinions with a partner.

3 Write a biography of someone you admire or write your autobiography!

USE OF ENGLISH
3

1 In **Paper** 3 you may have to expand a letter. Study this example. What changes do you have to make to do this task?

Dear Aunt Mary,

1 I/ write/ give you/ wonderful news.
I am writing to give you some wonderful news.

2 Richard/ ask me/ marry him/ I accept.
Richard has asked me to marry him and I have accepted.

3 I/ not know/ whether/ you/ remember him/ but/ you/ be/ introduce/ each other/ last year.
I don't know whether you will remember him but you were introduced to each other last year.

4 We/ get married/ 26th September/ Saint Agatha's church.
We are going to get married on 26th September at Saint Agatha's church.

5 We both hope/ your leg/ be better/ you/ can come/ wedding.
We both hope that your leg is better and that you will be able to come to the wedding.

6 It seem/ ages/ since/ we last see/ each other.
It seems ages since we last saw each other.

7 Anyway/ I/ have to/ say goodbye now/ lots/ other invitations/ send.
Anyway, I'll have to say goodbye now as I have lots of other invitations to send.

Lots of love,
Sally

2 Here and on the next page are two letters for you to expand.

Dear Sally,

1 I/ be/delighted/get/your letter this morning.
....

2 I/have/very clear/memory/Richard. He seem/such/nice/boy.
....

3 Congratulations. I hope/you/be/happy together.
....

4 Unfortunately/I/not be able/come/wedding.
....

5 At my age/I not think/I find/journey/easy.
....

6 All/same/I love give you/wedding present.
....

7 You/write/tell me/what/you/like/present?
....

8 My thoughts/be/with you both/the big day.
....

9 not forget/send me/photographs/piece/wedding cake.
....

All my love and very best wishes for the future,
Aunt Mary

Dear Jerry,

1 I write/say/how sorry/I be/hear/death/your grandfather.

....

2 He be/such/wonderful man. I/miss him/lot.

....

3 His sudden death/must be/shock/you/your family.

....

4 I remember have/long conversation/him/only/few days ago.

....

5 He used/be/active/garden/interested/everything around him.

....

6 I/really like/attend/funeral/pay/last respects.

....

7 If it be/just/family affair/I/quite understand.

....

8 Please/not hesitate/contact me/if/be/anything/I can do/help you.

....

Yours sincerely,
Miranda

SPEAKING

In groups of four, write a sketch (*a short play*) based on this cartoon. Then perform it.

U N I T 7 *The Natural World*

SPEAKING

1 Discuss these pictures with a partner.   3 What is your reaction to them?
2 When and where were they taken?

VOCABULARY

Complete the sentences using one of the words from the box.

ecology fallout pollution waste acid extinct reactor contaminated dumped environment

1 The world in which we live is our ....
2 Smoke, dirt and noise are all types of ....
3 If man continues to hunt whales, they will shortly become ....
4 Every day rubbish and chemicals are taken out to sea and .... It's disgusting and should be stopped.
5 In many parts of the world trees and lakes are being destroyed by .... rain.
6 At Chernobyl, in the USSR, there was an accident at a nuclear .... When it exploded, large areas of the surrounding countryside were .... and there was .... all over Europe.
7 .... is the science that studies the relationship between different life forms in nature.
8 When uranium is used up, it has to be kept in a safe place. It is extremely difficult to dispose of nuclear ....

 READING

1 Read the advertisement and decide what its aim is.

THANK GOD SOMEONE'S MAKING WAVES.

GREENPEACE

The natural world is under violent assault from man.

The seas and rivers are being poisoned by radioactive wastes, by chemical discharges and by the dumping of dangerous toxins and raw sewage. The air we breathe is polluted by smoke and fumes from factories and motor vehicles; even the rain is poisoned.

It's little wonder forests and lakes are being destroyed and everywhere wildlife is disappearing. Yet the destruction continues.

Governments and industries throughout the world are intensifying their efforts to extract the earth's mineral riches and to plunder its living resources.

The great rain-forests and the frozen continents alike are seriously threatened. And this despite the warnings of the scientific community and the deep concern of millions of ordinary people.

Despite the fact, too, that we can create environmentally-clean industries, harness the power of the sun, wind and waves for our energy needs and manage the finite resources of the earth in a way that will safeguard our future and protect all the rich variety of life-forms which share this planet with us.

But there is still hope. The forces of destruction are being challenged across the globe – and at the spearhead of this challenge is Greenpeace.

Wherever the environment is in danger, Greenpeace has made a stand. Its scientific presentations and peaceful direct actions at sea and on land have shocked governments and industries into an awareness that Greenpeace will not allow the natural world to be destroyed.

Those actions, too, have won the admiration and support of millions.

Now you can strengthen the thin green line; you can make your voice heard in defence of the living world by joining Greenpeace today.

Thank God someone's making waves.

2 Choose the best answers to these questions.

1 Which one of these statements is not made?
   A Drinking water is polluted.
   B Radioactive waste poisons the sea.
   C Sewage isn't processed.
   D Cars and factories poison the air.

2 The writer .... forests and lakes are being destroyed.
   A is surprised that
   B is unsure why
   C wonders why
   D understands why

3 Rain-forests are being destroyed because governments and industries
   A are unaware of what they're doing wrong.
   B are rich and powerful.
   C choose to ignore criticism.
   D basically care about the environment.

4 The earth's resources
   A should only be for people.
   B can be made to last longer.
   C will last forever.
   D belong to just humans and animals.

5 Governments and industries
   A don't know what Greenpeace thinks.
   B are forced to understand the problems by Greenpeace.
   C can easily ignore Greenpeace.
   D misunderstand what Greenpeace thinks.

3 Find the words and expressions in the advertisement that mean:

1 attack (*paragraph 1*)
2 rubbish (*paragraph 2*)
3 water and waste from toilets (*paragraph 2*)
4 strong-smelling air (*paragraph 2*)
5 to take by force or illegally (*paragraph 4*)
6 to be in danger (*paragraph 5*)
7 to use a natural force to provide natural power (*paragraph 6*)
8 limited (*paragraph 6*)
9 to protect (*paragraph 6*)
10 to oppose (*paragraph 7*)
11 a leading force (*paragraph 7*)
12 a strong effort of defence (*paragraph 8*)

 VOCABULARY
Word building

1 *Now you can **strengthen** the thin green line.*
Strengthen is a verb which is made from the adjective **strong**.
Work in pairs and complete this table.

ADJECTIVE	NOUN	VERB
wide		
strong		
deep		
weak		
short		
high		

2 Complete these sentences using one of the words from the table. Make any changes that are necessary.

1 They wanted to .... the harbour to allow oil tankers in.
2 These country roads are dangerously narrow. They need ....
3 Greenpeace has .... our understanding of the environment.
4 Industry is laughing at the .... of the new regulations.
5 Only people over a certain .... can join the army.

 LISTENING

You are going to hear an interview between Peter Whitehead, the presenter of a current affairs programme, and Frances Kelly, the leader of the Campaign for Clean Air. While you are listening, make notes about the dangers that the earth faces from these three gases:

1 sulphur dioxide
2 carbon monoxide
3 carbon dioxide

PRONUNCIATION

Saying the **th** sound and **the** 📼

1 Ways of pronouncing *th*

1 **Th** has two pronunciations in English: /θ/ as in **thin** and /ð/ as in **the**. Many students have problems with these two sounds!
2 Go back to the Greenpeace advertisement and find out which **th** words have the /θ/ sound and which have the /ð/ sound.
3 Listen to someone reading part of the Greenpeace text aloud and mark where he makes mistakes with the pronunciation of **th**.

> Despite **the** fact, too, **that** we can create environmentally-clean industries, harness **the** power of **the** sun, wind and waves for our energy needs and manage **the** finite resources of **the** earth in a way **that** will safeguard our future and protect all **the** rich variety of life forms which share **th**is planet with us.

4 Try this tongue twister!
Arthur's brother's thinner than Arthur's father.

2 Ways of saying *the*

1 The words that follow **the** can change its pronunciation.
If **the** is followed by a consonant, it is pronounced /ðə/, e.g. *the sun*.
If **the** is followed by a vowel, then its pronunciation becomes /ði:/ and we often use the linking pronunciation / j /, e.g. *the earth*.
2 Practise saying these examples from the text and group them according to how we say **the**. Where necessary, use the linking pronunciation / j /.
A the seas   C the rain   E the environment
B the air   D the power   F the admiration

LANGUAGE STUDY

The definite article

1 *The natural world is under assault from man.*
The can be used for many different reasons. Match each reason with an example sentence or phrase.

1 There was a man outside. **The** man was tall.
2 **The** moon and **the** world both go around **the** sun.
3 I can't find **the** pen I bought yesterday.
4 Where's **the** cat? (*the cat that lives in this house*)
5 Paul is in **the** garden.
6 She plays **the** piano well.
7 It was **the** best film I have ever seen.
8 **the** rich, **the** poor, **the** unemployed
9 **the** United States of America, **the** Queen of Spain

A with superlatives
B when only one exists
C when the object or person is mentioned for a second time
D when we make something definite by adding extra information
E with musical instruments
F with adjectives to describe a class or group
G when location means only one thing is being referred to
H with titles and place names that have the idea **of**
I when the object is known by everybody

2 When we do NOT use the article

Match the examples with their descriptions.

1	love/hate/beauty	A	most names of towns, cities and countries
2	Cats are beautiful.	B	uncountable nouns
3	petrol/sugar/milk/wood	C	countable objects in general
4	home/work/hospital	D	abstract nouns
5	New York/Brazil	E	some places/locations

3 Complete the following sentences with either a, the or nothing.

1 .... life is getting easier for .... rich.
2 .... accidents are generally caused by people driving too fast. This is certainly true of .... accident I had last year.
3 Caroline plays .... violin really well.
4 They gave Anna .... guitar for Christmas.
5 .... park has many examples of .... wildlife: .... birds, ... deer, and, of course, ... foxes.
6 Who's .... person who borrowed my umbrella?
7 .... pollution is destroying .... environment.
8 She is going to visit .... India and .... USSR.
9 We have nothing to fear but .... fear itself.
10 .... price of .... petrol is going up. .... petrol I bought yesterday was .... cheapest in .... area.
11 .... wood is much dearer than it used to be. In fact, ... wood I used to make .... shelves in the living room was £3 .... metre.
12 She's .... fascinating woman. Did you know she's .... leader of .... opposition party?

4 Correct these sentences. If you have to change them, use a, the or delete.

1 The most people in United States have two cars.
2 Mary works in an university.
3 Did you have the nice time at a school today, Amanda?
4 Beatles are most wonderful group I've ever heard.
5 What did you think of book I lent you?
6 She is going to be doctor.
7 They have two holiday homes, one in mountains and one at seaside.
8 All people who live in this town work at car factory.
9 Where's Mary? She is in sitting room talking on phone.
10 She's wearing jeans. In fact, they're jeans she wore last week.

VOCABULARY | Phrasal verbs

Substitute the verbs in **bold** with one of the phrasal verbs from the box.

> bring up   die out   get rid of   carry on   go ahead
> turn up   use up   look into   turn into   turn down

Make any changes that are necessary.

1 I am sorry to **mention** this, but would you mind turning the radio down?
2 When sulphur dioxide mixes with other elements, it **becomes** acid rain.
3 The company was told that it could **begin** the construction of a new plant.
4 If nations **continue** to dump nuclear waste at sea, the oceans will become poisoned.
5 The council has **refused** the request to build another car park.
6 The rhinoceros will **become extinct** if people continue to hunt it.
7 Government officials are **investigating** reports that the lake is being polluted by a chemical factory.
8 Oil, coal and gas are being consumed so quickly that supplies will shortly be **finished.**
9 Factory bosses should think carefully about where they **throw away** waste.
10 When they **arrived** at the demonstration, it had already finished.

READING

1 Read this article about pollution and see how much you agree with what the writer has to say on the subject.

Living in the modern world

Pollution is one of the greatest problems facing mankind. The nuclear accident at Chernobyl and the poisoning of the river Rhine by chemicals are just two recent examples of disasters affecting the environment. What can be done? Some people say there is no practical solution. However, I believe the problem can be dealt with on three levels: internationally, nationally, and, last but not least, on a personal level.

Let us begin by looking at the type of international action that can be taken. The first point I would like to make is that, when a disaster such as that at Chernobyl occurs, it affects millions of people. Radiation does not respect international borders. In my opinion, there should be strict safety regulations governing the construction of reactors. Furthermore, reactors should be regularly inspected by teams of international experts. Similarly, if a country wishes to get rid of nuclear waste by dumping it at sea, it should only be allowed once the matter has been thoroughly discussed by all the countries that would be affected. Environmental disasters can be avoided.

Let us now look at what can be done on a national level. Governments must be prepared to take action against pollution. For instance, air pollution could be reduced if car manufacturers and companies were made to fit effective filters on car exhausts and factory chimneys. These measures would in turn help to reduce the damage caused to lakes and forests by acid rain.

Lastly, what can we do as individuals? Firstly, I believe we should all be prepared to make changes to our lifestyles. Personally, I try and use public transport or my bicycle as much as possible. When I buy petrol, I make sure that it is the lead free variety. Secondly, we can protest against companies responsible for pollution by making our opinions known and hitting them in the pocket. For example, if the public boycotted products such as aerosols, which damage the ozone layer, then manufacturers would have to change their packaging policies. We would show them that we are not prepared to let them get away with destroying the environment.

To sum up, I have tried to show that there are steps that can be taken in the fight against pollution. It is a problem that can be solved given the right levels of commitment. However, only by acting as individuals first, can we expect governments to act in their turn.

2 Are these statements **true, false** or **not stated**.

1 Pollution gets a lot of publicity.
2 Many people accept pollution as a part of life.
3 The writer is a pessimist.
4 Chernobyl was nobody's fault.
5 The writer can't afford to use his car all the time.
6 Consumers have power.
7 We can all fight pollution.
8 What we do is more important than what governments do.

3 Now read the article again and answer these questions about its organization.

1 What does the first line of each paragraph do?
2 What words or expressions does the writer use to:
  A give his own opinions?
  B list his reasons and put them in order?
3 Several times the writer uses questions in the text. Find some examples of these questions. Why are they used?

LANGUAGE STUDY

make, let and allow

1 *... air pollution could be reduced if car manufacturers and companies were **made to** fit effective filters ...*
Study these sentences which show the relationship between **make, let** and **allow**. (**Make** here means **to force someone to do something**.)

Active   *He made her eat her carrots.*
Passive *She was made to eat her carrots.*

Active   *He did not let her leave the table.*
Passive *She was not let to leave the table.* WRONG
Passive *She was not allowed to leave the table.* CORRECT

Two rules
1 If we want to use **make** in this sense in the passive, we have to remember to add **to**.
2 We cannot use **let** in the passive. Instead, we have to use **allow to**.

2 Using **make, let** and **allow**, write as many sentences as you can based on these situations.

1 Anna wanted to go to the disco but her father told her she couldn't.
2 The teacher told Paul that he had to stay at school until he had finished the exercise.
3 The soldier did not want to jump into the river but the sergeant insisted.

● Think of your own childhood, schooldays or military service and tell a partner what your parents, teachers or officers made you or didn't let you do.

LANGUAGE STUDY
The passive

1 *... the problem **can be dealt with** on three levels ...*
Change the following sentences from the active to the passive.

1 Farmers spray the trees each week.
The trees ....

2 That factory is producing more and more pollution.
More and more pollution ....

3 Someone saw them dumping rubbish.
They ....

4 Demonstrators have broken into the oil refinery.
The oil refinery ....

5 The owners had hidden all the evidence by the time the police arrived.
All the evidence ....

6 A scientist was redesigning the reactor.
The reactor ....

7 A child can understand the problem.
The problem ....

8 The prime minister is going to open the enquiry.
The enquiry ....

9 We shall notify the police about this matter.
The police ....

10 Someone should have written to the newspapers.
The newspapers ....

2 In pairs or small groups, work out how the passive is formed with:

1 the present simple and past simple tenses
2 the present and past continuous tenses
3 the **going to** future
4 the present and past perfect tenses
5 modals like **can** and **must**
6 modals in the past like **might have**

WRITING
The opinion question

1 The article about pollution, which you read and analyzed, gives the writer's opinion on the subject. In **Paper 2: Composition** there is always one question which asks you to give your opinion on a subject. Success in doing this kind of composition depends on four things:

1 having sufficient topic vocabulary.
2 having sufficient ideas and opinions.
3 having the structures and expressions to use in this type of essay.
4 good essay planning and organization.

You are going to write an essay answering this question:
Even at the end of the Twentieth Century people are still dying of hunger. What can be done to solve this problem?

First of all, we shall look at topic vocabulary and then at a text which should help you with ideas.

2 Vocabulary
Join these split sentences.

1 They haven't got enough to eat because ...
2 The size of a population can be controlled ...
3 It didn't rain for two years and ...
4 All the animals ...
5 Wheat and rice are ...
6 Another word for help ...
7 There is a terrible **famine** so ...
8 If you get a loan from the bank, ...
9 The desert has become green ...

A is **aid**.
B two kinds of **crop**.
C died of **thirst**.
D through **contraception**.
E people are dying of **starvation**.
F you are in **debt** and you have to pay **interest**.
G the **harvest** failed.
H since **irrigation** was introduced.
I there was an awful **drought**.

3 Reading

This text should give you some ideas for the essay you are going to write on hunger.

When you have read it, match the pictures to the paragraphs.

GIVE BACK THE LAND

STOP USING MONEY AGAINST THE POOR

PUT FOOD FIRST

CONTROL THE CORPORATIONS

AIM FOR SOCIAL JUSTICE

4 In pairs, plan your composition.

When your teacher has checked your plan, write the composition.

Use the expressions in the article about pollution on page 80 to help you.

PARAGRAPH

1 Debt has been crippling the Third World over the last five years. Countries can be forced to sacrifice as much as half their export earnings as repayments on debts to Western banks. And, before the West offers new loans, it insists on drastic cuts in welfare spending which hit the deprived hardest. Debt repayments should never amount to more than ten per cent of a country's export earnings.

2 Hunger only affects the poor — there are no hungry countries, just bigger or smaller numbers of hungry people within countries. The government's commitment to social justice isn't the icing on the cake — it is the cake itself. The only way to end hunger is to reduce poverty and inequality, and make feeding people a priority.

3 Much of the world's cultivable land is owned by people with large farms — particularly in the Americas. Left to itself, this situation will worsen, not get better, since it is the large farmers who can borrow and afford mechanization and fertilizer. Land reform is not only essential for reasons of justice — it also increases food production, since smallholders farm much more efficiently than the big landowners. But sharing out the land will not work if inequality persists elsewhere in society.

4 The world is now a supermarket for the rich world's consumers — and the managers of that supermarket are the multinational agribusiness corporations. These companies control production prices, often holding small farmers under contract for their export crops. This way they can buy harvests at controlled prices while leaving the risks of bad weather and plant disease on the shoulders of the individual farmer.

5 Developing countries are still locked into a farming system created for the benefit of the rich world. Their best land and resources are used to grow cash crops for export rather than food. The trend away from crops for local consumption must be halted and farmers paid more for their harvests.

SPEAKING

Giving opinions, agreeing and disagreeing

1 Study these expressions and practise saying them aloud.

Giving your opinion	*I think ... I feel ... I believe ... In **my** opinion, ...* *From **my** point of view, ... As I see it, ...*
Strongly agreeing	*I **quite** agree. **Absolute**ly!*
Partly agreeing	*Well, I see your point but ...* *I agree up to a point but ...*
Disagreeing	*I am afraid I don't agree. That's not true.*
Strongly disagreeing	***What nonsense! What rubbish!***

2 With a partner, read and respond to these statements. Begin your responses by using one of the expressions we have just looked at in 1.

1 Smoking should be banned in all public places.
2 Men are much better drivers than women.
3 Nuclear energy will kill all of us in the end.
4 You can never trust a man with a beard.
5 People are old at 40.
6 Marijuana and alcohol are just harmless drugs.
7 People should live together before they get married.

● Make up some statements of your own and see how the class reacts to them.

3 Role play

In **Paper 5: Interview** you may have to take part in a role play. In this role play you are going to take part in a meeting to decide what to do about a local pollution problem. First, read about the situation. Your teacher will give you roles.

Techtronics is a large multinational company which produces chemical products. One of its factories is in Blackthorpe, a small town in the north of England. The factory is the biggest employer in the town and has over 1,200 workers. Recently, there have been a number of complaints because the amount of dirt coming from the factory chimneys seems to have gone up. Mr/Mrs Dobson, the mayor of Blackthorpe, has called a meeting of interested parties to find out more about the problem. Four other people are there. They are: Mike Smith, the manager of the factory; Marion Green, the leader of a local environmental group called Spearhead; Arthur McCarthy, trade union boss at the factory, and Jennifer Hunter, a local housewife. Their task is to try and find a solution to the problem.

You are **Mr/Mrs Dobson,** the mayor of Blackthorpe. You are in charge of the meeting and must make sure that everybody has the chance to speak. There is going to be another election soon and you want to solve the problem caused by the factory. You have met the American president of Techtronics and know that he will close the factory down if there is too much criticism. You think that the company should try and improve its image locally.

You are **Marion Green** from Spearhead. You are more worried about damage to the environment than the loss of jobs. Your scientists believe that the dirt is dangerous. You want the factory to fit new filters to its chimneys. You are worried about new reports of toxic fumes coming from pipes near a field where children play. You would like to organize a demonstration.

You are **Mike Smith,** the factory manager. You think the chimneys are dirty rather than dangerous. New filters would cost $3 million. The American company would close the factory down rather than spend that kind of money. Your boss says you can spend $300,000 on improving the company's image. You know there are fumes coming from pipes near a playing field. You are trying to get them fixed now.

You are **Arthur McCarthy,** the trade union boss at the factory. You aren't very worried about dirt from the chimneys. You think that jobs are more important. Blackthorpe is in an area of high unemployment. However, you think that Techtronics could do more for the town. The local amateur football team is looking for a sponsor and a new community centre is needed for old people.

You are **Jennifer Hunter,** a local housewife. You have written to Mike Smith but haven't had a reply yet. Your children, who play in a field near the factory, have been ill recently. Last week your washing was made dirty by the chimneys. Your husband is a worker at the factory.

USE OF ENGLISH

In the last unit, we looked at expanding a letter. Here is some more practice. Make all the changes and additions necessary to produce, from the following sets of words and phrases, sentences which together make a complete letter of complaint from Jennifer Hunter to Mike Smith.

Dear Mr. Smith

1 I write/complain/dirt/smoke/come/your factory/chimneys.
2 Two days ago/I decide/do/my washing.
3 I wash/sheets/put them out to dry/it/be/nice sunny day/there/be/breeze.
4 When I take washing in/I be/horrified/discover/it be covered in dirty marks.
5 I/assume/breeze I mention/carry/dirt/your chimneys.
6 If this be case/I must complain/strongest possible terms.
7 This be/not only because of my sheets/but because we have two small children/who be make/breathe same air.
8 Until this incident/I think/your chimneys/be safe and clean.
9 I already/write/local Member of Parliament/this matter.
10 Furthermore/I must warn you/I write/local newspaper tomorrow.
11 I look forward/receive your reply.

Yours sincerely,
Mrs Jennifer Hunter

U N I T 8 *Judging by appearances*

SPEAKING

It is said that it is possible to judge a person's character from their face. Study the photographs and say what they tell you about the characters of the people shown.

READING

1 Think of three things you would like to find out about the art of face analysis. Then read the article to see if your questions are answered.

2 Now read the article again and choose the best answers to these questions.

1 *Siang Mien*
  A was a secret art.
  B was known by emperors.
  C is quite recent.
  D is generally practised.

2 Chinese mothers think men with
  A big ears are exciting.
  B small ear lobes are kind.
  C flat noses are not interesting.
  D small ear lobes and flat noses can't be trusted.

3 A jade-face is best described as
  A flat at the bottom and pointed at the top.
  B pointed at the top and bottom.
  C pointed at the bottom but flat at the top.
  D oval.

4 People with eyes of different sizes
  A often have stepparents.
  B are usually unhappy.
  C are often divorced.
  D are supposed to be generous.

5 Princess Diana
  A proves the truth of *Siang Mien*.
  B has low ears.
  C was over 30 when she became famous.
  D has an ordinary face.

Secrets of the FACE

Is it really possible to judge someone's character from their face? The Chinese seem to think so. For over 2,000 years they have been practising *Siang Mien*, which is the art of judging character and predicting fortune from an analysis of the face. It developed in the ancient imperial courts of China and consisted of jealously guarded secrets that were passed from master to a few chosen apprentices. The secrets of face analysis were hidden away in special books which only a very few could look at.

These secrets cannot have been that well guarded and must have got out because practically all Chinese practise some form of face analysis. Mothers tell their daughters that men with flat noses and small ear lobes will make shy and rather dull husbands.

So how does this analysis work? Well, to start with, people's faces can be classified according to one of ten basic shapes, each of which has its own special name. A triangular face, for example, is called a *fire-face*. One which is square is known as a *wall-face*, while one which is diamond shaped is a *jade-face*. There are even *bucket-faces*!

Once the basic shape has been decided, then parts of the face such as the eyes, nose, chin and mouth can be analyzed in their turn. People who have not got conventional or beautiful faces should not worry, as ugly people tend to be lucky.

Anyway, let us see how *Siang Mien* works by using Princess Diana as a practical example. To begin with, we can say that she has got a *jade-face* which means that she must be strong-willed. This shape also belongs to people who are said to have had difficult childhoods. As you may know, the Princess's parents were divorced when she was a child and this time must have been a period of great unhappiness.

Turning to more specific features, we can see that one eye is a little larger than the other. It is a known fact that people with eyes of different sizes are often brought up by stepparents. They are also believed to be charming as well as being capable of great jealousy. We can see from this photograph that the top of her ears goes above the line of her eyebrows. People who have high ears such as hers are likely to become famous before the age of 30, while those who combine this with eyes of different sizes will be lucky.

3 tend to

According to the text, ugly people **tend to** be lucky. **Tend to** means **generally but not always**, e.g. *People from Scandinavian countries tend to have fair hair and blue eyes. They also tend to be quite calm and quiet.*

Now make some general statements about the people from your own country.

4 Discussion points

1 How far do you believe in this science?
2 Do you consider it to be convincing, ridiculous or amusing?
3 Could *Siang Mien* be dangerous in any way?

LANGUAGE STUDY

Predictions and guesses

1 In the article it says *Princess Diana has got a jade-face which means that she* **must be strong-willed**. **Must** is being used to make a deduction.
Match the example sentences of deductions and predictions with their definitions.

1 The killer will try to leave the country.
2 He can't be far away — the body is still warm.
3 She must be hiding somewhere in the area.
4 He must have been murdered between six and ten o'clock.
5 His wife can't have killed him. She was visiting her mother.

A A guess about a situation in the present   (*positive*)
B A guess about a situation in the past   (*negative*)
C A prediction
D A guess about a situation in the past   (*positive*)
E A guess about a situation in the present   (*negative*)

2 Search the text for examples of these forms and see how they are being used.

3 Make some predictions. Who do you think will win the next election in your country? Which country will win the World Cup? What will **you** be doing in ten years? What will your life be like then?

4 Make deductions about the situations in the pictures. If you are not so sure, use **might (not) do/have done** rather than **must** or **can't**.

PRONUNCIATION

 Students often confuse the different vowel sounds in **can** /kæn/, **must** /mʌst/ and **can't** /kɑːnt/.

1 Put these 12 words in the box in columns according to their vowel sound.

much cat match hum hat march ham cart harm hut cut heart	/kæn/ **can**	/mʌst/ **must**	/kɑːnt/ **can't**
	....	....	....
	....	....	....
	....	....	....
	....	....	....

2 Now listen to the 12 words and number them in the order you hear them.

3 Student A reads one of the following pairs of sentences aloud and Student B decides which is being said.

A Can / Can't | Tom ring you back?

B We don't have enough | stuff. / staff.

C Do you want it fried in | batter? / butter?

D I'm going to the | match. / march.

E Will you put your | cup / cap | away?

F She | can't / can | talk to you.

LANGUAGE STUDY

A further passive construction

*They are also **believed to be** charming.*
This means the same as *People believe they are charming.*

*She is **said to have had** a difficult childhood.*
This means that we think she had a difficult childhood but are not absolutely sure.
We can use this kind of passive construction with verbs like **say, believe, claim, think** and **know** to talk about the present and the past in a tentative way.

Change these sentences using this passive construction.

1 People **claim** the Mona Lisa is the world's most famous painting.
2 Experts **believe** it was a portrait of a nobleman.
3 They **say** her smile hides a secret.
4 Many **believe** it is Leonardo's masterpiece.
5 Scientists **know** he was a wonderful engineer too.
6 Historians **think** he was unhappy in old age.

VOCABULARY

Adjectives of personality

1 Fill the gaps with a word from the box. Only use each word **once**.

1 Janet is incredibly .... She always arrives on time and does her job well.
2 It's impossible to say anything to his grandmother. One word and she starts crying. She is so ....
3 I wonder why he is so .... He has got lots of money but he hates spending it.
4 When she was a child, her parents were incredibly .... Whenever she did the smallest thing wrong, they would send her to bed.
5 Ann is such a .... girl. She is always laughing and smiling.
6 Come on, Maria! You can't go on a country walk wearing high heels. Do be .... for once.
7 I'll give you a lift home if you're .... to me.
8 She was so..................... and understanding. When I told her my problems, I immediately felt better afterwards.
9 In westerns, the hero is always .... He always beats his enemies and can put up with any hardship.
10 That's the second plate you've broken this week. Why do you have to be so .... ?
11 I think he is an extremely .... boy. He laughs at stupid things and never concentrates in class.
12 Children are often really .... They hide behind their mothers when guests come.
13 Don't be .... , Cathy. You've got to learn to share things with other children.
14 She is 100% .... I'd leave my money, car, anything, for her to look after.
15 When I broke my leg, the nurse was so .... that she hardly hurt me at all.
16 Why do you get angry all the time? You are so ....
17 Bob is my best friend. He remained .... through all my problems.
18 He is such a .... person with his boring little job and his boring little wife.
19 He is terribly .... Once he has made up his mind, it is impossible to get him to change it even if it's obvious that he is wrong.
20 The general was really .... Just when the enemy thought it had won the battle, he played his best card.

> selfish bad-tempered tough crafty sensitive sensible
> strict trustworthy dull shy mean reliable stubborn
> silly nice cheerful sympathetic clumsy loyal gentle

2 All of these words are adjectives. We can make nouns from most of them. Use your dictionaries to find out what nouns can be made from these adjectives. Then write a short description of your character which includes both your good and bad points!

3 In pairs, use the pictures and descriptions below to work out your partner's character. When you have finished, compare it with the description your partner wrote about him or herself in 2. If you disagree, ask the rest of the class to decide on the truth!

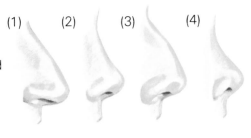

NOSE
long (1) = careful, worried
short (2) = cheerful, broadminded
high-bridged (3) = active, curious
short and snub (4) = secretive
large = aggressive, tough
wide = careless, fun-loving

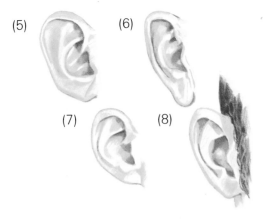

EARS
wide (5) = practical, sensible
large lobes (6) = independent,
                  strong-minded
no lobes (7) = dull, dependent
sticking out (8) = imaginative
pointed = ambitious, crafty
small = instinctive, sensitive

MOUTH
curving up (9) = gentle, naive
large (10) = generous, loyal
straight lips (11) = self-controlled
curved lips (12) = moody
small = trusting

EYES
slanting (13) = modest, tolerant
wide open (14) = friendly
close together (15) = energetic
deep set (16) = confident

VOCABULARY

Physical description and adjective order

1 When we describe somebody, we tend to follow this order in our description: height, build, age, hair, eyes, face, complexion, extra features, dress. Study this example.

> My cousin, Paul, is a tallish man in his mid thirties. He is a bit plump and has got long wavy brown hair. He has a round, friendly-looking face and small brown eyes. He has got a little scar on his cheek from an accident he had when he was a child. He wears glasses and has got a beard. He isn't very smart and tends to wear shabby clothes.

2 Height and build

1 When we use common adjectives like **short** and **tall**, we can modify them by adding **ish**. *She is tallish* means *she is fairly but not very tall*. We do this mostly in spoken English. Think of other adjectives that can be modified in this way.

2 Here are some other ways of describing build which may be new to you. Match the definition with the word.

Someone who is	frail stocky slim plump skinny	is	overweight. attractively thin. (old) and weak-looking. unattractively thin. shortish but well-built.

3 How would you describe the build of the following people?

Note We say **plump** rather than **fat** in a description of someone to be polite.

3 Age

1 In pairs, decide what ages these words and expressions describe.

   A elderly   **B** in your teens   **C** a youth   **D** a pensioner
   E middle-aged   **F** a toddler   **G** in your early/mid/late thirties

2 Tell your partner your age without being exact about it.

Note We use **elderly** as a polite way of referring to old people.

4 Face

1 Find people in your class who have got round, oval and square faces.
2 What are scars, wrinkles and freckles?
3 Who is sun-tanned and who is pale?

5 Eyes

When we describe people's eyes, we normally start with their size, followed by shape and colour, e.g.
She has got big round blue eyes.

SIZE + SHAPE + COLOUR

Put the following sentences into the correct order.

1 Susan has got brown/large/round/eyes.
2 Klaus has got blue/bright/eyes/small.
3 Mary has eyes/green/friendly/large.
4 Mariko has/almond-shaped/large/dark brown/eyes.

6 Hair

When we describe people's hair, we normally give length first followed by colour and style, e.g.
He has got short black curly hair.

LENGTH + COLOUR + STYLE

Match these adjectives with the pictures.

1 balding   2 straight   3 curly   4 bald   5 spiky   6 wavy

7 Clothes

The adjectives in the first column describe how people look. Working in pairs, and using your dictionaries if necessary, match the adjectives to their definitions.

1 casual   **A** old/worn a lot
2 scruffy   **B** carefully dressed
3 shabby   **C** well (expensively) dressed
4 smart   **D** informal
5 neat   **E** untidy/dirty

8
Write a short description of a famous person without saying who it is. Read the description to the rest of the class and see if they can guess who it is.

SPEAKING

Five people live in the same street, each in a different house. From the information you are given, work out where they live and what they look like.
Work in groups and see which group can solve the problem first.

1 Emily lives at number one next to a middle-aged person.
2 An elderly lady lives in between the two middle-aged people.
3 Anna has got straight hair. The man next door in number two has a moustache.
4 Brian is young and only has one neighbour.
5 Anna's female neighbour is rather overweight.
6 Diane has straight hair like her neighbour who also has wrinkles.
7 Charles is skinny and envious of his neighbour's curly brown hair.
8 The woman in her late thirties is worried about her neighbour's pale complexion.
9 Charles's younger neighbour is plump unlike his other neighbour who is the opposite.
10 The young man with the beard goes to the pub with the man who is bald.
11 One of Diane's neighbours is stocky.
12 Emily has a cousin on the street with wavy hair.
13 The youngest woman with straight hair walks with a limp.
14 Brian's cousin has got freckles.
15 The oldest woman wears glasses.

 LISTENING

You are going to hear a news item about a person who has disappeared.
You will hear the item twice.

1 Decide whether these statements are **true, false** or **not stated.**
   A The missing person isn't a woman.
   B The missing person is tall.
   C The missing person was probably carrying a yellow bag.
   D The missing person was definitely wearing jeans.
   E The missing person may have been wearing a jumper.
   F Someone thinks they saw the missing person after 8.30 p.m.

2 Complete the description of the man the police would like to interview. Include anything that might be important.

age: _____ height: _____

hair: _____ glasses: _____

dress: _____

car: _____

any other details: _____

_____

NUMBER _____

NAME _____

AGE _____

BUILD _____

HAIR _____

COMPLEXION _____

EXTRA FEATURES _____

LISTENING

Clive and Jenny both work in the same office. Last Friday, just for fun, they decided to reply to advertisements in the 'lonely hearts' column of a magazine. It is Monday morning and they are comparing notes about their weekend dates.

1 Read the 'lonely hearts' column advertisements and check that you understand them.

Male

PLUMP, fun-loving company director seeks warm, mature lady for companionship and cuddles.
FRIENDLY, leftish man into films, walks and history seeks bright woman to share fun times.
SHY, foreign language student seeks sensitive blonde to bring him out of his shell.
TOTTENHAM HOTSPUR FAN seeks sporty girl to join him at home and away matches!

Female

BRIGHT, professional woman, happy and successful, seeks honest and affectionate male to make her life complete.
GEMINI — attractive and articulate — seeks creative and compatible man.
CULTURE-LOVING lady seeks slim and attractive escort for opera and dinner parties.
SINCERE non-smoking vegetarian seeks meaningful relationship for now and for ever!

---

2 Listen to Clive and Jenny's conversation and decide who they made a date with.

3 Listen again to the coversation and match their descriptions of their dates to the illustrations.

4 Discusion points

1 Would you ever answer an advertisement in a 'lonely hearts' column?
2 If you were putting an ad in a 'lonely hearts' column, how would you describe yearself?
3 Can you match up the men and women in the ads above?

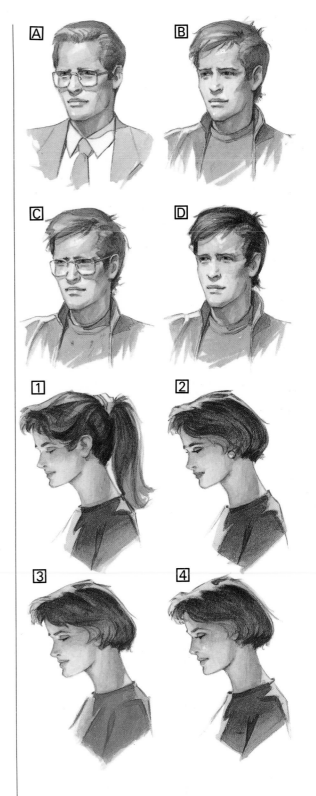

VOCABULARY

Word building

1 Working in pairs, and with the help of your dictionaries, complete the table.

ADJECTIVE	OPPOSITE	ADVERB	NOUN
happy	unhappy	happily	happiness
			sympathy
	unreliable		
		kindly	
loyal			
		honestly	
patient			
			responsibility
	insensitive		

2 What different ways are used to make the adjective negative?

USE OF ENGLISH
3

1 As we know from Unit 2, in **Paper 3** you may be asked to change a given word into the correct part of speech depending on its context.

Example: *Don't leave money lying around. He's* ....*untrustworthy*...... . TRUST

Explanation: The word **trust** is a noun. In this context, we need the adjective from this word, **trustworthy**. However, the context tells us that the adjective must have a negative sense, so we use **untrustworthy**.

To summarize, in order to do this exercise successfully, you have to:
1 decide which part of speech you have to use, noun, adverb, adjective and so on.
2 decide from the context whether the word you use will be used in a positive or negative sense.

2 Now do this exercise in exactly the same way. The table in **Vocabulary** above will help you with some of them.

1 The judge told him it was .... to drink and drive, and banned him for a year.   RESPONSIBLE
2 This poem shows the wonderful .... of the poet.   SENSITIVE
3 She divorced him because of his .... to the children.   KIND
4 The evening was .... spent playing cards and talking.   ENJOY
5 The keys were locked inside the car. .... , a side window was open.   LUCK
6 Due to the clerk's .... , we missed the train.   STUBBORN
7 Thousands of people are living in .... after the earthquake.   MISERABLE
8 The thing I hate about John is his ....   RELIABLE
9 Her boss accused her of being over- ....   AMBITION
10 She upset him with a .... remark about his big nose.   TACT

SPEAKING

Describing a photograph

As you know from Unit 3, in **Paper 5: Interview** you have to describe a photograph. We are now going to have a detailed look at this part of the exam.

1 Complete the commentary on this photograph using the words and phrases in the box.

This photo (1) .... a young mother and her two kids.
I (2) .... they must be from somewhere in South America.
(3) .... they're in a crowded market, although it's difficult to
(4) .... because you can't see much of (5) ....
    The mother has her hair up in a bun and a roundish face.
She (6) .... fed up but this (7) .... because she's
tired. (8) .... she's had a busy day shopping. The child with
its arm around her neck (9) .... a little boy. It seems he's
aware of the camera.
    The little girl (10) .... more than three. She is a little plump
but you can see that she really (11) .... her mother.
(12) .... her mother's mouth and the most beautiful almond-
shaped eyes. She is holding something in her hand ... I can't really
(13) .... It (14) .... be a charm or (15) ....
it's a crucifix.

takes after   tell   she has got   looks   shows   perhaps
might   the background   would say   can't be   looks like
could be   make it out   it looks as though   maybe

2 In the commentary **look** is used in different ways.
When do we use: **1** look? **2** look like? **3** look as though/if?

3 In pairs, discuss this photo and then write a description of it using the commentary on the first photo as a model.

UNIT 9 | *Teenage Cults*

SPEAKING   In groups, look at the pictures and tell the story. Then decide what the people might have said.

VOCABULARY

Clothes

Complete the sentences with an appropriate word connected with clothes.

1 These trousers are really *t*..................... . I'll have to go on a diet.
2 Mind you don't wash it in hot water. You don't want it to *s*..................... .
3 This jacket doesn't quite *m*..................... these trousers.
4 She wanted to make room in her *w*..................... so she threw away all her old clothes.
5 Go on! Buy that skirt. The colour really *s*..................... you.
6 These trousers are really too big. They look *b*..................... .
7 Passengers are advised to wear *l*..................... , comfortable clothing when flying.
8 You can't possibly wear that striped shirt with a tartan tie. They *c*..................... horribly.
9 Don't worry if these jeans are too big. We can always *t*..................... them *i*..................... at the waist and turn *u*..................... the legs.
10 I'd like a blouse to *g*..................... with this skirt. What would you suggest?

LISTENING

Listen to three short conversations which take place in a clothes shop and complete the grid as much as you can.

	CUSTOMER 1	CUSTOMER 2	CUSTOMER 3
What did they buy?			
What didn't they buy?			
Why not?			

SPEAKING

In small groups, discuss:

1 how important being fashionably dressed is to you.
2 what makes fashions change?
3 what different kinds of clothes are shown in the photographs.
4 if fashion is just a question of wearing different styles.

PRONUNCIATION

Rising intonation 📼

1 In each of the three conversations in the **Listening** one of the speakers repeats something that someone has just said. Listen again to the conversations and identify the repetitions. Say why they happen.

2 In pairs, practise showing surprise to these situations. Student A says something. Student B reacts, repeating what A says. Improvize!
   A You have decided to accept your teacher's offer of marriage.
   B You had a minor car accident on the way to school today.
   C You knocked over a cyclist (but she's OK).
   D You have decided to give up English and learn Russian instead.
   E You borrowed some money from your friend's wallet without asking.
   F You can't pay your friend back until the end of the month.

READING

1 You are going to read a British newspaper article which tries to explain why teenagers are attracted to certain teenage 'cults'. The writer puts forward seven explanations. Read the article on the next page and decide which explanations you think are the most and the least convincing.

2 Choose the best answers to the following questions.

1 In general, young people are most influenced by
   A their social class.
   B their friends.
   C pop stars.
   D their parents.

2 Which statement best sums up the global village theory?
   A Young people need to be independent.
   B People of the same age unite.
   C Efficient communication leads to copying.
   D Big business causes change.

3 The drug culture theory suggests
   A young people are alienated.
   B skinheads are relaxed.
   C nicotine isn't a drug.
   D everybody takes drugs.

4 Which of the following theories does the writer seem to accept the most?
   A The reaction theory.
   B The pop idol theory.
   C The class theory.
   D The capitalist domination theory.

5 The writer concludes that cults
   A make kids join them.
   B are evil.
   C provide an identity.
   D stay the same.

3 Discussion points

1 In small groups, see how much you know about hippies, punk and skinheads in terms of:
   • appearance
   • music
   • beliefs

2 Do you have groups like this in your own country?

Understanding Teenage Cults

Ever since the early 1950s there have been attempts to explain why youth cults happen. None of them has been entirely convincing.

The reaction theory Teenagers want to show how different they are from their parents and, perhaps more importantly, their older brothers and sisters. If the last fashion had long hair and wide trousers, then the next one will have short hair and narrow trousers. There seems to be a lot of truth in this.

The global village theory Because of films, records, television and radio, teenagers are aware of what their contemporaries are doing all around the English-speaking world. Almost as soon as there were hippies in San Francisco, we had them too. A problem with this theory is that the time has to be right for a style to be adopted. The main influence on teenagers remains their friends.

The teenage idol theory Teenagers imitate the people they look up to, chiefly film stars and pop performers. When David Bowie used eye shadow, so did many of his male fans. However, this only succeeds if the pop star is in tune with the way youth culture is already going.

The technology theory Many developments in teenage culture were possible only because of new technology. Electric guitars plus amplification meant you could have pop groups and pop festivals. The transistor radio made pop music inevitable.

The drug culture theory This theory suggests that the nature of a youth cult is determined by the drugs that it takes. Speed (*amphetamine*) equals aggression and energy — think of punks and skinheads. Pot (*cannabis*) equals relaxation and mysticism — think of hippies. Even "ordinary" society has its drugs such as alcohol and nicotine. But maybe the style came before the drug.

The capitalist domination theory Youth culture happened because commerce understood that teenagers had money to spend and worked out ways of making them buy more records, clothes and concert tickets. This does not account for cults that were anti-consumerist like the punks and hippies.

The class theory This is a sophisticated left wing theory. Youth cults assert the solidarity of young people who are victimized by society. Skinheads take aspects of working class culture to an extreme. They almost enjoy people looking down on them.

There is no simple explanation. My own research points to these general observations. Firstly, cults don't arrive fully-formed, flourish and then die. They are constantly changing and their message evolving. Secondly, teenagers only join a cult if it feels right, but most kids want to be something and cults give them something to be.

LANGUAGE STUDY

Conjunctions

Conjunctions are used to join nouns, verbs, adjectives or parts of a sentence together. Choose the most appropriate conjunction to complete the following sentences. Remember that the sentences must agree with the sense of the newspaper article you have just read.

1 Teenagers want to show they're different .... they react against their families.
   A because **B** but **C** so

2 .... do they react against their parents but against older brothers and sisters too.
   A Also **B** Not only **C** And

3 Young people know what's going on .... communications are so good.
   A yet **B** since **C** so

4 .... they are able to copy each other.
   A Even so **B** As well **C** That's why

5 .... teenagers copy pop idols, the stars have to understand what the young really want.
   A However **B** Although **C** In spite of

6 Pop music is popular .... modern technology.
   A owing to **B** because **C** due to

7 There are other drugs .... alcohol and nicotine.
   A as well **B** too **C** besides

8 Businessmen invented youth cults .... to exploit the young.
   A in order **B** therefore **C** also

9 .... , this does not explain cults such as the punks.
   A In addition **B** Nevertheless **C** Therefore

10 Skinheads feel victimized by society. .... , they form a culture of their own.
   A Consequently **B** In order to **C** And

VOCABULARY

Phrasal verbs

1 All of these phrasal verbs are used in this unit. Match the phrasal verb with the definitions on the right.

1 go along with   **A** cause someone to be disappointed
2 talk over   **B** put in order/put right
3 live up to   **C** be brave enough to accept or deal with something
4 sort out   **D** respect
5 put down   **E** agree with/support
6 look down on   **F** speak about something thoroughly
7 face up to   **G** have a low opinion of someone
8 let down   **H** keep to high standards
9 look up to   **I** make someone feel unimportant

2 Fill the gaps with the missing phrasal verbs from **1**.

1 Stop running away from the situation. It's time you .... it.
2 He promised to pick me up from the station but he didn't. That's the second time he has .... me .... this week.
3 She was never able to .... her mother's high expectations of her.
4 I don't know why you .... that boy. You agree with everything he says and copy everything he does.
5 Why do you .... her .... every time she speaks? I'm not surprised she has no self-confidence.
6 Don't be such a snob, Marcia. Just because she doesn't have as much money as you that's no reason to .... her.
7 After he had spent all evening .... the problem .... with his best friend, he felt much better about things.
8 You can't expect me to .... the plan before I've had an opportunity to study it carefully.
9 Oh, no! It's going to take ages to .... these documents .... Why doesn't he ever file anything?

READING

People often write to advice columns in magazines for help. Read this letter to Angela Strong and find out what the problem is.

Dear Angela,

I was horrified when I found out that my 12-year-old daughter had been arrested for stealing some make-up from a high street chemist. This happened because she had been dared by some older children from her school. She was so frightened that she started crying — which is what attracted the attention of the shop assistant. The police were called and she was given a telling-off at the police station.

Since this terrifying experience, she has been too afraid to go out on her own and cries all the time. My husband doesn't seem to care that much. He says that she shouldn't have stolen in the first place and was unlucky to be caught. Now it is over she must learn to live with it. But I feel a failure as a parent and am afraid that my child will turn to crime later on in life.

Yours sincerely,
Ashamed

103

USE OF ENGLISH

1 Make all the changes and additions necessary to produce, from the following sets of words and phrases, sentences which together make a complete letter of reply from Angela Strong.

Dear Ashamed,

1 I think/you should/follow your/husband/example/try/put/incident behind you/your family.
2 Your daughter/know/she/let you down/not/feel happy until/she feel/you/forgive/her.
3 Your feelings/guilt/be unjustified/you should/put/energy into/make/your child/feel better.
4 If I/be/you/I/not/worry/much/about/her/turn/to crime.
5 She/be/terrified/whole thing/and/be/put off/ever take/anything ever again.
6 Most kids/do/something like this/some stage/she be/just/unlucky enough/be/catch.
7 If she not/get over/experience soon/you can/always/take her away/short holiday/give her/change/scene.
8 Then she/can/face up to/relatives/neighbours.
9 I/be sure you/can/sort things out.

Yours sincerely,
Angela Strong

2 Fill each of the numbered blanks in the following passage. Use only **one** word in each space.

Dear Angela,

Six years ago, when I was a student, I was short of money. So once a week I .... (1) to go home to see my parents and get a decent meal. Although I had a good relationship with my mother, I never got .... (2) well with my father. I could never live up to .... (3) high expectations of me.
    One day I did a .... (4) terrible thing. I stole some money from him. I .... (5) started off by asking him if he .... (6) lend me ten pounds. He refused saying he had .... (7) given me enough and it was .... (8) I became more responsible with money. You know what it is like .... (9) a student. I'd run out of money and wanted to take a girl out. When he refused, I .... (10) him of being mean and we had a terrible row. He left the house and I was .... (11) angry that I stole ten pounds from his wallet.
    When he found out that the money was gone, he .... (12) who had .... (13) it and banned me from the house. .... (14) then I have returned but he has never really forgiven me and still looks down on me for .... (15) I did.
    My mother is very upset and I really .... (16) to work towards creating a happy relationship with my father for .... (17) our sakes. Half of me wants to say 'sorry Dad' while .... (18) other half still thinks he is ridiculous .... (19) having kept this attitude up for so long. How can I bridge .... (20) endless misunderstanding?

Yours sincerely,
Richard A

WRITING

Write a letter to Richard from Angela giving him advice. Remember that it should be written in an informal, friendly style. Look through Angela's letter to Dear Ashamed and find the language she uses to give advice. What other ways of giving advice do you know?

VOCABULARY

Participle adjectives

1 In the first letter to Angela Strong the writer said
*Since this **terrifying** experience she has been too afraid to go out on her own.*
Many verbs can be used to make adjectives from their present and part participles,
e.g. **to terrify, terrifying, terrified.**
*The experience was **terrifying**. She was **terrified** (by it).*

ACTIVE SENSE   PASSIVE SENSE

	-ed		-ing
We feel	bored tired depressed	because something is	boring. tiring. depressing.

2 Choose the right participle adjective to fit the sentence.

1 She was **horrified/horrifying** when she heard the news.
2 You look **depressed/depressing**. What's wrong?
3 The results were **disappointed/disappointing**.
4 His strange behaviour is **worried/worrying.**
5 Her table manners are awful. She's a **disgusted/disgusting** eater.
6 You'll find flying less **tired/tiring** than driving.
7 Don't be **bored/boring**, Freddie. I want to dance!
8 Sorry darling, I don't mean to be **bored/boring** and spoil your evening but can we leave now?

105

LANGUAGE STUDY
Reported speech

1 Richard in his letter to Angela Strong wrote
*When he found out the money was gone, he **asked me who had taken** it.*
In pairs, look at these reported speech sentences and decide what is wrong with them.

1 He told the problem was difficult.
2 She said him to turn down the music.
3 He asked her how much money did he take.
4 He asked whether he can help.
5 She explained to him the problem.

Now work out the basic grammar rules for:

A when we use **say** and **tell**, and how they are different grammatically.
B what happens to questions when we report them.
C what **usually** happens to tenses when they are reported.
D what happens to the word order of a sentence using **explain**.

3 Changes with modals
1 What do **may**, **can** and **will** become in reported speech?
2 What happens to **would, could, should, ought to, had better, might, used to** and **must** in reported speech?
3 Change this First conditional sentence into reported speech.
Helen: *If you do that again, I'll hit you.*
She told him ....

Note Second and Third conditional sentences stay the same.

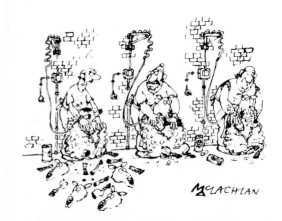

"I thought you said you'd done this before"

2 Tense changes
Complete this chart of tense changes.

DIRECT SPEECH	REPORTED SPEECH
1 Paul: She lives in London. *(present simple)*	Paul *said she lived in London* (..........*PAST SIMPLE*..........).
2 Mary: .... (...........................)	Mary told me she was working. *(past continuous)*
3 Karin: I've been to Spain. *(present perfect)*	She said .... (...........................)
4 .... (...........................)	Peter said he'd been living there for ages. *(past perfect continuous)*
5 Anna: I had made a mistake. *(past perfect)*	She told me .... (...........................)
6 Kate: We were watching TV. *(past continuous)*	She said .... (...........................)

NOTE It is not always necessary to make these changes. For example, if something that was said is **still** true then we can use the present simple instead of the past simple.

Alan: *I live in Germany.* → He said he lives in Germany.

4 Other changes

1 Change these sentences from reported into direct speech. Think carefully how you are going to deal with the words in **bold**.

A She said she was going to leave **the following day**.

B He said that **that** was the record he had bought **two days earlier**.

C They said the parcel would arrive **in two days' time**.

D He asked if anyone had come on **the previous day**.

E We told them their flat would be ready **the following month**.

F He said he had called **earlier** but nobody had answered the door.

G She asked him if **that day** was his birthday.

2 Now complete this table.

DIRECT SPEECH	REPORTED SPEECH
A this	....
B this/that	....
C today	....
D yesterday	....
E the day before yesterday	....
F before	....
G tomorrow	....
H the day after tomorrow	....
I next week/month/year	....

5 Reporting advice and suggestions

1 This is how you report advice.
She said, 'If I were you, I would take an umbrella.'
→ *She **advised** me to take an umbrella.*

2 This is how you report a suggestion.
She said, 'Let's play tennis.'
→ *She **suggested** playing tennis.*

> *suggest* + VERB + *ing* (GERUND)

or *She **suggested** that they (should) play tennis.*

Suggest is a complicated reporting verb to use because there are lots of possibilities. The best one to remember is **Suggest that someone should do something.**

3 Change these sentences with advice and suggestions into reported speech.

A 'If you take my advice you'll go by train,' Sue told Richard.

B 'How about watching TV?' Arthur asked.

C Julian: Why don't you go to the cinema, Gina?

D Doctor: You should take more exercise, Miss Brown.

E Grandmother: If I were you, Fatima, I'd wear a scarf.

6 Change these sentences from direct into reported speech and vice versa.

1 Carol: Don't make so much noise, Peter.
Carol told ....

2 Sue: If I were you, Richard, I'd go by train.
Sue advised ....

3 Paul said he was going to visit China the following year.
Paul: I'm ....

4 The porter told us the train had left five minutes earlier.
Porter: I'm sorry but ....

5 Robin: 'Why doesn't Sarah buy them this picture as a wedding present?'
Robin suggested ....

6 'Do you know where my tennis raquet is, Mum?' Sharon asked.
Sharon asked her mother ....

7 'If you're late tomorrow, I'm going to sack you.'
The boss warned him ....

8 He told us it was his birthday in two days' time.
'It's ....,'

9 'It's the first time I've flown.'
He said he ....

10 The doctor suggested that I should take more exercise.
I ....

Note Question 2 of **Paper 3** usually contains one transformation item like this.

LISTENING

1 Rachel has telephoned a radio phone-in programme for some advice. The person in the studio is Dr Howard who specializes in the emotional problems of young people.

Listen to Part A of the call and decide if these statements are **true** or **false**.

1 Mark is unemployed.
2 Mark left school a year ago.
3 Mark is no longer the same boy.
4 Rachel mentions three changes of character.
5 Rachel doesn't like his friends.
6 Rachel knows that Mark is taking drugs.
7 A television has disappeared from the home.
8 Mark likes listening to music.
9 Money is safe in the home.
10 Mark's father isn't at home very much.

- In pairs, discuss what you think is wrong with Mark.
  What advice would you give to his mother?

2 Now listen to Part B of the call. Note down the advice Dr Howard gives Rachel. In your opinion, does she give good advice?

- Imagine that you are writing to a friend about the programme. Write a short report of what Rachel told/asked the doctor and the advice/suggestions she provided.

WRITING

In Unit 7, we looked at the *Opinion question* in **Paper 2: Composition.** In this unit, we are going to look at two answers to the question
More and more young people are turning to drugs. Why is this so and what can be done about the problem?

1 Look at the answer on the next page and study the type of mistake that has been made.

There are some good ideas in this essay but there are quite a few mistakes. Some, such as numbers 2, 3 and 8, can be forgiven because the language rules are complicated. Others, such as 5, 9, 13 and 14, are much more serious. They are basic mistakes and could have been avoided! When you write an essay, it is essential that you check it for basic mistakes.

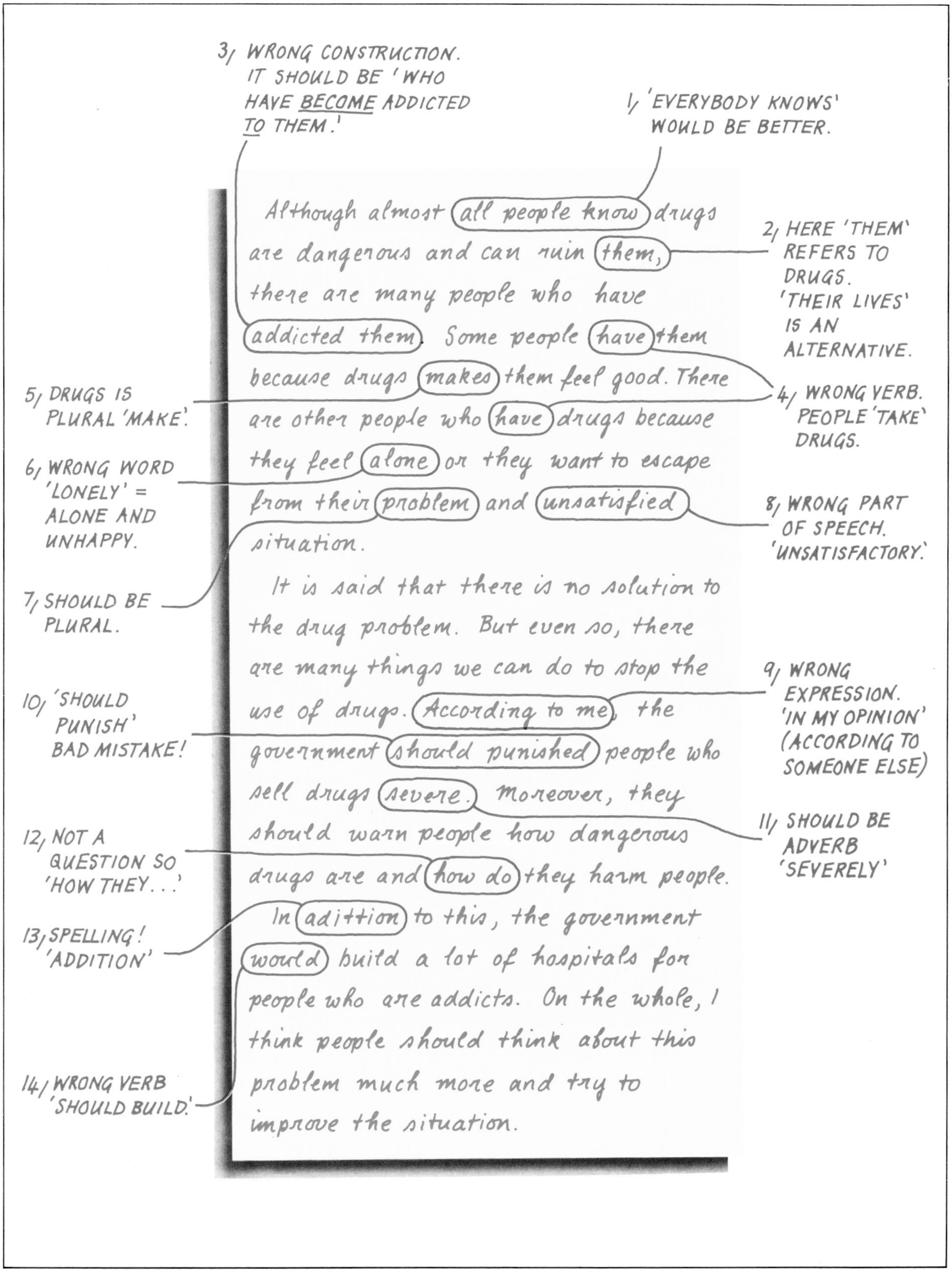

3/ WRONG CONSTRUCTION.
IT SHOULD BE 'WHO
HAVE <u>BECOME</u> ADDICTED
<u>TO</u> THEM.'

1/ 'EVERYBODY KNOWS'
WOULD BE BETTER.

Although almost (all people know) drugs
are dangerous and can ruin (them,)
there are many people who have
(addicted them). Some people (have) them
because drugs (makes) them feel good. There
are other people who (have) drugs because
they feel (alone) or they want to escape
from their (problem) and (unsatisfied)
situation.

It is said that there is no solution to
the drug problem. But even so, there
are many things we can do to stop the
use of drugs. (According to me), the
government (should punished) people who
sell drugs (severe.) Moreover, they
should warn people how dangerous
drugs are and (how do) they harm people.
In (adittion) to this, the government
(would) build a lot of hospitals for
people who are addicts. On the whole, I
think people should think about this
problem much more and try to
improve the situation.

2/ HERE 'THEM'
REFERS TO
DRUGS.
'THEIR LIVES'
IS AN
ALTERNATIVE.

4/ WRONG VERB.
PEOPLE 'TAKE'
DRUGS.

5/ DRUGS IS
PLURAL 'MAKE'.

6/ WRONG WORD
'LONELY' =
ALONE AND
UNHAPPY.

7/ SHOULD BE
PLURAL.

8/ WRONG PART
OF SPEECH.
'UNSATISFACTORY.'

9/ WRONG
EXPRESSION.
'IN MY OPINION'
(ACCORDING TO
SOMEONE ELSE)

10/ 'SHOULD
PUNISH'
BAD MISTAKE!

11/ SHOULD BE
ADVERB
'SEVERELY'

12/ NOT A
QUESTION SO
'HOW THEY...'

13/ SPELLING!
'ADDITION'

14/ WRONG VERB
'SHOULD BUILD.'

2 Working in pairs, look at another answer to the same question and try to correct it. See if you can find any mistakes which you think are serious!

(1)

The young people nowdays are in some ways lost. They don't expect much from life. Also they are living in difficults times. They keep trying to find out ways to enjoy themselves. In addition for them forbiden things is very attractive such as drugs alcohol etc.

So many of these youngs are getting addicted to drugs. Most of them start using drugs when they are adloescent. In that case they ar trying to solve their familiar problems. The main victims are those who is too weak to stand certain situations such as the lost of one of their parents or their

(2)

divorce. Drugs are very attractive at the first time. But after their "mask" falls and they become drug addicts.

I think both parents and goverments should do something very strong to the solution of this problem. The parents have to give freedom to their children to talk about their problem and doubts. The goverment should open a national debate in all places to discuss the drugs.

3 What can we learn from this? There are two main points:

1 When we have written a composition, we must read it through carefully to check for mistakes. In particular, we must check that the basic grammar is correct and that the different parts of sentences agree with each other.
2 We must get to know our mistakes. Lots of people make the same kind of mistake time after time. Look at your last four or five compositions and make a list of the kind of mistakes which you regularly make.

● Write your own answer to the question about drugs. Where you can, use expressions and ideas from the two compositions you have analyzed.

USE OF ENGLISH

1 Complete these sentences using a word based on **lose**.

1 Don't get upset. You have to learn to be a good ....
2 It took him many years to get over the .... of his wife.
3 Oh dear, are you .... ? Don't worry, we'll find your mummy.
4 I wish you wouldn't .... things all the time.
5 The .... keys turned up under a magazine.

2 Complete these sentences using a word based on **satisfy**.

1 Winning the championship was a .... experience.
2 I'm afraid your work is .... You will have to improve it or else!
3 I must express my .... with the service in your hotel. The room is dirty and the staff are extremely rude.
4 Now are you .... ? You have made your poor mother cry!
5 Would you mind .... my curiosity. How old are you?

3 Here is some more practice for the **Paper 3** activity where you have to read and process information.

A popular newspaper has run a competition to recognize and reward remarkable young people. The following five finalists have performed acts of bravery or kindness or overcome serious disabilities to help in the community.
Write three 60 word paragraphs explaining your choices for first, second and third prizes.

FIRST PRIZE:
£3,000
to help support a scheme of benefit to the community

SECOND PRIZE:
£1,000
either to a scheme of benefit to the community or to an individual over the age of 16 for outstanding bravery

THIRD PRIZE:
£250
support to a scheme or individual

Julius Craig, aged 18. Julius helps young cancer victims even though he has cancer himself. Now he spends time each week visiting hospitals and giving support to cancer sufferers and their families. His example has given hope to many people.

Jacinta Ryan, aged 6. Last winter she rescued her playmate, Wayne, aged 4, who fell into an icy canal near their home. She jumped into the water and held him up until help arrived.

Andrea Cooper, aged 18. Andrea has started a community centre for unemployed people and the homeless in her local church. She collects clothing and helps with temporary accommodation.

Dilip Singh, aged 9. He was hurt while beating off a group of youths who had tried to steal money from his uncle's shop. There have been a lot of racial attacks in his part of town.

Cora McBride, aged 21. Cora has started a scheme in Northern Ireland to encourage better understanding between Catholic and Protestant children. Children go on holiday together and work on community projects.

Paragraph 1
I think that .... should win first prize because ....
Paragraph 2
.... deserves second prize for ....
Paragraph 3
My choice for third prize is ....

UNIT 10 *Us and Animals*

1 Animals quiz

Look at the picture of the animals above and try to name them.
Then answer the questions.

1 What is the largest animal in the world?
2 What is the fastest mammal in the world?
3 What is the commonest mammal in the world?
4 What is the most poisonous snake in the world?
5 What is the largest bird in the world?
6 What is the rarest large mammal in the world?
7 Which is the creature most dangerous to man?

2 Our attitudes towards animals

Below are 15 animals that are often the object of our love and fear.
Which do you think are the most beautiful?

eagle	panda	elephant	cockroach	snake
crocodile	spider	mosquito	dolphin	lion
giraffe	seal	whale	rat	polar bear

When you have finished, compare your answers with a partner.

READING

1 Read the article about the work of Jane Goodall. Note down what human beings and chimpanzees have in common.

JUNGLE WARFARE

For 25 years now, Jane Goodall has been studying chimpanzees at Gombe in Tanzania. This has already become the longest project on animals living in the wild. However, she intends to carry on her research for the rest of her life as chimps can live for anything up to 50 years. In this way, she hopes to observe the progress of an entire generation of chimps from birth to death.

The most surprising discovery of the early years of her research was that chimps used tools. For example, they poked small branches into holes in trees in order to extract insects to eat. Before this discovery, people had thought that chimps weren't intelligent enough to use tools. Another distinction between chimpanzees and human beings had been eliminated.

There are, of course, many easily observed similarities. Chimps kiss and cuddle like humans. Furthermore, they are self-aware and can recognize themselves in mirrors which other animals are unable to do. Strong family relationships are seen to exist and even adolescent chimps run back to mother when they find themselves in trouble! What's more, chimps seem to have some kind of structured language in which they can express a certain number of abstract concepts.

However, not everything about chimps is so cosy and comfortable. Starting in the early seventies, Jane Goodall was horrified to observe a prolonged war waged by one group of chimps on another 'tribe' which had broken away some years earlier. This observation altered her perception of chimps, making them seem, in her eyes, even closer to humans. It had always been thought that humans were the cruellest of animals and that what made us unique was our habit of making war on one another. The chimps' war showed that this was not the case.

It appears that there was no reason for the conflict other than a perhaps natural hostility to aliens. Even though the younger males were the most aggressive of the group, they were sometimes joined by a single, aggressive female. Chimps in the enemy group were hunted individually and cruelly killed. The excitement and enjoyment Jane Goodall witnessed were very similar to that shown by human beings taking part in war or criminal activity. Despite the fact that a lion may kill a zebra for food or a bull fight to assert its dominance over the herd, this 'law of the jungle' must be distinguished from the behaviour of the chimps. It has been claimed that war was a key factor in developing human social organization and the selection of the strongest and the most intelligent. Jane Goodall believes that she may have witnessed this in its earliest stage of development.

During the war, some females left the losing side to join the aggressors. Although they were accepted, not one of their babies was allowed to live. This is a common pattern in other animals, and the adoption of infants from an alien group is unknown in other species apart from man. Nevertheless, older chimps may adopt younger brothers or sisters if the mother dies.

This may help us understand why stepfatherhood can be unsuccessful for humans and how difficult it may be to create artificial families. Child-beating is at its most common where stepparents are concerned. It may be just too difficult for most people to truly accept children that are not their own.

Goodall is currently studying how the early experiences of baby chimps affect them in later life — particularly how a badly-mothered chimp will become a bad mother herself. Such research may give us clues about human behaviour and motivation. She writes, 'Because chimps are less complex, it is easier to study these effects. The scars of childhood are less apparent where humans learn how to hide their feelings.'

2 Choose the best answers to these questions.

1 Jane Goodall wants to stay in the wild because
  A she wants to study a whole life cycle of chimps.
  B she feels she hasn't made much progress.
  C she wants to die with the animals she loves.
  D she wants to stay a record 50 years.

2 Which statement is not true about humans and chimps.
  A Both show affection.
  B Both enjoy war.
  C Both adopt freely.
  D Both use tools.

3 It seems that the chimps fought
  A to extend their territory.
  B because they didn't like strangers.
  C to win extra females.
  D because there was a food shortage.

4 Adoption
  A is unknown among chimps.
  B never occurs in nature.
  C occurs within chimp families.
  D often leads to child-beating.

5 It is useful to study chimp behaviour because
  A we can learn how to be better parents.
  B it is just like human behaviour.
  C it may help us understand ourselves better.
  D it is not as complex as our behaviour

LANGUAGE STUDY

The comparison of adjectives and adverbs

1 *It had always been thought that humans were* **the cruellest** *of animals.*
Work with a partner and decide if these sentences are correct. Where necessary, correct them.

1 She speaks good French.
2 James is more big than Mark.
3 She is the most good at English in our class.
4 She runs fast.
5 He plays tennis good.
6 His car isn't so good as mine.
7 Jane is very lazy. She works hardly.
8 You look coldly. Shall I shut the window?
9 They play chess much more badly than us.

2 Now answer these questions about the grammatical rules for making comparisons.

1 How do we make the comparative and superlative of a short adjective like **tall**?
2 How do we make the comparative and superlative of long adjectives like **beautiful**?
3 How do we make comparative sentences using **as**?
4 What happens to **good, bad** and **far** in the comparative and superlative?
5 How do we make adverbs from the following?
  A slow   **C** angry   **E** good
  B beautiful **D** hard, fast
6 What are the comparative adverbs for **good** and **bad**?
7 When do we use adjectives and adverbs after verbs like **look, feel, seem, sound, smell** and **appear**?
8 What's the comparative of **friendly** and **clever**?

3 Complete the sentences using the adjectives in *italics*.

1 Angela is .... person in the class. (*young*)
2 Corinne speaks good French but Lucia speaks it .... (*good*)
3 The bill isn't .... as I thought it would be. (*expensive*)
4 He bought .... petrol he could find. (*cheap*)
5 Don't kick the ball so .... You'll break a window. (*hard*)
6 Her teacher speaks .... than ours. (*slow*)
7 They live .... from school than I do. (*far*)
8 Your son's behaviour is .... in the whole school. (*bad*)
9 It was .... film I had ever seen. (*boring*)
10 You don't look very .... Cheer up! (*happy*)
11 She sings .... than anyone else in the choir. (*beautiful*)
12 He sounded .... than he did yesterday. By tomorrow he will have forgotten! (*angry*)
13 What's for supper? Something smells .... (*good*)
14 There isn't a room .... than this one. (*comfortable*)
15 She works ....(*quick*) than Julian but not .... than Alison. (*fast*)

4 Write sentences comparing two countries or towns that you have visited. Try and say something about the character of the people who live there as well as the place.

LANGUAGE STUDY
Contrasting ideas

1 In the article about Jane Goodall it says
*Some females left the losing side to join the aggressors. **Although** they were accepted, not one of their babies was allowed to live.*
There are two ideas in the second sentence:
They were accepted.
Not one of their babies was allowed to live.
Although is used to emphasize the contrast between the two ideas.

Let's look at other ways in which we can contrast ideas.

1 *She had a cold **but** she still played tennis.*
But shows that there is a contrast in the sentence. People don't normally play tennis if they have got a cold.

2 *Even though she had a cold, she still played tennis.*
Even though + SUBJECT + VERB

Even though emphasizes the contrast more than **although**.

3 *Despite (her) having a cold, she still played tennis.*
Despite + (POSSESSIVE ADJ.) + VERB + ing

Despite her cold, she still played tennis.
Despite + NOUN

Despite the fact she had a cold, she still played tennis.
Despite the fact + SUBJECT + VERB

4 *She had a cold. **However**, she still played tennis.*
However comes **between** the two ideas that are contrasted.

5 *She had a cold. **Nevertheless**, she still played tennis.*
Again, **nevertheless** comes **between** the two ideas that are contrasted.

2 In pairs, look at these sentences and, where necessary, correct them.

1 Although she is three years old, she can't walk.
2 Despite the restaurant was empty, the stranger came and sat opposite me.
3 However, the wine was bad the food was delicious.
4 Although it was a beautiful day, we had a marvellous day on the beach.
5 Even though he was unhappy, he was rich.

3 Now join these sentences using as many of the methods we have just looked at as possible.

1 It really enjoys going for walks. Their dog is very old.
2 They have a small flat. They have got a large dog.
3 They tried to housetrain the puppy. It didn't work.
4 Pigs are supposed to be dirty. Actually, they're quite clean.
5 The squirrels look tame. They may bite you.

● Invent sentences/situations of your own to show that you understand these different ways of making contrasts.

LANGUAGE STUDY

Sentences with **too** and **enough**

Study this sentence taken from the article about Jane Goodall. How could we rephrase it using **too**?

People had thought chimps weren't intelligent **enough** *to use tools.*

NEGATIVE VERB + ADJ. + enough + TO DO SOMETHING

Use **too** or **enough** to make sentences based on the following situations.

1 Annie was really tired last night. She didn't take the dog for a walk.
2 The birdcage was high up on the wall. The cat couldn't reach it.
3 The zebra was very slow. The lion caught it.
4 What a stupid dog! It will never learn that trick!
5 The children want to have rabbits as pets. They're only three and four.

SPEAKING

Describing a photograph

With a partner, discuss:

1 who the people in the photograph are.
2 where they are and what they are doing.
3 what the people are like.

WRITING

In the *Opinion question* in **Paper 2: Composition** you are often asked to comment on the rights and wrongs or the advantages and disadvantages of something. We are now going to look at how to go about answering this question.

1 On the next page you are going to read an answer to the question
'The killing of animals for their fur should be banned' Do you agree?'
Before you read it, try and guess the arguments that would be used by each side. What would those who support the use of fur say? What would their opponents say? Work in pairs.

Now read the answer and see if your predictions were correct.

(1)

People in the fur industry believe that the practice of killing animals for their fur should continue. On the other hand, many people want to ban it altogether. Which side is right? First of all, let us look at the arguments used to support the fur trade and then look at those of its opponents.

To begin with, the fur industry claims that fur is a natural form of clothing that man has worn since prehistoric times. Next, it is beautiful to look at and wear. In addition, the need for fur allows hunters to continue their traditional way of life, besides providing thousands of jobs in the fashion trade. Animals bred on farms lead much more comfortable lives than those in the wild which lead short and savage existences.

Opponents believe that there are now so many different kinds of

(2)

clothing that it is no longer necessary, or indeed justifiable, to kill animals for their fur. In addition, while the industry provides jobs, they are based on unacceptable cruelty. For instance, wild animals may take days to die in cruel traps. Moreover, even though conditions on farms may be good, they prevent animals living as nature intended.

On balance, I believe that the killing of animals for their fur should be banned. Despite the fact that fur is beautiful to look at and wear, man should learn to share the earth with other animals, not just exploit them. After all, there is now artificial fur which can give the look and feel of real fur without the cruelty.

2 Understanding the organization of the composition

1 Note down any topic vocabulary in this answer, e.g. *trap*.
2 Find the language in the answer which:
    A puts points in order.
    B says **and**.
    C balances points of view.
    D makes a conclusion.
3 What is the difference between **justified** and **justifiable**, and **accepted** and **acceptable**?

3 Working in pairs, plan an answer to this question
'Dogs make better pets than cats.' Do you agree?
Think of any specialized vocabulary you may need. Make a list of all the different arguments you are going to use.

• When your teacher has checked your plan, write the composition.

VOCABULARY

1 Phrasal verbs in this unit
Replace each of the words in **bold** with one of phrasal verbs in the box.

1 They had the dog **killed** because it was old and sick.
2 The farmer **found** some new born kittens as he was working in a barn.
3 Jenny has **thought of** a wonderful name for her new goldfish!
4 We had to call in the vet because a new disease **suddenly started** among our herd of cattle.
5 When you've finished supper, can you **continue** feeding the pigs?
6 No, you can't have a cat! It's no use complaining. Your father will **agree with** me.
7 Can I **depend on** you to feed the rabbit? You forgot yesterday.
8 Are you going to **suggest** a design for the stable?
9 The rat **attacked** the cat and bit it on the tail.
10 The puppy is covered in green paint! How did this **happen,** children?

> come across   come up with   put forward   come about
> back up   carry on   break out   turn on   put down   count on

2 Expressions with take+noun+preposition
Complete each sentence with an expression using **take**.

Example: *He took* ..*offence at* *what his uncle said.*

1 They took *p*.......... .... a demonstration against cruelty to animals.
2 Could you take *c*.......... .... my cat while I'm away on holiday?
3 She took *p*......... .... the poor little kitten, whose mother had left it, and gave it a home.
4 He takes a great deal of *p*........ .... the way his horse looks so he brushes its coat and combs its tail every day.
5 Julia is going to Kenya on business. I think she should take *a*.......... .... being there and go on a safari.

3 Preposition+noun+preposition combination
Complete the following sentences by adding the correct prepositions.

Example: *Susie went to the pet shop* ....*in*...... *order* ....*to*....... *buy some food for her goldfish.*

1 They didn't go to the zoo .... account .... the bad weather.
2 He was given a puppy .... place .... the dog that died.
3 The ambassador presented the zoo with the panda .... behalf .... the Chinese government.
4 The firemen rescued the kitten from the tree .... means .... a ladder.
5 .... addition .... her nine cats, she has three dogs.
6 He wrote a long reply .... answer .... the complaint about his dog.

SPEAKING

Complete the following questionnaire and then work out the results for the class as a whole.

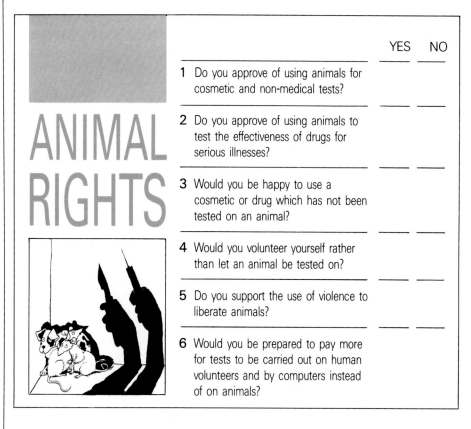

ANIMAL RIGHTS

		YES	NO
1	Do you approve of using animals for cosmetic and non-medical tests?		
2	Do you approve of using animals to test the effectiveness of drugs for serious illnesses?		
3	Would you be happy to use a cosmetic or drug which has not been tested on an animal?		
4	Would you volunteer yourself rather than let an animal be tested on?		
5	Do you support the use of violence to liberate animals?		
6	Would you be prepared to pay more for tests to be carried out on human volunteers and by computers instead of on animals?		

LISTENING

You are going to hear two people giving their opinions on vivisection (*experiments on live animals*). One is Professor Wright, a scientific researcher, and the other, Peter Savage, a member of the Free the Animals Movement. Read the following questions carefully before listening to the interview.

1 According to Professor Wright, why is there no alternative to experimenting on animals?
2 Which diseases does she claim have been conquered as a result of research involving vivisection?
3 Why does she say new drugs have to be tested on animals?
4 What, according to Peter Savage, is the problem of trying out drugs for humans on animals?
5 What is his explanation for the decline in killer diseases?
6 What point does he make about penicillin and aspirin?
7 What does he consider to be the most important argument against vivisection?

PRONUNCIATION 🔊

Sounds in sentences

1 Listen to these sentences and phrases taken from the **Listening** and note what happens to the parts that are underlined.

1 It's eleven o'clock ...
2 ... it's time for another edition of Crosstalk.
3 I have two guests to open the debate.
4 I must state categorically ...
5 ... in the old days ...
6 ... rats and mice ...

• Now practise saying the sentences and phrases by closely following the model.

2 How can we say the following story?

Mr West used to be crazy about photography. One day he took his car and went to a safari park. He stopped to take some pictures. Two ugly monkeys jumped on the car roof and bent the aerial. He got out of the car and tried to make them go away. Three enormous lions came and ate Mr West for lunch.

WRITING

Using your notes from the **Listening**, write a **for and against** composition on this question.
'Research which involves live animals should be banned.'
How far do you agree with this view?

SPEAKING

Paper 5: Interview has three parts which are linked by theme or topic. In part 1 you have to describe a photo. In part 2 you have to comment on a short text. In part 3 you either have to take part in a structured communication activity with other students or take part in a conversation with the examiner.

In previous units we have looked at the three parts separately. Now we are going to look at them together.

1 Describing a photo

Working in pairs, take it in turns to describe these two pictures to each other. Pretend to be students and examiners! When you are the examiner, make sure that you ask plenty of questions to keep the conversation going!

2 Commenting on a short text

Working in pairs again, take it in turns to say where the texts might have come from and who might have said or written them (and when). Finally, say what your reactions are to the passages.

A **Care of your cat**

1 *Eating*

Cats, with the exception of kittens, should be fed twice a day. Half a tin of cat food at each meal is sufficient. Kittens, on the other hand, should be fed more often to ensure proper growth. Cats in general will not overeat so do not worry about giving them too much food.

B Come on, Lucy! You wanted a rabbit, remember? So it's jolly well up to you to look after it properly and clean its cage out. You haven't done it for over a week now. Come on. Otherwise we'll have to find another little girl to be its mummy, won't we now?

C A DOG IS FOR LIFE NOT JUST FOR CHRISTMAS!

D Dogs! If you ask me, they're an absolute menace. They should all be put down! My next door neighbour has got a dog. Barks all hours. And last week it turned on the postman! Not only that, but they make such a mess everywhere, don't they? You should see the pavement outside our house. And if you say anything to the owners, they get all aggressive and start blaming you. Ought to put the owners down as well.

Note In the exam, you only have to comment on **one** text.

3 Structured communication activity

Work in groups of three and read about the cost and enjoyment factors for different kinds of pets. Then decide which kind of pet would be most suitable for the people mentioned below the chart.

- Write four paragraphs of not more than 30 words each explaining your choice of pet for each of the people described in the communication activity. You may have do something like this for the last part of **Paper 3: Use of English**.

	COMPANIONSHIP	RELAXATION	UPKEEP	COST
cat	***	***	**	**
fish		**	*	*
dog	****	**	***	***
rabbit	**	**	**	***
hamster			**	**
bird	***	*	*	**

Mr Edward Cohen, 68. Retired accountant. Recently widowed. Active man. Enjoys long walks. Has a house and large garden in the country.

Mr Kenneth Dukes, 52. An invalid. Confined to a wheelchair after a stroke. Has high blood pressure.

Emma and Gemma Jones, 8-year-old twins who argue a lot. They have a small garden. They would like a kitten but their mother is allergic to cats. They don't have much money.

Elsie Grey, an old age pensioner who lives in the eleventh floor of a block of flats. Her flat has good views and a sunny living room. She is lonely and does not go out a lot.

121

USE OF ENGLISH
3

1 Fill each of the numbered blanks in the following passage. Use only **one** word. Remember to read the whole story through first before you try to fill anything in and to study carefully what comes **after** the gap!
Here are five of the words to help you: *according, top, up, on, back.*

Sam is a puppy belonging to pub landlord, Steve Lock. A short time .... (1) Steve's friend John .... (2) helping to lay a carpet when he slipped and chopped .... (3) the top of his finger .... (4) a knife. The horrified landlord picked .... (5) the piece of finger and put it on the table .... (6) he bandaged his friend's bleeding wound. They had .... (7) that they could have the finger stitched .... (8) on when they got to hospital. .... (9), Sam the puppy had other ideas. The dog waited until the two men were .... (10) of the room and then jumped .... (11) the table and ate the finger. Fortunately, ... (12) to pub landlord Steve, his friend John .... (13) the funny side .... (14) the story. John says that the finger .... (15) hurts a little but that it should be all right .... (16) the end even if it is a little flat on .... (17). He is keeping his eye .... (18) Sam to make .... (19) that he doesn't come back for a .... (20) helping.

2 Finish each of the following sentences in such a way that it means exactly the same as the sentence printed before it.

1 The dog barked all night but we still managed to sleep.
 Despite ....

2 The cat can't catch the mice. They run too fast.
 The mice ....

3 Cats aren't as expensive to keep as dogs.
 Dogs ....

4 Man is the cruellest of all animals.
 There isn't ....

5 His canary sings better than mine.
 My canary doesn't ....

6 Is this the cheapest pet food you've got?
 Have you ....

7 Most of the animals survived the hard winter.
 Even though ....

8 I have never seen a dirtier-looking dog.
 This is ....

9 She couldn't afford the Persian cat.
 The Persian cat ....

10 The cheetah is the fastest animal in the world.
 No animal runs ....

UNIT 11 | *Your Cultural Heritage*

SPEAKING

1 Read the text about Cleopatra's Needle and find out:

1 where it came from.
2 how it was transported to England and what happened on the journey.
3 what now lies underneath it.

By the River Thames stands the obelisk known as Cleopatra's Needle. It was originally cut from a quarry in Aswan, stood for a time in Heliopolis and was again transported to Alexandria. After a couple of centuries, it fell over in the sand where it lay. In 1877, a British engineer performed the seemingly impossible task of transporting it to England. The Needle was put in a cylindrical container and towed by ship to England. After a hazardous voyage in which seven sailors drowned, it arrived in London where it was erected. Beneath it are various articles left for future archaeologists to find. They include the day's newspaper, some coins, a razor, a box of pins, four bibles in different languages, a railway time-table and 12 photographs of the most beautiful English women of the time!

2 Discussion points

1 Cities and museums in Europe and the USA are full of objects taken from other countries. Should they ever be returned to their country of origin? Do you think they were 'stolen'?
2 How important are history, language, tradition and works of arts in the country's culture? How easy is it for a country or region to lose its identity?
3 What do you think the people who buried the objects under Cleopatra's Needle were trying to say about their society? What would you choose to bury in a small box so future archaelogists would have an idea of what today's society is like.

123

READING

1 Read the facts about the origins of Carnival and then Joe Grayson's description of his trip to Trinidad with his girlfriend, Milly.

> ### CARNIVAL FACTS
> ◾ Ancient Roman festivals from pagan times were taken over by the Christians and became Carnival.
> ◾ The word *Carnival* comes from the Latin *carnem levare* which means *farewell to the flesh*. Carnival was the last time people could enjoy themselves before Lent.
> ◾ French colonists with their traditions of masked balls were responsible for taking Carnival to the New World.

2 Choose the best answer to these questions.

1 The European carnival
   A was invented in France.
   B had always been a Christian festival.
   C drew on different traditions.
   D was lent to the new world.

2 In Trinidad
   A the new festival just copied the French one.
   B carnival hardly changed.
   C everybody came from West Africa.
   D people used to be slaves.

3 The *can boulay*
   A does not start on Monday.
   B means something in French.
   C lasts a day.
   D celebrates slavery.

4 In Trinidad
   A steel pans are exported.
   B people act as drums.
   C drums used to be banned.
   D people make music by blowing into bottles.

5 Within the Caribbean, the Trinidadian carnival is
   A the noisiest.
   B the largest.
   C the longest.
   D the brightest.

3 Work in groups and tell each other about a festival from your own country or region.

Milly and I were really lucky to have Julius as our guide. We met him over a drink in a bar on the day we arrived. He had actually worked in England for 13 years before escaping back to the sun. He was proud of his island's history and filled us in on it as well as introducing us to Carnival.

As I'm sure you know, the black population of Trinidad used to be slaves. When they won their freedom, they started to develop their own version of Carnival. This partly copied the behaviour of their old masters but also drew on traditions from their own strong West African roots. Julius explained all the features of the Trinidadian version which make it so different: the special processions, the masked rituals, the stick dancing and drumming, all of which have transformed the event into what it is today. We certainly wouldn't have got so much out of our visit without him.

The first big event he took us to was an amazing procession with lighted torches which started at midnight on the Sunday, the day before Carnival. It is called the *can boulay* which comes from the French *cannes brulees* meaning burnt canes. The slaves would have to fight fires in the cane fields on the big estates. It was an incredible and somehow frightening sight, a reminder of the bad old days.

Julius told us all about a unique kind of Trinidadian band which doesn't use ordinary musical instruments. Instead, the musicians beat objects such as bamboo stems and bottles and spoons. This is because in the old days the white masters had been scared of the slaves communicating using drums, and so the beating of real drums was banned. The slaves had to make do with what they could lay their hands on! Another Carnival treat which Trinidad is famous for is its steel bands. It's incredible to think that such wonderful music can come from some old oil cans. Pans are made which are then beaten and tuned to notes on the musical scale. They let me have a go but all I managed to do was give Milly a headache!

Although all the Caribbean islands celebrate Carnival, Julius pointed out that none of them can match the scale of the Trinidadian festival. I believed him if the costumes were anything to go by. They were absolutely fantastic and take weeks to prepare. People dress up as vampire bats, devils with horns and tails and as African and even South American warriors. Julius told us that the South American warriors are based on a Venezuelan tribe which used to trade regularly in the southern parts of Trinidad. It makes you realize just how close the island is to South America.

All in all, it was an absolutely unforgettable experience and Milly and I would recommend it to anyone. If you go to Trinidad, we hope that you'll bump into Julius too.

LANGUAGE STUDY

used to and would

1 Joe Grayson says that *the black population of Trinidad used to be slaves* and that *in the old days the slaves would have to fight fires in the cane fields of the big estates.*
Both **used to** and **would** describe regular events in the past but they are not exactly the same in meaning.

Used to can describe:
1 past habits, e.g. *He used to smoke.*
2 past states, e.g. *They used to be slaves.*

Would is used to describe past habits or behaviour, e.g. *They would have to put out fires on the estates.*
You cannot use **would** to describe past states, e.g. you cannot say *She would be fat.* or *She would have brown hair.*

It is possible to use **used to** most of the time. However, we do not do this because of reasons of style. Look at this example and say why we do not use **used to** all of the time.

He used to get home at about six o'clock in the evening. Then he would sit down in his armchair, get out his pipe and sit puffing away at it. After that, mother would tell him that his tea was ready and he used to go into the kitchen to wash his hands.

- Why can't we say *His father would work at the car factory?*

2 Look at the pictures of life as it once was and life today. In pairs, discuss how things have changed.

LANGUAGE STUDY
Prepositions following adjectives

In the introductory text on Carnival it says that *French colonists were* **responsible for** *taking Carnival to the New World.*

The adjective **responsible** is often followed by the preposition **for**. If we follow a preposition with a verb, we have to put the verb into the gerund (*-ing* form).

Complete these sentences by following each adjective with an appropriate preposition. Sometimes there is more than one correct answer.

1 Are you interested .... antiques?
2 She was surprised .... how cheap the watercolour was.
3 Is he aware .... how long we have been waiting for the tour to start?
4 Pisa is famous .... its Leaning Tower.
5 When I was at school, I was really bad .... history.
6 We were extremely impressed .... the guided tour.
7 Hurry up! I'm worried .... missing the boat.
8 This festival is similar .... the one in Rio.
9 I'm really tired .... looking at monuments.
10 The flood was responsible .... damaging the statue.
11 She was terribly disappointed .... the tour.
12 This portrait of her is completely different .... that one.
13 We're not keen .... visiting the ruins.
14 I'm sorry .... being so late. I had to go back for my camera.
15 Sorry .... the delay. We should still get to the museum before it closes.

3 USE OF ENGLISH

Expanding a text

1 Read the tour guide's introductory speech and, in pairs, work out the route of the tour on the map of Cambridge.

2 Make all the changes and additions necessary to produce, from the sets of words and phrases, sentences which together make a complete speech.

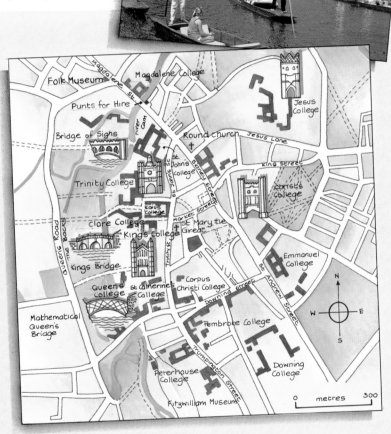

Good morning ladies/ gentlemen. Please allow/me/ introduce myself. My name/ be/ Amanda Southgate and I/ like/ welcome you/ wonderful town/ Cambridge/ behalf/ Culture Tours. I/ be/ your guide today/ it/ give/ me great pleasure/ introduce you/ most important sights/ this town.

We/ start/ tour here at/ Round Church/ , one/ few/ round churches/ England. After that/ we/ visit Trinity and Clare college/ then/ walk along the back of the colleges/ admire/ daffodils/ which/ be/ now/ in bloom. Then/ we/ visit/ King's College and its beautiful chapel. After/ brief look/ Queen's College/ we/ stop/ picnic lunch. Please may I/

remind/ you/ not/ walk/grass/ and/ keep/ footpath. Visitors/ not/be/allow/enter lectures or living accommodation.

This afternoon/ there/ be/ visit to/ Folk Museum/ which/ show/ how people/ use/ live in/ old days. Finally/ there/be/ opportunity/ you/experience/ trip/on a punt/which/ be/ kind/boat/ you push along

with a pole. I/not/recommend you/try/yourself/it/be easy/fall in /river!

One last thing/ I/ like/say before/ begin/ tour/, be/ if anyone/ should/ lost/, not/ forget/ be back here/ Round Church/ by 4.30 in order/ catch/ coach back. Many thanks/ be/ so patient/. Now let us/ begin/ tour.

WRITING
Making a speech

1 Make a note of all the expressions in the tour guide's speech that are useful in this kind of composition.

2 Make a list of constructions in the speech that use the infinitive, e.g. *Please **allow me to** introduce myself.* Why is the infinitive used?

3 Imagine that you are a tour guide and that you are giving an introduction to your city to a group of visitors. Where would you take them and what would you say?

VOCABULARY
remind, remember and forget

*Please may I **remind** you not to walk on the grass.*
Complete the following sentences with **remind**, **remember** or **forget**.

1 Do not .... to buy a guide book.
2 May I .... you that you are not allowed to smoke in here?
3 I shall .... that trip until the day I die.
4 Please .... me to your parents the next time you see them.
5 Can you .... her to send the postcards?
6 Passengers are .... to keep their valuables with them at all times.

2 Imagine you are going on holiday and a friend is going to look after your house or flat.
What instructions would you give them about watering plants, locking up, and so on?
Think of five things you would tell them to remember/not to forget to do.

LANGUAGE STUDY

Look at this verb pattern.
She reminded them to be back by 4.30.
SUBJECT + VERB + OBJECT + INFINITIVE

Transform these sentences using the same pattern.

1 'Would you like to come to the art gallery?' Sophie asked Ann.
   Sophie invited ....
2 I finally agreed with Leila's suggestion that we should go to the *son et lumière* show.
   Leila persuaded ....
3 'Why don't you visit the ruins this afternoon?' his mother said.
   His mother encouraged ....
4 'Whatever you do, don't walk on the grass,' the guide warned.
   The guide warned ....
5 'Stop smoking at once!' the curator shouted.
   The curator ordered ....

USE OF ENGLISH
Transformation exercise

1 Finish each of the following sentences in such a way that it means exactly the same as the sentence printed before it.

1 'If I were you, I'd take a picnic,' her landlady said.
   Her landlady advised ....
2 They spent 30 years putting in those windows.
   It took ....
3 'Don't forget to tip the guide,' she told John.
   She reminded ....
4 'Don't you dare touch that vase!' the curator warned the child.
   The child ....
5 People do not live in the castle any more.
   The castle used ....
6 You must not smoke in here.
   Smoking ....
7 It took three hours to go round the grounds.
   The tour ....
8 The chapel was decorated by Italian craftsmen.
   The king had ....

2 Fill each of the numbered blanks in the following passage. Use only **one** word in each space.

King's College Chapel

This chapel, which is set in the grounds of King's College, is .... (1) question the .... (2) beautiful building in Cambridge. It is .... (3) 500 hundred years old and is a magnificent .... (4) of late medieval architecture.

It was .... (5) by King Henry VI in 1446, but was not completed until the .... (6) century. This probably explains .... (7) use of different types of stone in .... (8) construction. The exterior is an elegant combination of stone and glass. We .... (9) best admire its beautiful stained-glass windows .... (10) the inside. It took craftsmen from Belgium over 30 years to put .... (11) in.

We can .... (12) see *The Adoration of the Magi*, an imposing painting .... (13) the artist, Paul Rubens, ... (14) was given to the chapel in 1961. The painting .... (15) the three wise men with the baby Jesus in the stable at Bethlehem. The chapel is also famous .... (16) its choir of boy singers .... (17) the regular recitals it gives. .... (18) Christmas, people .... (19) for hours to get a seat for the carol concert which .... (20) broadcast all over the world.

LANGUAGE STUDY
Adjective order

1 Complete these sentences by putting the adjectives in the correct order.

1 She is wearing a French/vest/cotton/green/a/ running.
2 George plays with a tennis/graphite/American/ racquet/black/a.
3 She was given plastic/Swiss/boots/a pair of/ski/ blue.

Now try to work out a rule for the order of these adjectives.

Although it is impossible to give a clear rule which will work in all circumstances, here is an acceptable order for adjectives.

number+opinion+size+shape+age+colour+ pattern+origin+material+purpose+noun

2 Lady Ffoulkes-Bracknell's house has been burgled! Lots of her most precious things have been stolen. Make any changes necessary to her letter to Inspector Jones of Scotland Yard.

Dear Inspector Jones,
   Many thanks for coming so quickly after my telephone call to you. Now that I have had time to see what the thieves took, here is a list of the stolen property:
1. English / an / writing / antique / desk / oak
2. eighteenth century / mug / silver / Bavarian / one / beer
3. clock / delightful / gold / silver / small / French / Louis XV / a
4. Italian / a pair of / pistols / ancient / duelling
5. tiger / looking / a / rug / dirty / skin
6. statue / tiny / stone / green / Columbian / a
7. rectangular / old / deep / trunk / ugly / a
8. two pairs of / striped / silk / pyjamas / blue and white
   I do hope that you are able to find my property as most of it is of sentimental value.
      Yours sincerely,
      Lady Anne Ffoulkes-Bracknell

LISTENING

You are going to hear the curator of a museum talking about some of the exhibits. Complete the table, answer the multiple choice questions and choose the right objects.

1 Complete the table.

	NAME	USE
object one		
object two		
object three	*flail*	
object four		

2 We can understand from the curator that
   A the tourists are late.   C it is raining.
   B the weather is poor.   D It is fine.

3 The museum
   A sometimes can't find out what objects were used for.
   B has some exhibits that are still used.
   C specializes in pretty objects.
   D eventually manages to find out what objects were used for.

4 Which of the pictures fits the description of object two?

5 Which of the pictures fits the description of object three?

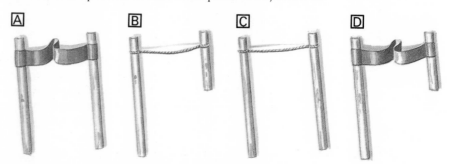

6 According to the curator, men who went poaching
   A were brave.   C risked deportation.
   B were often caught.   D did it for sport.

SPEAKING

Describing a painting

In **Paper 5: Interview,** as you know, one of the things you have to do is describe a photograph. These exercises will help you with this part of the exam.

1 Study this painting carefully, then read what a student said about it.

This is a painting of the countryside. In the front of the picture I can see two girls. They look very poor. They are wearing old clothes. Maybe they are sisters. I am not sure. Behind them there is the countryside. Maybe it is England. It looks like England very much. Typically English, I think. I think that maybe it has rained because I can see a lovely, um, rainbow, it is called, in the sky. I can see some animals in the fields behind the girls. The small girl is saying the other one something about the rainbow. It is a nice picture. It has been painted maybe a hundred years ago. One of the girls has got a musical instrument with her. Wait a minute! I think she is blind and the small girl is taking care of her.

2 In pairs or small groups, discuss how you could improve the student's description. Think about:

1 any obvious mistakes that have been made.
2 what you can say instead of **I can see...** and **maybe.**
3 what special words to describe paintings you could introduce.
4 what you could add to the description to make it more interesting.
5 how you could join up the observations better.

LISTENING

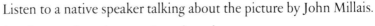
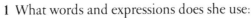

Listen to a native speaker talking about the picture by John Millais.

1 What words and expressions does she use:
  A instead of **I can see** and **maybe?**
  B to describe the position of objects within the picture?
2 What extra subjects does she include in her description?
3 How does she **move away** from the picture?

SPEAKING

In pairs, talk about this painting. Describe what is happening in it.

WRITING

1 In **Paper** 2 you may have to write a description of something. Study this example.

(1)

One of my favourite paintings is called 'The Fall of Icarus' by Peter Breughel. If you remember, Icarus and his father made themselves wings and learned to fly. Icarus ignored his father's warning and flew too near the sun. This melted the wax which held the wings to his body so he fell into the sea and drowned.

What is so interesting about this painting is that everyday life is going on while this disaster is happening. In the foreground there is a farmer totally unaware of what has just taken place. He concentrates on ploughing his field. Just behind him there is a shepherd boy looking up at the figure in the sky perhaps wondering what on earth it can be. Behind him, the cliffs curve away into the distance. In the background we can see the

(2)

rest of the bay and a few boats.

In fact, you have to look quite hard to see poor Icarus who is in the bottom right-hand part of the picture. You can see a splash and a pair of white legs sticking up as he disappears beneath the sea. Perhaps someone on the boat saw him but I doubt it. The only person who had a good view is the simple fisherman sitting on the shore in the bottom right-hand part of the painting.

In a way it's strange that the artist didn't put Icarus in the middle of the painting. I suppose what he is saying is that 'great' events often go unobserved and perhaps that life is more than a little absurd and ridiculous. What's more, it reminds us that we are often victims of our pride. Every powerful man or politician should have this picture in his office.

2 Now write about a picture you know well in the same way. Your composition must be between 120 and 180 words.

UNIT 12 | *Crime and Society*

SPEAKING | You and your scruples

Complete this questionnaire. If you wouldn't make any of the choices suggested, then add one of your own.

1 You can hear a terrible noise coming from your neighbour's house. It sounds as though he's murdering someone. Would you
a do nothing?
b call the police?
c go round yourself and see what was happening?
d ....

2 You discover a way of making free telephone calls anywhere in the world. Would you
a tell all your friends?
b keep the secret to yourself?
c inform the telephone company?
d ....

3 Imagine that you're a shop assistant and you notice one of your colleagues stealing from the till. Would you
a say nothing?
b tell the person to stop or else?
c inform the boss?
d ....

4 While you are parking your car, you accidentally scratch the paintwork of a new car next to you. Would you
a leave a note for the owner of the other car?
b hurry off?
c park as though nothing had happened?
d ....

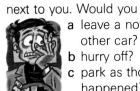

5 You are staying in an elderly person's home when you notice a painting on the wall. The old person doesn't know that it's a Rembrandt. Would you
a buy the painting for as little as possible?
b tell him what the painting was worth?
c offer him a fair price but not tell him everything?
d ....

6 A tramp smelling of alcohol asks you for money. Would you
a give him some, knowing he will spend it on alcohol?
b buy him a meal or a sandwich?
c refuse to give him any?
d ....

7 Your best friend's boyfriend/girlfriend invites you out for a date. Would you
a refuse the invitation and tell your friend?
b accept the invitation and keep it a secret?
c refuse it and say nothing?
d ....

8 Somebody pays you in cash for doing a job. Would you
a declare it to the taxman?
b keep the money without declaring it?
c not declare it but give the customer a discount for cash?
d ....

| ● Compare the results of your questionnaire with a partner.

READING

1 Before you read about Rose Jones, look at the photo of her and describe her in as much detail as possible. Then read the article and answer these two questions.

1 What reasons does she give for her life of crime?
2 Do you think her reasons are, in fact, reasonable?

A LIFE OF
CRIME

Looking at this little old lady, it is hard to believe that she has spent 20 of her 76 years in jail. Her crime has been pickpocketing. Just a short while ago she was caught practising her trade in Harrods — a favourite hunting ground for the pickpocket as it is frequented by the well-off. Her fingers aren't as quick as they once were and she was spotted by a sharp-eyed store detective more used to catching shoplifters.

Luckily for her, the judge let her off. All the same, crime certainly hasn't paid for Rose Jones. She lives in a damp, uncomfortable basement bedsit with no heating and no company except for her dogs and cats and the TV. Nevertheless, she believes that it is better there than in prison. During her many spells in prison, she met Ruth Ellis, the last woman to be hanged in Britain, and the notorious murderess, Myra Hindley, who would have certainly followed Ellis to the scaffold if hanging had not been abolished. Instead, she was given life imprisonment.

Rose blames her life of crime on her childhood and harsh upbringing. She feels that if her mother hadn't died when she was small, her life would have turned out differently. As it was, her father remarried and her stepmother was cruel to her. Hunger drove young Rose to steal food and she quickly graduated to picking pockets. She was only six at the time. When she was 11, she started doing menial jobs in big houses. She perhaps wishes she had taken that opportunity to go 'straight' but she didn't. She remembers taking a lipstick and a five pound note from some guests' luggage. When her mistress accused her of stealing, she denied everything and, for once, got away with it.

Her life 'inside' started when she was 17. Following a conviction, she was sent to a prison for young people. It was to be the first of many such visits. Yet, in all her long criminal career, Rose has never made any real money. Either she gave it away or she spent it on trivial things. Her husband stole the little money she had managed to save while she was in prison.

Nowadays, she has just about decided that her life of crime is over. After all, she finds it difficult to move around now without any support which makes her line of work rather difficult. In addition, the popularity of credit cards means that people tend to carry less cash around with them than they were once accustomed to. Rose thinks it is time she turned over a new leaf. But is it possible to break the habits of a lifetime?

2 Choose the best answer to these questions.

1 Rose was caught in Harrods
   A by someone well-off.
   B because she was clumsy.
   C while she was shoplifting.
   D by someone alert.

2 She started stealing
   A because she was told to.
   B for money.
   C for excitement.
   D from necessity.

3 Myra Hindley
   A wasn't as bad as Ruth Ellis.
   B deserved to be hanged.
   C benefited from a change in the law.
   D was hanged for murder.

4 When Rose was a servant,
   A she could have led an honest life.
   B she resisted temptation.
   C she stole some clothes.
   D she was punished for stealing.

5 Picking pockets nowadays
   A is less profitable.
   B is more difficult.
   C has new rewards.
   D is a job for a young person.

3 Discussion points

1 Is Rose a victim of society or just another criminal?
2 Crime among young children is on the increase all over the world. Whose fault is this? The parents? The teachers? The politicians?
3 What do you think should be done with small children who commit crimes?

LANGUAGE STUDY

Conditional sentences using **if**

1 *If Rose's mother hadn't died when she was small, her life would have turned out differently.*
Correct these sentences.

1 **First conditional:** *If it will rain, we will play tennis.*
2 **Second conditional:** *If he would have a haircut, he would look nicer.*
3 **Third conditional:** *If she had have phoned you, I would have told you.*

2 Which sentences express the idea of:

A something is quite likely to happen in the future.
B an unreal situation completely in the past.
C something in the past that affects the present.
D an established fact.
E something possible but unlikely.

1 If you heat water to 100 degrees centigrade, it boils.
2 If he studies hard, he will pass the exam.
3 If you smoked less, you would save a lot of money.
4 If you had kept the receipt, I would change the skirt.
5 If he had scored the goal, we would have won the match.

3 Change the verbs in brackets into the most appropriate form of the conditional.

1 What you (*do*) if you (*be*) in my situation?
2 Behave yourself, Lucy. If you (*do*) that again, you (*have*) go to bed.
3 Their marriage only lasted three months. If he (*be*) less mean, she (*not leave*) him.
4 Good, everybody's ready. If we (*leave*) now, we (*miss*) the rush hour traffic.
5 If you (*smoke*) less, you (*have*) much more money. But I don't think you ever will.
6 If we (*lock*) the car window, we (*not give*) them the opportunity to break in.
7 When Alice (*get*) here, you (*show*) her to her room?
8 I know it's a delicate situation, Inspector, but what you do (*say*) if I (*give*) you a little present?
9 If you (*press*) that button, a receptionist (*come*) to help you.
10 The film was marvellous. If you (*come*) with us, you (*enjoy*) it too.
11 Imagine, darling. What we (*do*) if your husband (*have*) an accident?
12 If I (*be*) the prime minister, I (*bring back*) capital punishment.

'Would you say your husband had any Swiss enemies?'

 PRONUNCIATION 📼

1 How do we say the following sentences in normal speech?
What do we have to contract?
Which parts of the sentence should be stressed.

1 I will do it if you want me to.
2 If he had not come, we would have had a good time.
3 If I were you, I would see a doctor.
4 If only I had not said it!

2 Listen and identify which conditional construction is being used in the eight sentences.

	FIRST	SECOND	THIRD	MIXED
1				
2				
3				
4				
5				
6				
7				
8				

 LANGUAGE STUDY
Verbs followed by prepositions

1 *Rose's mistress **accused her of stealing**.*
Complete these sentences of verb preposition combinations.

1 You accuse someone ....*of*...........
2 You forgive someone ....
3 You arrest someone ....
4 You discourage someone ....
5 You blame someone ....
6 You punish someone ....
7 You prevent someone ....
8 You convict someone ....
9 You congratulate someone ....
10 You warn someone ....

doing something.

2 Make all the changes and additions necessary to produce sentences from the following sets of words and phrases. Make sure that you choose the correct prepositions to go with each verb.

1 Her employer/accuse/her/steal/money.
2 Rose/blame/parents/not/bring her up/properly.
3 His mother/punish him/be rude/to their neighbour.
4 The lock/prevent/burglar/break into/house.
5 The jury/convict him/murder/his wife.
6 The shopkeeper/forgive/child/steal/sweets.
7 His son/be/arrest/sell drugs/to teenagers.
8 Her nephew/be/discouraged/talk/the police.
9 The judge/congratulate/police/catch/gang.
10 She/warn/children/play/park/after dark.

 VOCABULARY

Phrasal verbs

Replace the words in brackets with a phrasal verb from the box. Make any other changes which are necessary.

The police are 1 (*investigating*) an incident which took place this afternoon. Two masked men 2 (*robbed*) a security van outside the national bank and 3 (*escaped*) with half a million pounds. Their getaway car 4 (*knocked down*) one of the guards as they 5 (*went towards*) the motorway.

She had 6 (*invented*) a wonderful alibi and managed to 7 (*make everyone believe her lies*). The police only 8 (*discovered*) the truth because a jealous lover 9 (*betrayed her*) to the police.

The children are suspiciously quiet. I wonder what they are 10 (*doing*). I think I'll go and have a look.

He 11 (*lost control of his emotions*) and cried. He confessed everything to his father. His father 12 (*didn't punish him*) because he believed the boy was genuinely sorry.

The alarm bell 13 (*started to ring*) when the gang tried to 14 (*enter*) the bank.

find out   look into   run over   go off
get away with   break down   hold up
be up to   break into   make for
let off   make up   take in   give away

Different types of crime

1 What are the crimes described in these situations? The words are given in the box.

1 He threatened to send the love letters to her husband unless she gave him £500.
2 The telephone box had been smashed and there was graffiti all over the walls.
3 An old man has been attacked and robbed in a city street. He is recovering in hospital.
4 Department stores lose millions of pounds each year through goods being stolen off the shelves.
5 Thieves broke into the house while the family was away on holiday.
6 The young woman was sexually attacked as she walked across the dark park late at night.
7 He watched with satisfaction as the fire he lit burnt down the factory. 'That'll make them wish they'd never given me the sack,' he thought.
8 It was a perfect copy. It was so good, in fact, that it could even fool an expert.
9 The bank believed her to be trustworthy. They had no reason to suspect that she had transferred thousands of pounds to false accounts.
10 'If you want to see your child again, put $50,000 in an old suitcase and wait for further instructions.'
11 George gave the man £50 in return for a small packet of heroin.
12 It was a beautiful day. The sun was shining and people were sitting outside the cafe enjoying the sunshine. Then the bomb went off.
13 'If only I hadn't brought these watches through customs,' she thought as she sat crying in the police station.

burglary   arson   vandalism   terrorism   forgery
blackmail   smuggling   fraud   mugging   rape
kidnapping   drug pushing   shoplifting

2 What do you call the criminals who commit these crimes?
The crime is **burglary,** the verb is **to burgle.** What other verbs can be made from this list of crimes?

SPEAKING

Paper 5 Structured communication activity

You are on the parole board of a prison which is so overcrowded that you must release two prisoners. Study the descriptions of five possible candidates for release and make a decision on whom to set free.

1 **Alan Jones:** Guilty of murdering his wife by slowly poisoning her. Described by neighbours as a kind and gentle person. His children love him. His wife had lots of affairs and pushed him to the limit.

2 **Janet Green:** Found guilty of shoplifting for the tenth time. She is a homeless tramp who likes to spend the winter in prison. It is early December and the weather is very cold.

3 **Miranda Morgan:** A drug addict guilty of selling heroin to teenagers. Has already tried two unsuccessful drug treatment programmes. Has a two year old child who will have to go into care if she goes to jail.

4 **Mick Brown:** Guilty of vandalism and football hooliganism. 19 years old and below average intelligence. Aggressive and gets violent when drunk. One previous offence for drunken driving.

5 **Cynthia Carter:** English teacher guilty of smuggling her two cats into England. This is against quarantine regulations. The customs officers would like an example to be made of her.

 USE OF ENGLISH

For the last part of **Paper 3** you may have to write an answer based on your interpretation of graphs or diagrams.

The Chief Constable of an English county has to write a report on serious car accidents in his county. Study the table and his notes. Then continue his report making recommendations for the future. Write between 120 and 180 words.

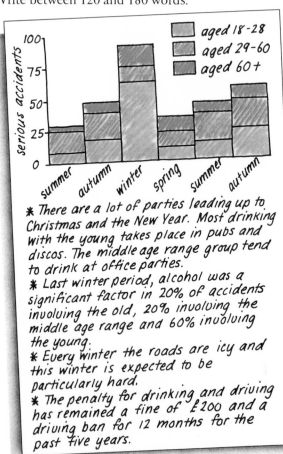

* There are a lot of parties leading up to Christmas and the New Year. Most drinking with the young takes place in pubs and discos. The middle age range group tend to drink at office parties.

* Last winter period, alcohol was a significant factor in 20% of accidents involving the old, 20% involving the middle age range and 60% involving the young.

* Every winter the roads are icy and this winter is expected to be particularly hard.

* The penalty for drinking and driving has remained a fine of £200 and a driving ban for 12 months for the past five years.

REPORT

Over the past eighteen months the number of accidents has ....

The groups most at risk are ....

The main reasons for accidents seem to be ....

I predict that this winter ....

In order to reduce the number of accidents this winter we should ....

VOCABULARY

Paper 1: Reading comprehension Section A

Choose the word or phrase which best completes the following sentences.

1 When they got back from holiday, they found their house had been .... by burglars.
   A broken into   B broken up   C broken down
   D broken off

2 The criminal thought he had .... the perfect crime.
   A made   B done   C completed   D committed

3 Some friends at school .... him to steal the sweets.
   A dared   B threatened   C let   D made

4 He'll always be the same — a leopard never changes its ....
   A pattern   B stripes   C coat   D spots

5 The crime .... seems to be going up and up.
   A percentage   B wave   C figures   D rate

6 You must always .... us the truth.
   A confess   B tell   C speak   D say

7 Wilson had .... an alibi for the time of the robbery.
   A made over   B made do   C made into
   D made up

8 Oh, no! My wallet has been ....
   A robbed   B picked   C stolen   D theft

9 The police are said to be looking .... the matter.
   A for   B into   C up   D over

10 The defence asked the court to take the prisoner's age .... consideration.
   A up to   B into   C in   D over

11 She was sent to jail for .... for the murder.
   A life   B live   C living   D lifetime

12 It is said that .... makes a thief.
   A possibility   B choice   C chance
   D opportunity

13 He .... to drive in the bus lane even though he knew it was illegal.
   A decided   B risked   C avoided   D kept

14 What are the children getting .... ? They're very quiet.
   A on with   B up with   C off with   D up to

15 Bank managers should be completely .... people.
   A trusting   B trustworthy   C trustful
   D trusty

16 If you park there, you'll have to pay a ....
   A fee   B fine   C ticket   D fare

17 The blackmailer .... to send the photographs to the police.
   A enjoyed   B threatened   C suggested
   D denied

18 The police hate it when judges .... criminals.
   A let down   B let up   C let in   D let off

19 You can't smoke in here. It's .... the law.
   A according   B anti   C against   D opposite

20 The spy was shot for ....
   A treachery   B betrayal   C traitor   D treason

21 He .... the crime because the witness died.
   A gone away with   B got over   C got away with
   D got off with

22 The forgery was so clever you could not .... it apart from the real thing.
   A tell   B say   C check   D choose

23 The judge .... him not to do it again.
   A said   B explained   C threatened
   D warned

24 They caught the entire gang .... for the boss.
   A apart   B but   C aside   D except

25 Drunkenness is .... for many road accidents.
   A guilty   B responsible   C faulty   D cause

139

SPEAKING
Discussing texts

1 Study these passages. Then say where you think they might have come from and who might have said or written them to whom and when. Finally, what is your reaction to the passages?

A Go on, Jerry. I wish you weren't so boring all the time. Come on, have another drink! We've only got to get to the next village. You'll be all right as long as you drive slowly. Anyway, there won't be any coppers around at this time of night, will there?

B Driving while under the influence of alcohol is a serious offence. For this, the court fines you £200 and bans you from driving for one year. For failing to report an accident, the court had contemplated a period of imprisonment. However, on taking your age and previous good record into consideration, we have decided on probation. Nevertheless, you had better watch your step, young man, otherwise you will go to jail.

C So you want to borrow the car again, Jerry. That's fine provided you promise to be careful. I wish you didn't mix with that boy, Wayne, though. He's a terrible influence on you. Mind what you drink unless you want to lose your licence!

D Yes, it was a really awful time. I wish I'd listened to my dad before. He was marvellous though considering I wrecked his car and everything. Wayne was in plaster for a couple of months. In a way, it was his own fault, wasn't it? If only he hadn't forced me to have that drink.

---

2 These texts go together to form a story.

1 What order should they appear in?
2 Can you imagine what might have happened between the texts?
3 What do you think Wayne, Jerry and the father are like?

LANGUAGE STUDY
Ways of saying **if**

1 In the passages there are four different ways of saying **if.** See if you can find them.

2 Complete these sentences using each variation of **if** once.
   A We'll have a picnic .... , of course, it rains.
   B I'll go .... she goes!
   C I'll take you to the airport .... you pay for the petrol.
   D You'd better hurry .... you'll miss your train.

3 How can you explain the difference between the answers to A and D?

LANGUAGE STUDY
Forms of **wish**

1 In Passage A Wayne says
I wish you weren't so boring all the time.
Answer the questions which follow each example.

1 *I wish I had a million pounds.*
   A Is he talking about the past, present, or the future?
   B Does he think he's likely to have a million pounds?
2 *I wish I had blue eyes.*
   A Is she talking about the past, present or future?
   B Is her wish unlikely or impossible?

We use **wish + past simple** when we want something in the present to change. Such a change is either unlikely or impossible.

3 *I wish I had worn gloves.*
  A Did he wear gloves?
  B How does he feel now? What do you think happened to him?

We use **wish + past perfect** when we regret in the present what we did in the past.

4 *She wishes he would stop smoking that awful pipe.*
  A Is she talking about the present, the future or both?
  B Does she really believe that he will stop?
  C How does she feel about the situation?
  D Can we use this construction to talk about ourselves?
5 *I wish the train would come. I'm freezing to death.*
  A Is he talking about the present, the near future or both?
  B Does he want the train to hurry up?
  C Does he really believe the train will arrive soon?

We normally use **wish + would** either when something is annoying us and we would like it to stop, or when we want something to happen sooner rather than later.

6 *I wish I could swim.*
  A Can he swim?
  B Would he like to?

We use **wish + could** when we want to talk about ability.

Note We can often use **if only** instead of **I wish**, e.g. *If only I'd worn gloves.*

"Look, lady, all the wishing in the world isn't going to change anything."

2 What might you say if you were the people in the following situations? Make sentences using one of the forms of **wish** we have just looked at.

1 Liz is unhappy because she has got a small flat.
2 Alex has been trying to lose weight but his diet hasn't made any difference.
3 Thieves have stolen Candy's fur coat. It wasn't insured.
4 You work with someone who whistles horribly all day long.
5 Anita drank too much again last night. She has got a terrible hangover.
6 She wants to take the top off a bottle of aspirin but she can't open it.
7 Katie is sitting by the telephone. She is waiting impatiently for Angus to ring.

● Write some sentences about **yourself** using each of the forms we have looked at.

 LISTENING

1 Listen to two people discussing a traffic accident and answer the **true** or **false** questions.

1 Mark is a very alert child.
2 His eyes were injured in the accident.
3 He is probably going to stay in hospital for a while.
4 He was knocked over by a car outside his school.
5 The driver of the car had been drinking.
6 A teacher gave Mark first aid until the ambulance arrived.
7 Jackie Brown was picking Mark up from school.
8 Mark wanted to buy some sweets.

2 There are several characters in this story. Put them in order according to who you think was the most responsible for Mark's accident. Discuss your answers in groups.

3 Imagine that you are characters in the story. Make as many sentences using **wish** and the third conditional as you can.

USE OF ENGLISH

Fill each of the numbered blanks in the following passage. Use only **one** word in each space.

A blind bank robber who was desperate for money was given a 12-month suspended sentence. David Worrell had .... (1) put his white stick on the counter before .... (2) a note to the cashier saying he .... (3) shoot her if she did not hand over the cash. The court heard .... (4) Worrell had lost his previous job because of his condition and had been .... (5) down for many more.

Worrell, ... (6) pleaded guilty to attempted robbery, queued up and passed a note .... (7) £2,000. He wanted to use the money to start his .... (8) disco business. The cashier .... (9) the alarm and refused to .... (10) over any money. .... (11) if he had got away a young blind person would have been .... (12) to identify. When he tried to .... (13), he walked straight into the bank's glass doors .... (14) than through them. He was later arrested.

Between the incident and his trial, Worrell had succeeded .... (15) starting his own successful discotheque. .... (16) judge said, 'This sort of offence would .... (17) result in a substantial term of imprisonment. You are a man of good character, with an .... (18) severe physical disability but .... (19) this you have been able to generate .... (20) prosperous business.'

WRITING

The opinion question

1 Two students wrote answers to the question. *'It is often said that serious crime could be reduced if judges gave stricter sentences.' How far do you agree with this view?*
Working in pairs or small groups, read both compositions and decide which one gives the better answer to the question. Decide which one has:

- the better ideas.
- the better range of expressions.
- the better vocabulary.

---

(1)

The number of serious crimes has increased in the past few years. Most of these crimes are committed for economic and social reasons. What can justice do to reduce them?

Each country has its own laws which is why the same crime can be sentenced in different ways. The first reason why judges should give stricter sentences is because more and more criminals are no longer afraid of being punished. They know that prisons are overcrowded and that most of them will be released early for good behaviour. Therefore justice should be more consistent and give sentences which will immediately frighten criminals.

The second reason is that in certain countries capital punishment has been abolished.

(2)

This special sentence could be re-introduced for very difficult cases. For example, a terrorist responsible for the deaths of innocent people should not be kept alive.

On the other hand lots of crimes are committed because of poverty and unemployment. Delinquency cannot be cured by stricter sentences. Some people need to be directly helped in their lives at school, work and in the family.

To sum up, for shocking crimes capital punishment should be used but carefully. Anyway, justice should be more competent and precise in order to take care against mistakes.

(1)

I do not think that stricter sentences would by themselves reduce serious crime. But I want harder and longer punishment because it shows that someone has done something wrong and will maybe keep people from doing the same thing.

What we have to do is ask ourselves what our morality is. We could do a lot so that our children do not grow up in a world without rules, order and morality. This is difficult but very important.

We can do a lot for criminals, both during and after their time in prison. We have to educate them about what is right and wrong and make

(2)

them understand. I know that this is sometimes done but we have to look after them even after they have left prison. Give them a job and somewhere to live. More things for them would cost more but they could be paid for by reducing the comfort in prison. It is not necessary for them to have videos or colour TV etc.

I can sum up by saying that I want stricter sentences together with more work to make them more functional in today's society.

2 Take the best elements from both compositions and write your own composition on the same topic. If you have any problems, refer to the composition work in Units 7 and 9.

3 USE OF ENGLISH

Finish each of the following sentences in such a way that it means exactly the same as the sentence printed before it.

1 You're going to end up in prison if you don't change your ways.
   Unless ....

2 My advice to you is to call the police.
   If I ....

3 The policeman told us to fit new locks on the door.
   He suggested ....

4 He did not wear gloves so the police caught him.
   If ....

5 It is a pity she didn't insure the stereo.
   She wishes ....

6 Thieves broke into our house while we were on holiday.
   Our house ....

7 Would you like me to call the police?
   I'll call ....

8 If I had known all the facts, I would not have rung the police.
   As I ....

9 Jerry didn't steal the jewels. He didn't know where the key to the safe was.
   Jerry can't ....

10 You can borrow the car, but you've got to fill it up with petrol.
   Provided ....

Beyond belief

SPEAKING

Find out from your partner if he/she:

1 believes in ghosts.
2 is at all superstitious.
3 has ever had, or knows someone who has had, a
  supernatural experience.
4 believes in telepathy or premonitions of the future.

LISTENING
The Chaffin Will affair

1 Listen to the story and find out what the
connection is between a will, a coat, a bible and
a ghost!

2 Listen to the story again and decide if these
statements are **true** or **false**.

1 Marshall doesn't seem to have been a generous
  person.
2 The first will had been written before 1906.
3 The strange events took place in 1925.
4 The ghost appeared to Mrs Chaffin.
5 The ghost sometimes didn't tell the truth.
6 The note was found in an overcoat pocket.
7 The bible belonged to Mrs Chaffin.
8 Each son finally inherited a third of the property.

● Can you come up with a logical explanation for
  what happened?

READING

1 Doris Stokes was a famous medium. She claimed
she was able to contact the spirits of the dead. Read
her story quickly and find out:

1 what she thought about her imaginary friends.
2 how imaginary friends helped her.
3 when she had her first psychic experience.

Imaginary friends

BY DORIS STOKES

'My mum warned me that I'd end up in a mental hospital.'

We have all heard of children who have imaginary playmates. I get lots of letters from parents about them and I always say the same thing: don't say there is no one there. What you are putting down to imagination could be a spirit child.

One dad wrote to me to say he was getting very worried about his child. He told me his son had an imaginary friend called Robbie, and was forever saying things like, 'Don't set off yet. Robbie's not in the car.'

I told him, 'Your child can actually see that boy, love. Don't say anything. He'll either grow out of it and go on to more worldly things or he'll develop into a very good medium.'

I was about six or seven when I first saw the spirit children. I'd had rheumatic fever and had to be in a pushchair. I don't know how, but I knew that other people could not see Christopher and Pansy. I saw them a lot. And you know, I never could do maths — it was a mystery to me — but Christopher and Pansy helped me pass my exams!

So there's nothing frightening about children having imaginary friends, especially if they've been very close. I remember one little lad telling his mum, 'You don't have to come up and turn the light off tonight. Grandma will do it.'

His mum watched him go upstairs on his own that night and the lights went off! It scares the life out of some parents. But you just have to accept that his grandma loved him very much. She'd always tucked him in. It was a routine.

Most children are psychic up to the age of 11 or 12. My first psychic experience happened when I was four. I woke up to a commotion outside in the street.

There was a fire in the house nearby, and all the neighbours were crying. They kept saying, 'Poor Tom, what a terrible way to die.' As I peered from between their legs, I saw they were bringing out a stretcher with little Tom on it, and Tom was also walking beside it. I told my dad I'd seen Tom and he said, 'If you did, love, then you did.' You see, I'd seen Tom's spirit walking beside him.

My mum warned me that I'd end up in a mental hospital. I did. Nearly 40 years later I was a nurse in one!

2 Choose the best answers to these questions.

1 Imaginary playmates
   A can worry parents.
   B are imaginary.
   C make parents write to Doris.
   D are usually spirit children.

2 Children who have psychic experiences
   A are generally frightened by them.
   B always see friends.
   C either see friends or grandparents.
   D can see someone who's been close.

3 Doris's spirit friends
   A were invisible to everyone.
   B were older than Doris.
   C taught her to do maths.
   D got her through her exams.

4 Doris claims that
   A children over 12 aren't psychic.
   B children tend to lose their powers after 12.
   C children are only psychic until 12.
   D a few children are psychic at some point.

5 When Doris said that she'd seen her friend Tom, her mother
   A thought Doris was going mad.
   B became psychic herself.
   C thought Doris was psychic.
   D knew Doris was going to become a nurse.

3 Discussion points

1 What do you think about Doris's stories and powers?
2 Do you know of any mediums in your own country?
3 What is the place of such powers in conventional religion?

VOCABULARY
Ways of looking

Doris Stokes says *she peered through someone's legs.*
Peer is a way of looking.
Using these dictionary definitions, complete the sentences which follow with a way of looking.

gaze /geɪz/ to look steadily for a long or short period of time
peer /pɪə/ to look very carefully or hard, especially if it is hard to see
look /lʊk/ to turn the eyes so as to see, examine or find something
see /siː/ to use the eyes, have the power of sight
stare /steə/ to look fixedly, with wide open eyes, as in wonder, fear, anger or deep in thought
glance /glɑːns/ to give a rapid look
watch /wɒtʃ/ to look at some activity/event

1 They sat on the bench and .... the tennis match.
2 He quickly .... over his shoulder to see if anyone was following him.
3 She wound down the car window and .... at the sign through the fog.
4 Do you think you could .... at the engine for me? It doesn't seem to be working properly.
5 Have you ever .... a ghost?
6 The child .... at the woman's strange hat for a good five minutes.
7 They stood on the top of the hill and .... at the beautiful river.

LANGUAGE STUDY
Abbreviating clauses

1 Doris Stokes says *I'd seen Tom's spirit **walking beside him.***
This is the same as *I'd seen Tom's spirit. It was walking beside him.*
Study these next two examples. What are the differences between them?

1 We saw them. They were opening the door.
   → *We saw them opening the door.*
2 She felt a hand. It touched her face.
   → *She felt a hand touch her face.*

2 Join these pairs of sentences in the same way.

1 We felt the ground. It started to shake.
2 Anna noticed a strange smell. It was coming from a cupboard.
3 Did you hear their dog? It was barking all night?
4 We listened to their footsteps. They were coming closer.
5 The policeman caught the thief. He was climbing through the window.
6 The children watched the farmer. He was milking the cows.

 LISTENING

Juliet, Malcolm and Yolanda are discussing reincarnation. Listen to their conversation and answer the following questions.

1 Of the three,
   A only Juliet believes in reincarnation.
   B nobody is completely convinced about reincarnation.
   C only one believes in reincarnation.
   D Malcolm is the most open-minded.

2 Juliet gives information about .... of Jane Evans' previous lives.
   A three
   B four
   C five
   D six

3 Which of the following statements is not mentioned as a criticism of Jane Evans' past life in France?
   A She forgot to mention basic domestic details.
   B She was often inaccurate.
   C Many of the facts were already well-known.
   D She couldn't remember the merchant's name.

4 Gretchen Gottlieb
   A used to be called Dolores.
   B spoke English.
   C died like the Jewish girl.
   D had never studied German.

5 In the case of Gretchen Gottlieb,
   A researchers managed to check the facts.
   B her answers were sometimes illogical.
   C her German showed a few mistakes.
   D the researchers felt they were being tricked.

 PRONUNCIATION

1 When Juliet says she has been reading a book about reincarnation Malcolm comments *Reincarnation! You surely don't believe in all that.* Notice the way he says **reincarnation.** His voice rises then falls. This **tune** is often used to express disbelief.
Listen to the recording again and stop the cassette every time you hear this particular tune. Try to copy the intonation.

2 Listen to these six phrases. Is the speaker showing surprise, showing disbelief or making a simple statement?

1 His own daughter.
2 His own daughter.
3 His own daughter.
4 By car.
5 By car.
6 By car.

 LANGUAGE STUDY
no sooner and **not only**

1 In the **Listening** Juliet says *No sooner had she told the story **than** some archaeologists found the cellar.* This means the same as *She had no sooner told the story than some archaeologists found the cellar.*

*Not only did she make a lot of mistakes **but she also** avoided using verbs.*
This means the same as *She not only made a lot of mistakes but she also avoided using verbs.*

1 What happens if we begin a sentence with **no sooner** or **not only**? Try to make a rule.
2 Why might we use this type of construction in conversation or when writing?
3 Do you know of any other phrases which can be used in this kind of construction?

2 Finish each of the following sentences in such a way that it means exactly the same as the sentence printed before it.

1 The moment she arrived she started to complain.
No sooner ....

2 He both sings and dances.
Not only ....

3 Never have I eaten such an awful meal.
I ....

4 No sooner had the match begun than fighting broke out.
When fighting ....

5 Not only is this exercise tedious it is also hard.
This ....

6 We had hardly put up the tent than it started to rain.
No sooner ....

VOCABULARY
Extreme adjectives

1 Juliet says
*There are some **fascinating** stories in this book.*
Fascinating means **very interesting**.
In the box there are pairs of adjectives similar to **interesting** and **fascinating**. Match them up.

GORGEOUS   COLD   BOILING   HUGE

STARVING   TINY   BIG

TERRIFIED

TIRED   FASCINATING

SURE

FRIGHTENED   INTERESTING   HUNGRY

BAD   POSITIVE

FREEZING   WONDERFUL

AWFUL   HOT

BEAUTIFUL   EXHAUSTED   SMALL   GOOD

• Can you think of any other pairs of adjectives that operate in the same way?

2 Look at these sentences and decide which ones are right and which are wrong.

1 It's very cold.
2 It's very freezing.
3 It's absolutely freezing.
4 It's absolutely cold.
5 It's really cold.
6 It's really freezing.

• How can we modify **ordinary** adjectives like **cold** and **extreme** adjectives like **freezing**

• When can we use **very, absolutely, really?**

3 Complete these sentences using an appropriate adjective from the box.

1 After the walk, we were .... as we had not eaten all day.

2 The room was really .... He had to stand on the bed to close the door.

3 Can you close the window? It's .... in here!

4 Don't eat in that restaurant! The food is
....

5 'You look great after your holiday!' 'Yes, I feel
....'

6 He was so .... when he saw the spider that he fainted.

7 What a .... dress! It's the most beautiful one I've ever seen!

8 The book was so .... that she read it in one go.

9 They live in a .... house. It's got ten bedrooms and six bathrooms.

10 I didn't sleep at all last night. I feel totally
....

11 I'm absolutely .... he used to be a policeman.

12 I'm not really very .... I had a big breakfast.

WRITING
The Mysterious Hitchhiker

1 In Unit 4 we looked at telling a story. Here is some more practice.
Read the two versions of the same story and note what the differences between them are. Think about vocabulary, grammar and style.

2 In pairs, write the end of the story of the second version using words and expressions you have learnt in this unit.

3 Write a composition on this subject.
You were walking through the countryside one day with a friend when you came across a ruined mansion. Describe what happened.

Version 1

ONE NIGHT a friend of mine was driving past one of the cemeteries outside Rome. By the side of the road, he saw a girl of about 18 who was hitchhiking. He stopped to pick her up and, as she looked cold, lent her his jacket.

She told him where she wanted to go and he took her to a block of flats in a small street. As she got out, she held out the jacket but Carlo told her to keep it and that he would see her another time. She smiled and went into the building.

A few days later, Carlo went back to find her. When he told an old woman the girl's description, she told him that the girl used to live there but had died a couple of years before.

Three months later Carlo went to the cemetery to put some flowers on his mother's grave. As he was leaving the cemetery, he noticed his jacket on another gravestone. When he picked it up, he saw the photograph of the girl he had given a lift to.

Version 2

ONE COLD WINTER'S EVENING, Carlo, an old friend of mine, was driving past one of the huge cemeteries just outside Rome. It was freezing cold and he happened to notice a young girl hitchhiking by the side of the road. Even though it was winter, she was just wearing a thin dress.

Carlo pulled up and opened the passenger door to let her in. Her lips were blue with cold so he gave her the jacket he was wearing to put over her shoulders. After a few moments' silence, he asked her where she wanted to go and she whispered her instructions. He glanced at her and noticed for the first time that she was extremely beautiful. She had a delicate pale face with long blonde hair and large green eyes. He wondered what she had been doing standing by the side of the road and guessed that she looked so sad because she must have had a row with her boyfriend who had left her there.

They drove on in silence, the girl making little gestures to show him which route to take. They finally turned into a narrow street in an old part of town. As soon as the girl got out, she took off the jacket and held it out to Carlo. Carlo refused to take it because she still looked cold and he wanted an excuse to see her again. She smiled mysteriously and disappeared through a dark doorway, without saying a word ... .

149

READING

1 In Unit 5 we looked at the techniques you can use for answering the multiple choice questions. As a final check, see if you can put this procedure into the right order.

> ▢ Make your choice. Don't rush and watch out for 'traps'.
> ▢ Read the text again, slowly and carefully.
> ▢ Identify the parts of the text for which there are questions.
> ▢ If in real doubt, guess the answer from the most likely of the alternatives.
> ▢ Read the text through quickly for a general understanding.
> ▢ Eliminate the obviously wrong alternatives.
> ▢ Read each question and its four alternative answers.

2 Now apply the procedure to this text. The multiple choice questions are on the opposite page.

Understanding the mysteries of intuition

by Graham Greene

I can well believe in telepathy, for it has been part of my life since childhood. My mother had the gift of picking up thoughts from my elder sister. The two used to play it as a game at parties, and I can still see no way in which they could have cheated.

My mother would leave the room and the guests would decide between them, with no intervention from my sister, some action for my mother to perform when she was summoned back into the room. My mother would gaze closely for a moment at my sister and then would make the action we had chosen, moving a cushion or a chair, perhaps taking the lid off a box. I never saw her fail.

My own first experience of what might be a kind of telepathy I have already described in *A Sort of Life*. I would have put it down to mere coincidence if it had not been repeated twice under roughly the same circumstances, each involving a tragedy at sea and a loss of life. The first occasion was during an Easter seaside holiday at Littlehampton when I was seven years old. I dreamt of a shipwreck and I can still see clearly one image of the dream. A man is scrambling up the staircase of a ship and a great wave is coming down to swamp him. Next morning we heard the news of the *Titanic* sunk that night.

Of the second dream of a wreck about ten years later, I have also written. I can recall no details and have lost the dream diary which I was keeping during a course of psychoanalysis in London. Perhaps writing down the dream cancelled the memory of it. Again, my dream coincided with a real wreck, this time of the *Rowan* in the Irish Sea when, I seem to remember, that a whole orchestra lost their lives.

Always the sea, always lives lost. But the third occasion was not a dream. I was in my flat in Antibes one morning, some six or seven years ago, with nothing to worry me when around breakfast time I was overcome by a deep depression and an anxiety agonizing in its acuteness. I have a witness, for a friend came to lunch with me and I told her what I feared, that something terrible had happened to one of my family. To distract me, she turned on the radio for the one o'clock news. A plane coming from Corsica had crashed that morning into the sea off Cap d'Antibes a few miles away and there were no survivors. On board was General Cogny whom I had known and liked in Vietnam.

1 In the party game Greene describes
 A he played no part.
 B his sister would have to guess.
 C his sister would have to mime.
 D his mother often guessed wrongly.

2 Greene describes
 A one accident.
 B two dreams.
 C three dreams.
 D four incidents.

3 Greene claims the first dream
 A involved lots of people.
 B was after the sinking of the *Titanic*.
 C was just a coincidence.
 D can't have been a coincidence.

4 The second dream he describes
 A was never recorded.
 B is still completely clear.
 C had no connection with real life.
 D happened in his teens.

5 On the third occasion
 A he was eating breakfast.
 B he was alone.
 C his prediction was not accurate.
 D a relative was involved.

USE OF ENGLISH 3

Fill each of the numbered blanks in the following passage. Use only **one** word in each space.

Most ghost stories are set in mysterious, old houses .... (1) castles. The ghosts themselves, ... (2) spirits wander the earth at night, are usually the .... (3) of some horrible crime. This is not always the case as the .... (4) story shows.

When my friend, Paul, was a schoolboy, he often .... (5) to chat to Mr Scott, an elderly gentleman .... (6) on his own. Mr Scott was a keen gardener. He .... (7) always be looking after his lawn or his flowers and Paul was .... (8) the habit of saying a few words to him over .... (9) fence.

.... (10) summer's evening, as Paul was .... (11) his way home from school, he saw, as usual, Mr Scott in his garden. The old man was busily weeding his .... (12) beds. When he saw Paul, he invited him into the garden with a wave of his hand. Slowly, they strolled .... (13) round, admiring the various flowers. Then, to Paul's surprise, Mr Scott bent .... (14) and picked a bunch of his finest dahlias. 'Here boy,' he said. 'Give these to your mother.'

No .... (15) had he arrived home than he presented the flowers to his mother. He then told her that they were with Mr Scott's compliments. His mother's face went red .... (16) anger. '..................... (17) wicked boy!' she shouted. 'How .... (18) you say such a thing! I bumped .... (19) his daughter in the supermarket this morning. She told me that the poor old chap had passed .... (20) in his sleep last Friday.'

VOCABULARY

Choose the word or phrase which best completes the sentence — A, B, C or D.

1 His bad behaviour was put .... his upbringing.
   A up with **B** off **C** by **D** down to

2 You shouldn't .... at people. It's rude!
   A watch **B** glance **C** stare **D** peer

3 Can you .... me to your parents when you next see them?
   A excuse **B** remind **C** forget **D** remember

4 Tomorrow morning we are going to .... mushrooms.
   A pluck **B** select **C** choose **D** pick

5 I am .... the habit of reading in bed.
   A in **B** on **C** of **D** from

6 She .... the answer in his ear so nobody else could hear.
   A told **B** shouted **C** whispered **D** confessed

7 Take the wine downstairs and put it in the ....
   A attic **B** cellar **C** loft **D** cave

8 We watched the cat .... the tree.
   A climbed **B** climb **C** had climbed **D** was climbing

9 When his grandmother died, he came .... a fortune.
   A into **B** up with **C** by **D** across

10 Sometimes she sleepwalks and you can find her .... through the house.
   A strolling **B** wandering **C** walk **D** stepping

11 There wasn't enough .... to convict the suspect.
   A evidence **B** suspicion **C** proof **D** prove

12 It was .... hot that we took off our jackets.
   A very **B** so **C** really **D** absolutely

13 We weren't taken .... by his story.
   A in **B** up **C** on **D** out

14 He .... her into buying a new car.
   A convinced **B** talked **C** persuaded **D** made

15 Their parents .... to let them go to the party.
   A did not **B** denied **C** refused **D** prevented

Remember that there will be 25 items in this section of the exam.

"Hang on, didn't four of us carry him here?"

UNIT 14 *Destination USA*

AMERICAN LINE.
United States Mail Steamers.

BETWEEN
LIVERPOOL AND PHILADELPHIA.

The First-class Full-powered Iron Steamships

Pennsylvania | Indiana | Abbotsford
Kenilworth | Ohio | Illinois

LIVERPOOL TO PHILA...

Calling at QUEENSTOW...
This is the only TRANS-AT...
The Steamers are fitte...

...ed Rates. ...een two and
Provisions, but without Wines or Liquors.

SPEAKING

1 Working in pairs or small groups, describe and discuss these pictures.

1 Where had these people come from?
2 Why had they left their homes?
3 How do you think they felt?

2 Discussion points
1 Have you ever considered emigrating?
2 What circumstances would make you leave your own country?
3 If you had to, which country would you emigrate to and why?
4 Do you have relatives who have emigrated?
5 How easy or difficult would it be for a foreigner to settle down in your country?

READING

1 Read the text, study the US immigration graph and answer the questions.

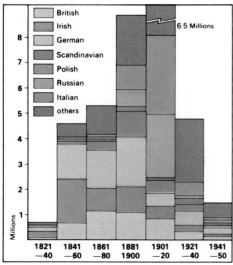

Immigration in the 19th century.

Legend:
British
Irish
German
Scandinavian
Polish
Russian
Italian
others

6.5 Millions

Y-axis: Millions

X-axis: 1821—40, 1841—60, 1861—80, 1881—1900, 1901—20, 1921—40, 1941—50

1 How many people emigrated from Europe between 1815 and 1914?
2 When was the Irish potato famine?
3 How many foreign-born Americans were there in 1890?
4 What was the number of black slaves in 1860?

THE MELTING POT

The USA is a land of immigrants. Between 1815 and 1914, the world witnessed the greatest peaceful migration in its history: 35 million people, mostly Europeans, left their homelands to start new lives in America. Why did these people risk everything by leaving their homes and families to see what the New World had to offer? How had the Old World let them down? There are both *push* and *pull* factors which we should consider.

Al Pacino — his family came from Italy.

First, what forced emigrants to make the momentous decision to leave? One major cause of the exodus among European peasants was the rise in population which in turn led to *land hunger*. Another was politics. Nationalism saw increased taxation and the growth of armies, and many young men fled eastern Europe to avoid being conscripted. Also, the failure of the liberal revolutions in Europe caused the departure of hundreds of thousands of refugees.

Physical hunger provided another pressing reason. Between 1845 and 1848, the terrible potato famine in Ireland ended in the deaths of one million Irish people and the emigration of a further million who wished to escape starvation. Following the collapse of the economy of southern Italy in the 1860s, hundreds of thousands decided to start afresh in America.

Religion also encouraged millions to leave the Old World. We should remember that the Pilgrim Fathers had wished to escape the ungodliness of England, while the Russian Jews of the last century sought to escape persecution and death in their native land.

Ronald and Nancy Reagan in Ireland discovering his roots.

In short, people chose to leave their homes for social, economic and religious reasons. As a result, by 1890 among a total population of 63 million, there were more than nine million foreign-born Americans.

But what were the attractions? First of all, there was the promise of land which was so scarce in Europe. Next, factories were calling out for labour, and pay and conditions were much better than back home. Men were needed to open up the West and build the long railroads, and settlers were needed to populate new towns and develop commerce. There was the space for religious communities to practise their faith in peace and comparative isolation.

This immigration meant that by around the 1850s Americans of non-English extraction had started to outnumber those of English extraction. As we know, there were losers. To start with, there were those unwilling immigrants, the slaves who had been used as a source of cheap labour for the tobacco plantations of the South. Nor should we forget the equally awful fate of the American Indians. By 1860 there were 27 million free whites, four million slaves and a mere 488,000 free blacks.

Nowadays, the USA is still seen by millions as the Promised Land. Gone are the days when you could buy US citizenship for one dollar. Yet, even though entry is strictly limited, refugees continue to find freedom and people from poorer countries a better way of life. As always, it remains a magnet to the ambitious and the energetic who are ready to commit themselves to the land that gives them a second chance.

2 Choose the best answers to these questions.

1 What is not given as a reason for emigration in the text?
   A The search for religious freedom.
   B The search for adventure.
   C Avoidance of military service.
   D Economics.

2 The lives of 19th Century European peasants were difficult because
   A there was no shortage of land.
   B of peace.
   C the population had gone down.
   D there were too many of them.

3 Which of these things was not an attraction of the USA?
   A Employment.
   B A healthy life.
   C Availability of land.
   D Business opportunities.

4 Which fraction gives the closest estimate of the number of non-native born Americans in 1890?
   A A third.
   B An eighth.
   C A half.
   D A quarter.

5 The story of the American Indians is
   A sadder than that of the slaves.
   B the saddest tale of all.
   C not as sad as that of the slaves.
   D as sad as that of the slaves.

LANGUAGE STUDY
The gerund and the infinitive

1 Study these two sentences.
*They **chose to leave** their homes for social, economic and religious reasons.*
*Immigrants **risked losing** their lives in the West.*

If we want to follow **choose** with another verb, we must put the second verb into the **infinitive**.
We can't say *They chose emigrating.*

If we want to follow **risk** with another verb, we must put the second verb into the **gerund**.
We can't say *They risk to lose their lives.*

2 Complete these sentences putting the verb in brackets into either the **infinitive** or **gerund**.

1 Have you ever considered .... (*emigrate*)?
2 The customs officer refused .... (*let*) him into the country.
3 They denied .... (*enter*) the country illegally.
4 The government agreed .... (*allow*) the refugees over the border.
5 They threatened .... (*deport*) her on the next flight.
6 He avoided .... (*cross*) the bridge by swimming the river.
7 The tourist offered .... (*hide*) her in the boot of his car.
8 Would you mind .... (*show*) me your passport, sir?
9 Have you finished .... (*fill in*) that form?
10 He pretended .... not (*understand*) the regulations.
11 Immigration officials tend .... (*be*) suspicious.

3 Now make a list of those verbs in the exercise that are followed by either the infinitive or gerund. Can you add to the list?

+ infinitive	+ gerund
choose	*risk*

4 Look at these pairs of sentences. Decide where there is:
● little or no change in meaning.
● an important change in meaning.

1 It started to rain. It started raining.
2 He remembered to close the window. He remembered closing the window.
3 I like to play tennis. I like playing tennis.
4 My car needs working on. I need to work on my car.
5 They stopped to look at the map. They stopped looking at the map.
6 She tried to learn Japanese. She tried learning ten new words a day.

5 Put the verbs in brackets into the **gerund** or **infinitive**. Sometimes, both may be possible. Look carefully at the context you are given.

1 Don't forget .... (*go*) to the travel agent's, will you? The plane tickets need .... (*pick up*).
2 I shall never forget .... (*see*) her for the first time.
3 Oh, no! It's starting .... (*rain*).
4 I like .... (*play*) tennis but I wouldn't like .... (*play*) with her. She's such a bad loser.
5 Lucia started .... (*study*) English six years ago.
6 He remembers .... (*drive*) up to the crossroads but nothing else after the accident.
7 Do try .... (*make*) less noise. I'm trying .... (*concentrate*).
8 Have you ever stopped .... (*wonder*) why she behaves like that?
9 We really need .... (*do*) some shopping; we're running out of everything.
10 I've tried .... (*jog*) and aerobics, but I still can't lose weight.
11 I'm terribly sorry but I forgot .... (*post*) your letters.
12 Did you remember .... (*do*) your homework?
13 I'll stop .... (*lend*) you money if you waste it on cigarettes.
14 I can't get this table through the door. Have you tried .... (*take off*) the legs?

3 USE OF ENGLISH

Judith is on holiday in New York. She is talking to Mr O'Rourke. Complete the dialogue by filling in the blanks numbered 1 to 6. But read the whole conversation first.

JUDITH:	With a name like O'Rourke, you must be Irish.
MR O'ROURKE:	That's right, my dear. I sure am.
JUDITH:	(1) ....?
MR O'ROURKE:	Well, my great great grandfather came here more than 130 years ago.
JUDITH:	(2) ....?
MR O'ROURKE:	Life was so terrible in Ireland. There just wasn't enough to eat.
JUDITH:	(3) ....?
MR O'ROURKE:	No, he came with two of his brothers but one died on the voyage.
JUDITH:	(4) ....?
MR O'ROURKE:	Yes, I have. My wife and I went back to visit our old village ten years ago.
JUDITH:	(5) ....?
MR O'ROURKE:	It was the most unforgettable experience I have ever had. I met lots of distant cousins.
JUDITH:	(6) ....?
MR O'ROURKE:	Yes, we have kept in touch. In fact, some of them are coming over to spend the Easter vacation with us.

VOCABULARY
Phrasal verbs in this unit

1 Match the phrasal verb on the left with its synonym on the right.

1 set up	**A** persuade
2 take up	**B** make a home
3 go up	**C** disappoint
4 carry out	**D** establish
5 talk into	**E** increase
6 settle down	**F** adopt/start something new
7 let down	**G** become popular
8 catch on	**H** perform

2 Complete the sentences using each phrasal verb **once** only. Make any necessary changes to the sentences.

1 This new game is really ....; everybody is playing it.
2 You shouldn't make threats if you're not going to .... them ....
3 Why do prices keep ....?
4 The shop assistant .... me .... buying this new suit and I really hate it already!
5 It's time you .... and started a family.
6 This business was .... 100 years ago.
7 When she retired, she .... gardening so she wouldn't get bored.
8 I'm sorry to .... you .... but I can't take you to the airport after all.

3 When you have finished the unit, go through it and see what context these phrasal verbs have been used in.

LANGUAGE STUDY
Saying numbers

By 1860 there were twenty-seven million free whites, four million slaves and a mere four hundred and eighty-eight thousand free blacks.

In pairs, look at the following sentences and, where necessary, correct them.

1 She lived for hundred years.
2 The population of the USA is over two hundred millions.
3 Five thousands of people visit the gallery every day.
4 My telephone number is twenty four, thirty three, eight hundred and ninety five.
5 I would like one dozen of eggs please.
6 The code for London is nought one.
7 Dozens of people walked out of the film.
8 The book is one hundred eighty pages long.
9 Altogether that's three pounds and sixty five.
10 The average family has two comma four children.
11 The drawer is an eight of an inch too wide.
12 There were thousands of people at the party.
13 The Battle of Waterloo was in one thousand eight hundred and fifteen.
14 My car goes thirty miles for one gallon of petrol.

LISTENING

Listen to the numbers and write them down.

1 Phone numbers
A .... B ....
2 Account numbers
A .... B ....
3 Decimals
A .... B ....
C ....
4 Fractions
A .... B ....
C .... D ....
5 Dates
A .... B ....
C ....
6 Amounts
A .... B ....
7 Scores
A Lendl won the tennis match ....
B Italy beat Holland ....
8 Large numbers
A .... B ....
C ....

 PRONUNCIATION 📼

1 Listen to the phone numbers and account numbers again and try to copy the rhythm and intonation. How are the numbers broken up?

2 In pairs give each other these telephone numbers over the phone.

1 635 4551
2 289 6412
3 010 33 4842 6780

Now change roles.

4 045 75551
5 010 36 5 421 5331
6 4524

 VOCABULARY
British and American English

There are some differences between British and American English but don't worry too much, the language is mostly the same!

1 Match the American English words on the left with the British English words on the right.

1	cable	A	holiday
2	diaper	B	note
3	apartment	C	chemist
4	truck	D	plaster
5	fall	E	biscuits
6	vacation	F	bill (*in a restaurant*)
7	band-aid	G	lift
8	purse	H	telegram
9	check	I	petrol
10	cookies	J	nappy
11	drug store	K	tap
12	freeway	L	handbag
13	gas	M	underground
14	bill (*paper money*)	N	lorry
15	elevator	O	autumn
16	candy	P	motorway
17	subway	Q	sweets
18	faucet	R	flat

2 Change these sentences from American into British English.

1 Can you go to the drugstore, honey? We need some diapers for the baby and a band-aid for my finger.
2 Last fall, I was driving along a freeway when I ran out of gas. Luckily, a truck driver stopped and gave me a ride.
3 Our apartment is quite near the subway station.
4 They sent us a cable inviting us to spend our Christmas vacation with them.
5 It's my turn to pay the check. Pass me my purse; I've got a $20 bill in it.
6 Cookies and candy are bad for our teeth.
7 Nothing works round here! Not only is the elevator broken, but so is the faucet in the bathroom!

● Can you think of any other words that are American English?

SPEAKING

Structured communicative activity

Here is some more practice for the last part of **Paper 5: Interview.** You have a free day in New York. Working in small groups and, using the information below, plan a day's sightseeing together.

METROPOLITAN MUSEUM OF ART

 Opening times
Tues 10 am—8.45 pm
Wed-Sat 10 am—4.45 pm
Sun and public holidays
10 am—4.45 pm
Closed Mon
The Metropolitan
Museum of Art — America's largest museum of art and the third largest in the world, only the British Museum and the Hermitage in Leningrad being larger — was founded in 1870 on the private initiative of a group of New York citizens who believed that their city, with a population then approaching a million, ought to have an art museum of its own.

EMPIRE STATE BUILDING

 Although now exceeded in height by the World Trade Center, the Empire State Building, erected in 1931, is still the principal emblem and landmark of New York. From its two observatories (viewing terraces) on the 86th and 102nd floors there are incomparable views over Manhattan, extending in clear weather to other parts of the city and the neighbouring state of New Jersey.

LITTLE ITALY

 Immediately NW of Chinatown is another of New York's smaller ethnic enclaves, Little Italy, now increasingly losing its identity as a result of the northwest movement of the Chinese population.

In Mulberry Street are many Italian restaurants (one of the best known being Paolucci, No. 149, in a building dating from 1816) and Italian-style cafés (the best known of which is Ferrara, established in 1892, at 195 Grand Street, around the corner from Mulberry Street). There are also numerous Italian shops and men's clubs in Little Italy.

MACY'S

 Broadway and 34th Street
Opening times
Mon, Thurs and Fri
9.45 am—8.30 pm
Tues and Wed
9.45 am—6.45 pm
Sat 9.45 am—6 pm
Sun noon—5 pm

CENTRAL PARK

 Central Park is the principal "lung" of New York City, with an area of 340 ha (840 acres), 5% of the total area of Manhattan. It extends for 4 km (2½ miles) from 59th to 110th Street, with a breadth of 500 m (550 yd) between Fifth Avenue and Central Park West, the continuation of Eighth Avenue.

LISTENING

In **Paper 4** you will have to complete three or four comprehension tasks. The listening passages could take the form of interviews and dialogues, radio broadcasts, announcements and instructions or parts of lectures on any topic.

Each passage will be played **twice.** There is a short pause between each time the tape is played.

EXAMINATION ADVICE

■ When the examination paper is given out, you only have about a minute to look at it. This minute is very important! Make sure that you read the questions before you hear the tape. This means that you will know what you have to listen out for.

■ Don't worry if the language of the tape is difficult. The questions you have to answer will test understanding at the level of students at First Certificate.

■ At the end of each section, make sure that you read the questions for the next passage you are going to hear.

■ **Always** write in ink. **Never** write in pencil.

■ **Never** try to make notes and fill in the question paper afterwards. You will not have time.

---

1 Listen to the guide giving details about the Statue of Liberty and fill in this table.

DATE ON THE TABLET(1)	_____
NAME OF THE SCULPTOR (2)	_____
MATERIAL (3)	_____
STATUE FINISHED (4)	_____
HEIGHT OF STATUE (5)	_____
HEIGHT OF STATUE AND PEDESTAL	
(6) _____ FEET, (7) _____ METRES.	
WEIGHT (8)	_____
WHEN DEDICATED (9)	_____

2 Gus is telling his friend Andy about the rules of American football. Listen carefully to their conversation and answer the following questions.

1 A field goal is worth
  A six points.
  B one point.
  C three points.
  D two points.

2 In American football, you can pass the ball forwards
  A as often as you like.
  B never.
  C twice in a *play*.
  D once in a *play*.

3 A *play* is
  A thirty seconds.
  B when the teams block and tackle.
  C the time between two scrimmages.
  D when the ball is passed between players.

4 How many examples does Gus give of when the ball can change hands between teams?
  A 2.
  B 3.
  C 4.
  D 5.

5 Gus thinks that American football is
  A easy to understand.
  B twice as difficult to understand as cricket.
  C half as difficult to understand as cricket.
  D easier to understand than cricket.

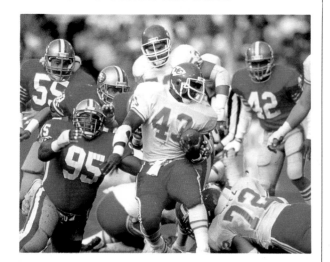

3 Listen to two friends discussing the Mormons and decide if these statements are **true** or **false**.

  1 Gina is no longer a Mormon.
  2 Mormonism is a Christian religion.
  3 It dates from 1727.
  4 Smith was visited by Mormon.
  5 There are similarities with the Old Testament.
  6 The plates were written in Hebrew.
  7 Mormonism quickly became popular.
  8 The plates may have come from Israel.
  9 The dead can be included in the church.
10 Mormons have more than one wife.

3 USE OF ENGLISH

1 The word in capital letters at the end of each of the following sentences can be used to form a word that fits suitably in the blank space. Supply the correct form of the word.

Example: *The inspector heard the man's **confession.***
        CONFESS

Note This exercise revises vocabulary which has appeared in this unit.

1 It was a .... episode in the country's history.   SHAME
2 They celebrate their .... on 4th July. DEPEND
3 The refugees found .... over the border. SAFE
4 The king's .... organized a revolution. OPPOSE
5 My aunt is an .... officer.   MIGRATE
6 He missed the .... of his train by a minute.   DEPART
7 The .... was won in the last minute of the game.   CHAMPION
8 It was a complete .... due to poor planning.   FAIL
9 Their .... has lasted a lifetime. FRIEND

2 Fill each of the numbered blanks in the following passage. Use only **one** word in each space.

Baseball, rather than American football, is the national game of the USA. So, it is quite .... (1) that Americans are proud of it and .... (2) it extremely seriously. It is hardly surprising .... (3) that English claims that the game was based on rounders succeeded .... (4) upsetting a lot of people. Particularly, as rounders is a .... (5) game for people not tough .... (6) to play England's national sport, cricket!

The argument .... (7) so much controversy that a special commission was set .... (8) in 1905 in America to establish the truth. Not surprisingly, it decided that baseball had .... (9) born in New York in 1839.

.... (10) then baseball has been .... (11) up all over the world. In recent years, South American countries .... (12) come to dominate the amateur game. Cuba has .... (13) won the championship no .... (14) than 18 times.

The game has also caught .... (15) in Australia and Japan. So much .... (16) that these countries can now field quite impressive teams. These developments resulted in one of the .... (17) ever blows to American sporting pride at .... (18) Los Angeles Olympics of 1984, ... (19) the Japanese managed to beat the Americans 6-3 .... (20) the championship final.

WRITING
The rules of the game

1 Read all about the rules of baseball on the next page and label the diagrams.

2 Decide whether these statements are **true** or **false**.

1 The *diamond* is the most important part of the field.
2 During the game, there are 18 players on the field.
3 The text describes three ways of being out.
4 You score a run by running round all four bases.
5 The batter can hit the ball anywhere he likes.
6 Balls have to be pitched inside the *strike zone*.

3 Analysis
1 How is the text organized? What is the topic of each of the paragraphs?
2 Make a list of the expressions the writer uses for saying what players can and can't do.
3 What is the specialized vocabulary associated with baseball?

4 You are going to take a group of foreigners to a sporting event in your country. Write a short speech in which you explain the rules of the game to them.

Before you begin, try and make a list of any specialized vocabulary you may need. For example, do the players need any special kind of equipment?

THE GAME I'M GOING TO TRY TO EXPLAIN IS BASEBALL. It is played on a large field which has a diamond shaped area in one corner where the main action takes place. The area just outside the diamond is called the infield and the rest is named the outfield. The diamond has a base at each corner which is where the name baseball comes from.

Anyway, two teams of nine players each take it in turns to bat while the other fields. The object of the game is to score more runs than the opponents. A run is scored by the batter safely making his way all the way round the bases without being out. Doing this with one hit is called a *home run*.

Play starts when the fielding team is ready and the batter is in position. The pitcher then delivers, that is, throws the ball to the batter who tries to hit it. If the batter misses the umpire shouts *strike* and, if he misses three times, he is out and another member from his team takes his place.

If the batter manages to hit the ball then he has to drop the bat and try and run to a base. However, he must hit the ball into *fair territory*, in other words not behind the foul lines. Only a single runner can occupy one base. If a fielder catches the ball in the air, touches the base with the ball before the runner gets there, or succeeds in touching the runner between bases while holding the ball, the runner is also out.

The batter does have some advantages. The pitcher isn't allowed to deliver the ball outside the strike zone and, if he delivers four bad balls, the batter can move to the next base. Naturally, it is absolutely prohibited to throw the ball at the batter!

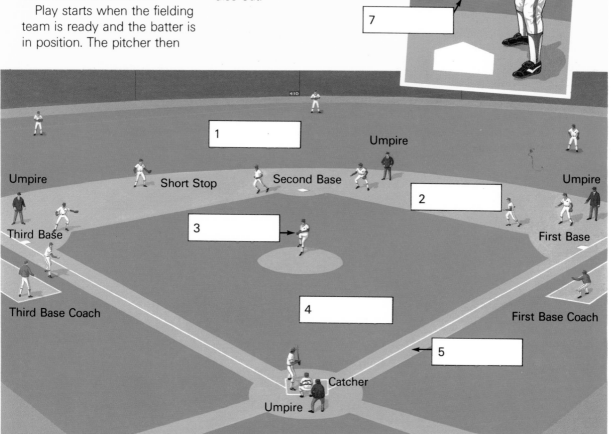

163

UNIT 15 | *Our Common Future*

SPEAKING | What does the future hold for us?

1 Complete this questionnaire individually and then discuss your answers in pairs or small groups.

1=impossible   **2**=unlikely   **3**=possible   **4**=quite likely   **5**=bound to happen

In or/by the year 2025 ...

1	there will have been a catastrophic nuclear accident or war.	1 2 3 4 5
2	people will be living in cities on the moon.	1 2 3 4 5
3	English will still be the international language.	1 2 3 4 5
4	Canada and the USA will be one country.	1 2 3 4 5
5	a cure for AIDS will have been found.	1 2 3 4 5
6	Madrid will be the new fashion capital of the world.	1 2 3 4 5
7	most families will have a robot to help with the housework.	1 2 3 4 5
8	the USA will have had at least one black president.	1 2 3 4 5
9	women will be completely equal with men.	1 2 3 4 5
10	Brazil will be a new superpower.	1 2 3 4 5
11	life expectancy in industrialized countries will be 100.	1 2 3 4 5
12	cash will have disappeared. Everything will be paid for by credit or cash card.	1 2 3 4 5

2 Discussion points

1 Which predictions are the most/least likely to come true?
2 Who is the most optimistic/pessimistic person in your group?
3 As a group, think of three other things you think will be or will have come true by the year 2025.

VOCABULARY

Work and New Technology

Complete the following sentences with a word or expression to do with **work.**

1 A c..................... is an electronic calculating machine.
2 A computer programmer writes s..................... which is used to control the operations of the h..................... .
3 A w..................... p..................... is a kind of small computer which is mainly used for office work and writing letters and reports.
4 She sent her secretary on a t..................... c..................... to learn how to use the new computer.
5 Typing, shorthand and word processing are useful office s..................... .
6 A r..................... is a machine which can move and do some of the work of a human being.
7 The car company is planning to introduce new technology into the factory. This means that 60 workers will be made r..................... as they will no longer be needed.
8 Their t..................... u..................... is negotiating with management in an effort to save the jobs.
9 The workforce is threatening to go on s ....
10 In England, people without jobs can go on the d..................... ; the government pays them a little money every week.

PRONUNCIATION

Word building

Look at the words that can be formed from the verbs **employ, compete** and **qualify.**
In pairs, decide where the stress falls in each word.
Also, work out what part of speech each word is, i.e. noun, verb or adjective. There may be **more** than one noun or adjective in each group.

1 employ	em*p*loy= *VERB*	unemployment=
	employed=	unemployable=
	employment=	unemployed=
	employable=	employee=
	employer=	
2 compete	compete=	uncompetitive=
	competitive=	competition=
	competitor=	
3 qualify	qualify=	qualifications=
	qualified=	unqualified=
	disqualify=	disqualification=

USE OF ENGLISH

The words in capitals at the end of each of the following sentences can be used to form a word that fits suitably in the blank space. Supply the correct form of the word.

1 He was turned down for the job because he wasn't .... QUALIFY
2 In parts of the country the .... situation is terrible. As many as 20% of the working population is without a job. EMPLOY
3 The world of computers is extremely .... COMPETE
4 In many countries the .... get the dole. EMPLOY
5 She left school with good .... QUALIFY
6 The factory was .... so the management tried to cut costs by making some workers redundant. COMPETE
7 He is completely .... Not only is he lazy but he is dishonest too. EMPLOY
8 Their best designer went to work for a .... COMPETE
9 More than a thousand workers are .... here. EMPLOY
10 Three firms are in .... for the same contract. COMPETE

READING

1 Quickly read this article and decide:

1 who you think wrote it.
2 how the writer feels about computers and new technology.
3 if you agree with his view of the future.

The menace of the

MICRO

Hardly a week goes by without some advance in technology that would have seemed incredible 50 years ago. Over the past 20 years computers have completely revolutionized our lives. Yet we can expect the rate of change to accelerate rather than slow down within our lifetimes. The next 25 years will see as many changes as have been witnessed in the past 150.

These developments in technology are bound to have a dramatic effect on the future of work. By 2010, new technology will have revolutionized communications. People will be transmitting messages down telephone lines that previously would have been sent by post. A postal system which has essentially been the same since the Pharoahs will virtually disappear overnight. Once these changes are introduced, not only postmen but also clerks and secretaries will vanish in a paper-free society. All the routine tasks they perform will be carried on a tiny silicon chip. As soon as this technology is available, these people will be as obsolete as the horse and cart after the invention of the motor car. One change will make thousands, if not millions, redundant.

Even people in traditional professions, where expert knowledge has been the key, are unlikely to escape the effects of new technology. Instead of going to a solicitor, you might go to a computer which is programmed with all the most up-to-date legal information. Indeed, you might even come up before a computer judge who would, in all probability, judge your case more fairly than a human counterpart. Doctors, too, will find that an electronic competitor will be able to carry out a much quicker and more accurate diagnosis and recommend more efficient courses of treatment.

In education, teachers will be largely replaced by teaching machines far more knowledgeable than any human being. What's more, most learning will take place in the home via video conferencing. Children will still go to school though, until another place is created where they can make friends and develop social skills through play.

What, you may ask, can we do to avoid the threat of the dole queue? Is there any job that will be safe? First of all, we shouldn't hide our heads in the sand. Unions will try to stop change but they will be fighting a losing battle. People should get computer literate as this just might save them from professional extinction. After all, there will be a few jobs left in law, education and medicine for those few individuals who are capable of writing and programming the software of the future. Strangely enough, there will still be jobs like rubbish collection and cleaning as it is tough to programme tasks which are largely unpredictable.

If we accept that people have the need to work, then an option might well be to introduce compulsory job sharing and to limit the length of the working week. Otherwise, we could find ourselves in an explosive situation where a technocratic elite is both supporting, and threatened by, vast numbers of the unemployed. Whether the future is one of mass unemployment or greater freedom and leisure will depend on how change is managed over this difficult period and how the relationship between work and reward is viewed.

2 Choose the best answers to these questions.

1 Changes
   A occur daily.
   B will deeply affect our lives.
   C are dangerous to society.
   D will take place five times faster than before.

2 By 2010
   A postmen will have lost their jobs.
   B bookshops will have disappeared.
   C people will no longer send letters.
   D it will be cheaper to send messages.

3 Which is not one of the writer's predictions?
   A Professionals won't escape change.
   B Doctors won't be as efficient as computers.
   C Professionals will know less than today.
   D Computers could make fairer judgements.

4 Children
   A won't be taught in schools.
   B won't have contact with teachers.
   C will learn more than at present.
   D will learn life skills at school.

5 People are advised to
   A join a union.
   B change their jobs.
   C become cleaners.
   D prepare for the future.

6 The biggest problem we shall face is
   A filling up people's free time.
   B dealing with the unemployed.
   C changing attitudes.
   D dividing work up fairly.

More complex ways of talking about the future

1 The future perfect

*By 2010, new technology **will have revolutionized** communications.*

1 The future perfect can be more easily understood if we remind ourselves how the present perfect is used. Look at these three sentences.

A *She went to Germany five years ago.*
B *She has been to France.*
C *He has lived here for ten years.*

In sentence **A** we know when she went to Germany so we use the past simple. (*definite past*)

In sentence **B** we know that some time in the past she was in France but are not told when. In this case, the present perfect has to be used. (*indefinite past*)

In sentence **C** the present perfect is used in a different way. It means he started to live here ten years ago and he still lives here. (*unfinished past*)

With the present perfect, we consider the past from the viewpoint of the present. The future perfect is used in the same way as the present perfect except the past is considered from a point in the future.

By 2010 new technology will have revolutionized communications.

FUTURE TIME + will have + PAST PARTICIPLE

- Will technology revolutionize communications?
- Will this happen before, in or after 2010?
- Do we know exactly when it will happen?

2 Expand these sentences using the future perfect.

A I/will/finish/this exercise/in five minutes' time.
B By/end/century/doctors/will/find/cure/AIDS.
C They/will/arrive/by ten o'clock this evening ...
D ... but they/be/tired/hungry/because/they/will not/sleep/or/eat.
E By next April/I/be/out of work/six years.
F A super-intelligent computer/will/be/invent/by/year/2000 ...
G ... and human labour/will/be/replace/robots.
H ... but they still/will not/find/a way/replace cleaners.

2 The future continuous

*People **will be transmitting** messages down telephone lines ...*

Match the descriptions of the uses of the future continuous with the example sentences. Which sentence describes:

1 an activity completely covering a period in the future
2 a future arrangement
3 a guess about something happening in the present

A It's six o'clock. Dad will be listening to the news.
B I'll be taking the 11.30 train.
C We'll be working in New York for the next two months.

3 The future after introductory time expressions

*Once these changes **are** introduced, not only postmen but also clerks and secretaries will vanish in a paper-free society.*

1 Study what happens when two sentences expressing the future are joined by using an introductory time expression.
   Doctors will find an answer to AIDS. They will be able to cure people.
   → *As **soon as** doctors **find** an answer to AIDS, they will be able to cure people.*

   After the time expression, a form of a present tense has to be used.

2 Now join the sentences using the words in capital letters. Make any other necessary changes.

   Example: *Children will still be going to school. Scientists will be trying to invent machines to teach them at home.* WHILE
   → *Children will be going to school while scientists **are trying** to invent machines to teach them at home.*

   A Office workers will have jobs. New technology will make them redundant. UNTIL
   B Robots will have been introduced. Factory workers will go on strike. AS SOON AS
   C Computers will act as judges. They will be programmed with all the information. ONCE
   D Oil will have run out. Scientists won't have discovered an alternative source of energy. BEFORE
   E Super-intelligent computers will be invented. Technicians will need to maintain them. IMMEDIATELY
   F All these changes will take place. Our world will be transformed. AFTER

4 Write a paragraph predicting what your life will be like by or in the year 2000. What will you have done? Will you be married and have children? Where will you be living? What will your job be?

WRITING | The opinion question — a final look

1 *Many countries around the world have problems with unemployment. Young people in particular are often unable to find work. What can be done about this problem?* Imagine that your answer to the question is the one below. You have five minutes to go before the end of the exam and now you must **check** your answer. In pairs, read the composition carefully and correct any mistakes you find.

(1)

Unemployment among young people is increasing constantly. The reason is that industry try to reduce the number of employees who are replaced by computers or person able to manipulate these computers.

I think the problem is that company look mainly after well-qualified people with a lot of experience because they expect to make serious business and don't give the chance to university students to introduce themselves.

On the other hand in the work area young people tend to specialise too much in one

(2)

limited area and haven't got any other knowledge. I think students should take an orientation that will allow them to get several kinds of job and mainly studies in connection with technologie, public relations, commerce and social activities.

Another fact is that student are quickly self-satisfied. Once they don't get a job in this specialisation don't go on looking for another job and choose the easier way "unemployment".

2 Look at the grading system that your compositions will be marked against. What mark would be fair for the composition you have just checked through?

MARK	GRADE	DESCRIPTION
18-20	Excellent	Natural English with just a few unimportant mistakes. Answers the question thoroughly.
16-17	Very good	Good use of vocabulary and structure. Range of structure better than simple sentences. Mistakes are non-basic.
12-15	Good	A simple but accurate answer. Fairly natural English without too many mistakes.
8-11	Pass	Reasonably correct English but a little unnatural and clumsy.
5-7	Weak	Not a pass. Vocabulary and grammar are not good enough to answer the questions properly.
0-4	Very poor	Difficult to understand. Mistakes show a lack of basic knowledge of English.

3 Know yourself

Look through the most recent compositions you have written and think about these questions.

1 What are your biggest problems? For example, do you do well when you write simply? Do you do badly if you try to express complicated ideas?
2 What are your 'favourite' mistakes? For example:
  - spelling.
  - tenses.
  - agreement of subject and number or person and tense.
  - punctuation and problems with handwriting.
3 In general, what mark would you give yourself for your compositions? Be honest!
4 What should you do in the examination? For example, should you try and write simple accurate English so that you are just able to pass, or should you be a little more ambitious? Ask your teacher what he or she thinks.

4 Final advice

1 Remember the First Certificate Examination is not a philosophy examination. Do not try to express ideas that are too complicated for your level of English.
2 Do not rush into writing. Spend at least five minutes planning your composition.
3 Leave at least five minutes at the end of each composition to check for mistakes.
4 Write slowly and clearly so that you do not have to copy out the composition again. This is a waste of time as you may just copy out mistakes again. Spend this time checking your work.

5 Write a composition on this topic in 45 minutes.
Is new technology a blessing or a curse?

LISTENING

You are going to hear an expert being interviewed about the future of the world's cities. The interview is divided into two parts. Complete the tasks for each part of the interview.

Part one
Listen to the interview and complete the notes.

1 In 1950, ... of ten of the biggest cities were in developed countries. By 2000 they will have .... out of ten.

2

1950	Position in top 10	Population
New York	....	*12 m*
London	....	....
Calcutta	*10*	....
Tokyo	*3*	*6 m*

2000	Position in top 10	Population
New York	....	....
Calcutta	....	....
Tokyo	....	....

3 In the year 2000, the world's two largest cities will be Mexico City with a population of .... million and São Paulo.

Part two
Listen to the second part of the interview and decide if these statements are **true** or **false**.

1 It is getting difficult to commute to London.
2 There is a trend of people leaving London.
3 Movement from London can be exaggerated.
4 Most insurance companies are based outside London.
5 People are happier living in the country.
6 One company had to close its London office.
7 Since then the company has doubled its productivity.
8 Farming land is being developed for accommodation.

 USE OF ENGLISH
A final look

1 Fill each of the numbered blanks in the following passage. Use only **one** word in each space.

Night had finally come. She knew that .... (1) now all the humans who worked in the factory would have gone to their .... (2) in satellite city. She realized that she would .... (3) to be careful. The robot guard passed by .... (4) four minutes. .... (5) it disappeared around the corner, she jumped up from behind the low wall .... (6) she had been hiding and ran .... (7) the narrow corridor towards .... (8) main factory workshop. Her heart was .... (9) so fast she was certain that the robot guard .... (10) be able to hear it. Then, ... (11) before she had time to realize, there in front of her was the enemy. Here was the monster that .... (12) stolen the jobs of half the workforce.

The computer looked .... (13) innocent as it stood silently in the middle of the office. She walked .... (14) up to it with hate .... (15) her heart and told .... (16) that she was going to teach it a lesson it would never forget. .... (17) her pocket she took a .... (18) screwdriver and a hammer. As she approached it, ... (19) a strange mechanical cry came from the front of the creature, the lights came on .... (20) around her and the sirens began to wail.

2 Sentence transformation

This exercise tries to cover most of the important sentence transformation patterns you are likely to face in the examination.

Finish each of the following sentences in such a way that it means exactly the same as the sentence printed before it.

Try and identify which particular point is being tested.

1 I haven't been to the cinema for ages.
It's ....

2 The garage is servicing my car on Monday.
I'm ....

3 He couldn't reach the button because it was too high.
The button ....

4 They understand more than we do.
We don't ....

5 'Why don't you apply for the job, Anne?' said Sue.
Sue suggested ....

6 I haven't seen him for three years.
The last time ....

7 He is extremely rich but very mean.
In spite ....

8 I didn't know the answer because I hadn't read the book.
If ....

9 I'd prefer us to go to the cinema.
I'd rather ....

10 Nobody has told him yet.
He still needs ....

11 The lesson was so boring she fell asleep.
It ....

12 Bob finds his new contact lenses uncomfortable.
Bob isn't ....

13 His mother wouldn't allow him to go out.
He ....

14 You don't need to finish that this evening.
It ....

15 You'll be ill if you continue to smoke.
Unless ....

16 You'd better not touch that switch.
If I ....

17 Janet has made the necessary arrangements.
The ....

18 'What time does the manager come back?' the customer asked.
The customer wanted ....

19 This fruit is a new experience.
It is the first ....

20 What a pity I broke the vase.
I wish ....

21 Remind me to water the plants.
Don't ....

22 It's a good idea to take the train.
You'd ....

23 It took us three hours to open the door.
We spent ....

24 I'd rather you didn't smoke in here.
Would ....

Note Remember that in **Paper 3** you will only be tested on **ten** items.

3 Complete the following sentences with one appropriate word connected with the subject of **work**.

1 Make sure you fill in the application .... clearly.

2 It was a difficult .... because they asked her some tough questions. However, they still offered her the job.

3 Sarah did a three month .... course to learn how to do the job.

4 Instead of working until he was 65, he took early ....

5 More and more people are losing their jobs. .... is very high.

4 Supply, in the space in each of the following sentences, the correct phrase made from the verb **look**.

1 The cause of the fire is being .... by experts.

2 We had to .... the number in the telephone directory.

3 Can you .... the engine .... ? It doesn't seem to be running properly.

4 She can't wait to go to college. She's really .... it.

5 It's wrong to .... on people less fortunate than ourselves.

READING

There was an essay competition for children with the title *The world I would like to see in the year 2000.*
Read the texts and find out which child:

1 doesn't mention nuclear war.   A B C D
2 seems to be the most concerned about the environment   A B C D
3 seems to feel most responsible for the future.   A B C D
4 seems most interested in economic solutions to world problems   A B C D
5 discusses agriculture the most   A B C D

In the Year 2000

A Anna Lindsop, aged 14

My ideal world would have no nuclear arms. No bombs, ships, tanks and planes. There would no longer be the threat of the bomb to massacre the innocent wildlife as well as ourselves. If by chance a war did brew up, it would be fought with constructive words instead of weaponry. Weaponry that would cause holocaust and sleepless nights.

With the saved money, I would spend it on clothing and feeding the public and helping Third World countries fend for themselves. I would help them to grow crops and sow the land quickly with machines. I would help them to dress wounds, so that they can enjoy life as we do.

It would be a much better place if everyone was kind and considerate to others, no matter what their colour or religion. I'm not saying that everyone should be a Christian, Jew or a Methodist. I'm just saying that they should respect other religions, not mock them or be aggressive.

B Graham Gomez, aged 12

In the year 2000 I would like to see Britain and the rest of the world in harmony. If the world was at peace, then the majority of the people would be happy. I would not want a communist state but I would want most people given the same amount of money in their pay packet. At least enough for them to live comfortably and have a small treat every now and then. Somehow the world's money would have to be divided out among the countries so that poor countries wouldn't exist any more. I can't really believe that people who want to argue with hate in their voice really exist.

C Samantha Corrigan, aged 12

Atom bombs are being made as easily as someone makes a cup of tea or coffee. I would love the world to be at peace. Maybe in the year 2000 a miracle might be performed and the problem of unemployment might be solved as well as crime and vandalism.

We are tomorrow's generation. We will make it whatever it is. If it is horrible, it will be our fault. Will a matter of years change everything?

D Anthony Twist, aged 14

A place which will be peaceful; where my children and their children in turn may live in happiness and prosperity. No guns, tanks or other instruments of war. No living under the threat of a nuclear holocaust, just a caring society. Caucasoid, Mongoloid and Negroid all working together in harmony and having equal opportunities to advance through life. No unemployment and a good healthy standard of living for all.

A clean healthy environment: less noise, no pollution, no lead in petrol which can cause brain damage in young children, new public baths, larger parks, decent housing and protection for wildlife in danger.

But my main desire is to see people less materialistic, less selfish, less violent and more loving than they are now.

USE OF ENGLISH

Reading and processing information

1 Write four short paragraphs summarizing what the children think, starting with the introductory words you are given.

A Anna Lindsop seems to be most worried about ....
better place if ....
(maximum 40 words)

B Graham Gomez seems to think the way to solve the world's problems is by

....
(maximum 25 words)

C Samantha Corrigan seems afraid of ....
Social problems such as ....
on ....
(maximum 50 words)

D Anthony Twist imagines a world where everybody ....
environment by ....
However, his greatest concern is that ....
(maximum 60 words)

2 Write a short composition describing what **you** would like the world to be like in the year 2000.

Tapescripts

for all the Listenings except for the ones on pages 160-1 in Unit 14.

UNIT 1

PAGE 12 1 Checking in

Ground steward: Afternoon, madam. Could I have your ticket, please? Thank you. Would you like smoking or non-smoking?

Marisol: Non-smoking. I would like a window seat too.

Ground steward: Let me see now. No, I'm sorry. We've got no seats left in the non-smoking area. We've got some left in the smoking area.

Marisol: No, no, no. I wanted non-smoking, please.

Ground steward: I see. Let's have a see. Yes, I've got one. It's an aisle seat. Is that all right?

Marisol: An aisle seat? What's an *aisle* seat? Sorry.

Ground steward: It's on the end of the row of seats — it's where the people walk up and down. You know?

Marisol: Oh, yes. Yes, that's OK.

Ground steward: Oh, right. OK, then I can give you Seat P3. Would you put your luggage on the scales, please? I'm awfully sorry, madam, you're two kilos over.

Marisol: Two kilos! But I thought you were allowed 22 kilos. I weighed my luggage before I left home and I had 22 kilos.

Ground steward: No, I'm sorry, Madam. It's ... the limit is 20 kilos. But, look, why don't you take something out of your baggage and put it in your hand luggage? And then you'll be OK.

Marisol: Oh! OK, thank you very much.

Ground steward: Oh, no problem. Let's see. Now here's your boarding card and your ticket.

Marisol: Thank you.

Ground steward: Bye bye.

Marisol: Bye bye.

2 The captain's announcement

Captain: Good afternoon, ladies and gentlemen. This is Captain Anderson speaking. On behalf of myself and the crew, I'd like to welcome you on board this Air Magnesia flight to London. May I apologize for the short delay in our departure. This was caused by a problem with one of our tyres but everything's all right now and we should be able to make up for the lost time. We shall be flying at an altitude of 30,000 feet and our estimated time of arrival is 19.30 local time. Weather conditions are good but we may experience a little turbulence for the first 30 minutes so I would suggest you keep your safety belts fastened. During the flight, dinner will be served and our cabin crew will be ...

3 Buying duty free

Stewardess: Duty free?

Marisol: Yes, please. What sort of perfume do you have?

Stewardess: We've got three kinds: Blue Lady, Jennifer and Seduction. Is it for you?

Marisol: No, it's for a lady of about 50.

Stewardess: Well, Jennifer might be a bit young then.

Marisol: I see. What's the difference between the other two?

Stewardess: Well, Seduction's quite a bit more expensive.

Marisol: Can you tell me how much they cost?

Stewardess: Seduction starts at £9 for a small bottle. For the same price you could have a medium sized bottle of Blue Lady.

Marisol: I'll take the Blue Lady at £9.

Stewardess: Anything else?

Marisol: Yes, could I have two hundred Winchester, please?

Stewardess: I'm afraid we've just run out.

Marisol: Oh, in that case, I'll have a carton of Churchill's.

Stewardess: Here you are. Is that all?

Marisol: Yeah.

Stewardess: Now, that'll be £18.50.

Marisol: Can I pay in pesetas?

Stewardess: Yes, that'll be fine.

PAGE 13 4 The lost luggage

Official: So you've arrived from Spain and you've lost your luggage.

Marisol: Yes, that's right. I've lost all my things.

Official: Now, don't you worry. Bags usually turn up quite quickly, you know. You kept your receipts, didn't you?

Marisol: Yes, of course.

Official: Good. Right then, could you describe the bags to me, please?

Marisol: Yes, there is a suitcase and a holdall.

Official: What's the suitcase like?

Marisol: It's red and it's got a brown leather strap around.

Official: Bright red?

Marisol: No, dark.

Official: Anything else you could say to describe it?

Marisol: It's quite large.

Official: I see.

Marisol: And it's got the address of where I am staying in England on the label.

Official: Good. And the holdall? Is it a bag or a case?

Marisol: A bag. And it's dark blue with red handles.

Official: Fine.

Marisol: Again, it's quite big. The sort of thing tennis players use. Do you know what I mean?

Official: Yes.

Marisol: You will find them, won't you?

Official: I'm sure we will. OK, if you'd just like to wait over there for a few minutes. I'll go and have a look to see if your stuff is on the trolley. Keep your fingers crossed.

UNIT 2

PAGE 16 1 What's on at the cinema

Recorded voice: This is the Criterion cinema bringing you details of the very best in screen entertainment in North London. On Screen 1 we have the adult, action-packed adventure thriller *Raw Deal* starring Arnold Swarzenegger. Performances are at 2.45, 5.15 and 7.45. Showing on Screen 2 is *Crocodile Dundee 2* with Paul Hogan. This wonderful comedy has performances at 3.00, 5.30 and 8.00. Finally, on Screen 3 another chance to see that romantic classic, *A Room With A View*, with performances at 3.45 and 8.15. May we remind patrons that smoking is only permitted in Screen 1. All tickets are priced at £2.60, with children half price. This is the end of the recorded announcement.

2 Jeff and Emma decide what to do

Jeff: What would you like to do then?

Emma: Well, there's not much on TV, is there? Do you fancy a movie?

Jeff: Fine, but I don't feel like going all the way into town. What's on locally?

Emma: Well, I rang the Criterion earlier and they've got *Raw Deal* — you remember we saw something about it on TV last week.

Jeff: No, I don't fancy that. Too much blood and guts.

Emma: I agree. Oh, there's also *A Room with A View*. Why don't we go and see that?

Jeff: We could but I've seen it.

Emma: Well, so have I.

Jeff: Sorry, I'd forgotten.

Emma: But it was so good I'd love to see it again.

Jeff: Oh, I would too but not just yet. I only saw it a short while ago.

Emma: OK. How about *Crocodile Dundee 2*?

Jeff: *Crocodile Dundee 2*! Why didn't you say so? I loved the first one.

Emma: It was all right. Still, I'd rather we went to that than any of the others. There's a performance at eight.

Jeff: Eight! Well, then it's time we left.

Emma: Don't panic. That's when the performance begins. There'll be adverts and trailers and things before the film actually starts. *Crocodile Dundee* won't start till at least eight-thirty. We've easily got an hour.

Jeff: But I'm starving. I haven't eaten since lunchtime.

Emma: I haven't either. Let's grab something on the way. A hamburger or something.

Jeff: Right. I'll get my coat. Have you seen the keys to my car?

Emma: Weren't they on the mantlepiece?

UNIT 3

PAGE 33 Surviving in the snow

Presenter: Now, I'd like to move on to the next item. The weather certainly seems to have taken a turn for the worse and it looks like we're in for some heavy snowfalls in the next few days. Now, of course, every year there are cases of motorists who break down and get caught out in really bad weather. Tragically, some die and this is even more tragic when we consider that most of these deaths could be avoided. Now we have in the studio this evening Julie Mitchell from the Canadian Automobile Club and she's going to tell us how to stay alive if we get caught out in the snow and our car breaks down. Hi, Julie.

Julie: Hi.

Presenter: So what should we do?

Julie: Well, the first thing that you should remember is that your car is your most important piece of survival equipment you have if you get caught in a drift. So don't leave it unless you can actually see the place you want to get to. People have died when they needn't have because they have gotten impatient, left their cars and got lost in the snow.

Presenter: So, rule number one is stay in your car unless you can see where you're going.

Julie: Your destination.

Presenter: Right. Anything else we should remember?

Julie: Oh, certainly! First of all, use your common sense. If you have to drive and know you're going to hit bad weather, make sure you have blankets, a sleeping bag and a shovel in case you have to dig yourself out, and ideally food and hot drinks.

Presenter: Is there anything we can do to help ourselves if we're stuck, apart from keep warm, that is?

Julie: Oh, sure. You've got to keep warm but you've also got to keep the car well ventilated — there have been cases of drivers suffocating in their cars — so have the window on the side away from the wind open a little, say half an inch or so.

Presenter: OK. What about using the car heater to keep warm?

Julie: Oh, I'm glad you asked me about this because this can be fatal unless you take extreme care. The risk of death from exhaust fumes is high. The cold takes hours to kill you but exhaust fumes can kill you in a matter of minutes. Before you run your engine, make sure the exhaust is completely free from snow. Otherwise, the fumes will escape into the car. Anyway, only run the engine for ten minutes every hour and every time make sure the exhaust is free.

Presenter: Any final tip?

Julie: Yes, if you know you're setting off in bad weather, ring up your destination just in case something happens on the way. That way, if you're late, your friends will know something is wrong and will be able to tell the police to go out and look for you.

Presenter: Thanks Julie for coming in and I hope our listeners out there … .

PAGE 40 Survival games

Mike: Well, I just sort of watched the telly really. Did a bit of laundry. Had a drink. That was about it.

Phil: I don't blame you. The weather was awful, wasn't it? That drizzle. Cold as well … I was fed up. What did you do, Kim?

Kim: Well, I had quite a good time, actually. I went on one of these, you know, survival games weekends.

Mike: You what!

Kim: You must have heard of them. These survival games.

Mike: What do you do?

Kim: Well, you … Oh, I'm not going to tell you 'cause you'll only take the mickey.

Mike and Phil: No, no. Go … Tell us. Tell us.

Kim: Do you really want to hear?

Mike and Phil: Yeah.

Kim: Well, the idea of it is to capture an enemy flag. You're split into two teams and … see! I told you. You're laughing already.

Mike: No, no. Come on. Let's hear the whole lot.

Phil: You spent the weekend playing soldiers?

Kim: Well, we only had ink pellets. It wasn't real bullets.

Phil: Ah, pathetic! What happens? You fire them at other people?

Kim: Yeah, you have about 40 minutes. It lasts 40 minutes and you've got to try and — well, like I said — capture the …

Phil: Isn't that a bit dangerous? Well, what do you fire them at?

Kim: No, no. You get this visor thing to wear to protect your eyes.

Mike: What and bang bang you're dead?

Kim: Yeah, then they're out once you've got them. Once you've been hit by an ink pellet. It's good fun. Well, it's great. It's better than sitting around watching telly. I was out in the open air, running around.

Mike: I don't know about that.

Phil: I don't know. It's quite nice being out.

Kim: Yeah, it was very invigorating.

Mike: What were the others like then? Were they all little kids playing Cowboys and Indians?

Kim: No, they were fairly normal people. Young. There was more men than women which was nice. It was just innocent fun for the weekend. It was good.

Phil: Did you go with anybody, like did you go with a friend or anything?

Kim: Yeah, I went with Tricia, a girl I worked with.

Mike: Ah, Tricia! She was doing it as well.

Kim: Yeah. We just thought we'd try it.

Phil: I can't imagine her doing it.

Kim: We're going to go again. We really enjoyed it. You should come along.

Phil: Kept stopping to do her make-up.

Mike: World War Three. You going to do it again?

Kim: Yes!

UNIT 4

PAGE 44 An alternative Cinderella

Narrator: Once upon a time there were three sisters who lived with their widowed father. The two eldest ran a beauty parlour and a clothes shop. They were both interested in finding a rich husband. The youngest daughter, whose name was Cinderella, looked after the house. Her father had refused to set her up in business as he wanted someone to look after him. Cinderella did not mind too much as she was doing a correspondence course in accountancy and marketing.

One day Cinderella decided to enter a competition in a woman's magazine because it offered some good cash prizes. If she won one of them, it would help her finance the setting-up of her own hamburger restaurant.

Around that time the newspapers were full of stories about a big party that was going to be held at the palace. It was said that the prince, a real playboy, wanted to find a wife and settle down. From the moment they heard about the ball, the two eldest sisters spent days and days trying to make themselves look beautiful. As for Cinderella, she wondered what all the fuss was about and didn't have the slightest interest in going to the ball.

One morning, while she was doing some work for her accountancy course, there was a knock at the door. She opened it and saw an extraordinary woman standing there with a ridiculous looking tiara on her head. The woman, who called herself Fairy Godmother or FG for short, told Cinderella that she'd won first prize in the magazine competition she'd entered.

The prize was a 'charm course' worth hundreds of pounds as well as books and records. Cinderella wasn't really that keen on doing the course but she realized she could probably make a small profit if she sold the prizes. However, in return for the prizes she would have to dress up in lots of fine clothes and be driven to the palace where she'd spend the night at the ball and be photographed for the woman's magazine.

The big day arrived and a shiny Rolls Royce came to pick her up. The man from the car hire firm said he was only on duty to midnight. Moments later a woman arrived bringing a fur coat and a diamond necklace which would be Cinderella's just for the evening. When she turned up at the palace, she noticed that one of the servants was stealing food from the buffet tables. The palace itself was cold and draughty, and the king himself was a man with a sad smile. Cinderella felt sorry for the man and told him why the food was disappearing so fast. The king then told her about his financial problems. He was almost bankrupt and he had organized the party in the hope that he might find a millionaire's daughter for his son. Cinderella suggested lots of ways of making money: reorganizing the kitchens, opening the palace to the public and so on.

By this time it had turned midnight. The car hire man drove away and the woman came to collect her fur coat and necklace. The king showed Cinderella around the palace and they eventually came back to the ballroom where the party was still going on. The prince, who by this time was hopelessly drunk, took one look at Cinderella and asked her to dance. She kicked off her glass slippers, which were killing her, and joined him on the dance floor. Soon afterwards, she left the palace and hitch-hiked home.

The following day the newspapers were full of the big story about the prince who had fallen for a beautiful mysterious woman who had disappeared. Her glass slippers, which she had left behind, were the only clues that would lead him to her. When Cinderella read the news, she was absolutely furious. Nevertheless, she saw quite a bit of the prince because she started work at the palace as financial adviser. In no time at all the palace was making a profit again. Naturally, Cinderella refused to marry the prince but she did help him cut down on his drinking and involved him in useful social work in the community.

PAGE 50 An expert on folk and fairy tales is interviewed

Interviewer: Cinderella is one of the most famous fairy stories in the world, isn't it?

Expert: Yes, that's right. In fact, about, there are about ... 350 versions of the tale have been recorded worldwide.

Interviewer: Presumably, they vary quite a bit.

Expert: Oh yes, indeed. In the German version of the tale, for instance, the sisters, well the stepsisters that is, are, are described as being 'fair of face but ugly in spirit'.

Interviewer: Whereas in the English version they're just plain ugly.

Expert: That's right. And in the Italian version of the tale Cinderella only wears rags to cover up her beautiful clothes underneath.

Interviewer: But these are only minor differences, surely?

Expert: Well, if you go further afield, then the story changes quite a lot. In the Indian story help doesn't arrive from a fairy godmother but rather from a magic tree, or rather from a part of it. Which of course we can see in our version in the form of the fairy godmother's wand.

Interviewer: And why do you think the story is so popular?

Expert: Well, I think it has to do with the fact that it's a fight between good and evil, it has a happy ending and, perhaps most important of all, it deals with ordinary people.

Interviewer: Just one last question before we discuss Dick Whittington. Why is it that Cinderella wears glass slippers?

Expert: Ah! Well now. One theory is that the story came into English from the French version of the tale. Now, of course *vert* (V E R T) meaning green and *verre* (V E R R E) meaning glass both have the same pronunciation.

Interviewer: So the translator got a bit mixed up.

Expert: Precisely.

Interviewer: Well, let's turn to Dick Whittington. Now, this isn't exactly a fairy story, is it?

PAGE 51 Dick Whittington

Interviewer: Well, let's turn to Dick Whittington. Now, this isn't exactly a fairy story, is it?
Expert: No. No, that's correct.
Interviewer: There is some truth in it, then?
Expert: Oh yes, there really was a Richard Whittington known as Dick to his friends, but he wasn't born poor and he didn't come up to London to seek his fortune, although he did make a lot of money. He was, in fact, the son of a wealthy knight, Sir William Whittington.
Interviewer: Oh really. But what about the cat? Where does that fit in? A cat can't have made him rich, surely?
Expert: Ah, but it did. It's not one of the four-legged variety, though. You see, Whittington made his fortune transporting coal by ship. And, believe it or not, these ship were commonly referred to as cats.
Interviewer: Is Dick Whittington a story which is only known in Britain ...

PAGE 52 A tall story

Carol: I heard this wonderful story the other day which I must tell you.
Arthur: Oh my god, not another one of your stories.
Carol: You're going to hear it anyway so ...
Arthur: Go on then, I'm all ears.
Carol: Well, you see there's this woman and she's driving off to meet a friend in town one day. She's in a bit of a hurry and she doesn't notice the cat asleep in the driveway. Anyway, you can guess what happens next.
Arthur: I think I can, yes.
Carol: She's backing out of her driveway when she hears this little cry as she goes over something.
Arthur: The cat.
Carol: Right first time.
Arthur: Go on.
Carol: Anyway, so she gets out of the car and sees the cat lying there
stone dead. And she doesn't know what to do. She's already late for her meeting with her friend and she's thinking 'Where am I going to put Java?'
Arthur: What's Java?
Carol: Oh, Java's the name of the cat. Well, she can't leave it there and she can't put it in the dustbin 'cause the kids might see. Anyway, to cut a long story short, she looks in the car and sees this plastic bag from a rather smart department store.
Arthur: I don't believe a word of this.
Carol: No, it's all true. Cross my heart. So she puts the cat in the bag and drives off to meet her friend. Well, when she's parked the car, she decides to take the bag with her into the department store where she's meeting her friend. You see, she thinks her friend will have some clever idea about what to do with the cat.
Arthur: You've got to be kidding!
Carol: No, no. She goes into the shop, oh, and spots a rather nice-looking handbag on the counter and puts down the plastic bag for a sec to have a quick look at it. Can you guess what happens next?
Arthur: No. I hate to think.
Carol: She puts the handbag down and looks for the plastic bag. It's gone, of course. And just then she hears this scream and commotion out in the street. She goes to the door and sees this middle-aged woman lying in the street — she'd fainted — with the plastic bag with poor old Java in it beside her on the
pavement. You see, she was a shoplifter and, when she'd got outside, she hadn't been able to resist having a peep at what was inside the bag.
Arthur: Ridiculous. Still, it makes a good story.

UNIT 5

PAGE 57 Julie talks about her holiday plans

Friend: What are you doing this summer for your holiday, Julie?
Julie: I'm going off with some friends. We're going to the Lake District for about ten days or so.
Friend: Oh, are you camping?
Julie: No, we'll be staying in youth hostels most of the time. We're going to do a lot of walking but we'll be able to get to a youth hostel by the end of each day.
Friend: Oh, tell me, what will you be taking with you then?
Julie: Well, a pair of really good walking boots for a start and quite a lot of clothing. You can never be sure what the weather's going to be like. It can be lovely one moment and grotty the next. When you're up high too, it can even snow on a summer's day!
Friend: Sounds a bit dangerous. Do you have to take any special equipment or anything with you?
Julie: No, not really. Oh, we'll take those survival blankets which you can wrap yourself up in, you know, just in case but apart from that nothing special.
Friend: Oh yeah, I know. One of those silver things you see them wearing at the ends of marathons.
Julie: That's it. Oh, a map and compass, of course, sleeping bags for the youth hostel, waterproof jacket and trousers, oh and a camping gas stove and kettle so we can brew up. But no tent. I took one last year but I needn't have bothered. I didn't use it once.
Friend: So you've done this sort of thing before.
Julie: Oh, yeah. This'll be my fourth visit to the Lakes. How about you? Have you got any plans?
Friend: Well, I'm not sure. I might be going to Greece or Turkey ...

PAGE 63 Anita tells a friend about her holiday.

Friend: Welcome back, Anita. Did you have a good time?
Anita: Ah, it was great, thanks. I feel so relaxed.
Friend: Well, don't worry, it won't last. We've been incredibly busy the last two weeks. But tell me about the holiday. You were on a boat, weren't you?
Anita: Yes, it was a sailing holiday but the boat had a crew who looked after you and so on. You didn't have to do anything strenuous if you didn't want to.
Friend: What were the crew like?
Anita: Oh, absolutely fantastic. There were half a dozen of them in all. Well, the captain was a real character called Nico. He must've been about 50 and he had this wonderful grey beard. He was tremendous. I've got sone photos. I'll bring them in to you when I've got them back.
Friend: What about the other people?
Anita: Oh, they were fine. There was one old girl who was about 70 but she was very lively and then a couple in their early twenties but most of us were in our late thirties, early forties. We all got on really well together, oh, except of course there had to be one complete pain in the neck, Donald, a divorced computer salesman who kept on using all the sailing jargon and being very macho. Oh, he thought he was wonderful. He

spent the whole two weeks walking round holding his stomach in. Anyway, I'd rather not go on about Donald.

Friend: What were the sleeping arrangements like?

Anita: Fairly comfortable but the cabins were a bit small and stuffy.It didn't matter, though, 'cause we all slept out on the deck which was marvellous, watching the shooting stars.

Friend: Sounds as though you had a lovely time.

Anita: Oh, I did. The food wasn't that great but the wine was OK and you could have as much as you wanted.

Friend: And the men?

Anita: Well, I met this absolutely gorgeous boy called Savvas. Oh, just like a Greek god he was. Anyway, he promised me he's going to write ...

UNIT 6

PAGE 66 Rosie talks about her life

Interviewer: Rosie, you agreed to draw two social circles. Now, would it bother you at all to go into them?

Rosie: Well, I suppose it could be a bit embarrassing but, well, I'll try to be as straightforward as I can.

Interviewer: I guess the first question that anyone would ask is, what happened to Simon?

Rosie: I was afraid you'd ask that. Well, to cut a long story short, I'd been going out with him since I was 16. When he was 18, he went away to university and, when he was away, I fell in love with Clive.

Interviewer: Where had you met Clive?

Rosie: Clive was Simon's best friend from school. I'd known him a long time.

Interviewer: And he'd been going out with Lucy?

Rosie: Yes, that's right. Well, they split up over something silly and the following weekend there was a party on, and Clive and I went together 'cause Simon was away. Well, it seemed the natural thing to do. Then quite simply we realized we loved each other.

Interviewer: How did Lucy and Simon take this?

Rosie: Well, Simon was really upset for a while but he soon found a new girlfriend at university. I think he got over it pretty quickly really. As for Lucy, well, she was furious because she said it had only been a lover's quarrel and that I'd pinched Clive off her.

Interviewer: Well, in a way hadn't you?

Rosie: Yeah, I know it sounds awful and I felt rotten at the time but I couldn't help myself. Later on I made it up with Lucy and we still see each other from time to time.

Interviewer: And what about Simon and Clive?

Rosie: Well, they fell out completely and haven't spoken to each other since.

Interviewer: And what about your parents? There seems to have been something of a change there.

Rosie: Well, my dad really liked Simon — he was going off to study to be a doctor and he's quite smart and was always polite — whereas Clive was unemployed at the time and wore an earring and things. Well, there were some terrible rows. Dad even refused to come to the wedding. We're just about talking to each other now but relationships are very tense still. Since Sophie was born, I've been getting on much better with my mum. I get on really well with Tom, my father-in-law, and I've grown much closer to my auntie Cathy.

Interviewer: Why's that?

Rosie: Well, I was brought up to think of her as the black sheep of the family. She'd been a bit wild when she was young and got kicked out of her home and I think she could understand what I'd been through.

Interviewer: And your grandmother?

Rosie: Oh, she passed away two years ago.

PAGE 70 Harriet Williams talks about her childhood.

Harriet: As you know, I was born in India. My father had a terribly important job — he was in charge of building projects for an entire region and supervised the construction of dams, roads, bridges and suchlike. I didn't see much of him as a child as he was often away. And when he was home, the house would be full of engineers with plans and papers.

The house I remember very clearly. You wouldn't call it a mansion but it was extremely large and painted white with a veranda and lovely grounds for me to play in. We had servants and all the years we were there my mother never lifted a finger to do anything. I had a number of nannies and, being the only daughter, I was spoilt by everyone. My two elder brothers, poor lambs, were packed off to boarding school in England at the age of seven and I was brought up with a tremendous sense of my, and my family's, self-importance.

In the summer the women and children would go to the hills but the men worked on through the heat on the plains. And it was during the summer that my father fell ill and could not continue with his job. We had to return to England. That was in 1920 and I remember being very seasick on the journey home.

In India everyone talked about going home but the reality for me was a terrible shock. When we landed, it was cold and grey and I was surprised at seeing so many white faces around me. I realized I wasn't special anymore. We travelled first class up to London but it was nothing compared to travelling first class in India. And I was so disappointed in our house. It seemed to cramped and dingy. I felt that I had really come down in the world. We only had one servant and she didn't live in. My mother tried to do the cooking — oh, she did her best but at first she made a terrible mess of everything.

But the worst thing about coming back was what happened to my father. From being responsible for major projects and hundreds of people he suddenly became just one of many working in the ministry. He never got used to it and somehow seemed to physically shrink in the last few years before he retired.

As for myself, oh, we had always had the best in India but in England we had to make do with ordinary things. In India I had my clothes made and I remember, I am ashamed to say, being terribly upset at having to buy clothes from a shop, off the peg as it were. I thought this was awfully common. And at first I expected to be waited on hand and foot but gradually I came round to the idea of doing some of the housework.

Looking back on it, it seems incredible how dramatically my life changed. Actually, I think the change did me good because my upbringing in India had made me into such a little snob and coming home to England taught me what ordinary life was really like.

UNIT 7

PAGE 77 Peter Whitehead interviews Frances Kelly

Peter Whitehead: The Campaign for Clean Air has just issued a report on air pollution and we have in the studio Frances Kelly of the CCA who's going to tell us something about the dangers we face from air pollutants.

Frances Kelly: Hello.

Peter Whitehead: Let's start with sulphur dioxide which causes acid rain. I thought the government was doing something about that.

Frances Kelly: Well, they are but slowly. Sulphur dioxide emissions from power stations are still going on and the resulting acid rain is still killing off fishes and plant life in lakes and destroying the forests. And we in Britain are among the worst culprits when it comes to this kind of pollution.

Peter Whitehead: What are the other pollutants?

Frances Kelly: Carbon monoxide and carbon dioxide. Carbon monoxide, which is mostly produced by motor vehicles can, even in small doses, cause sickness and a slowing of the reflexes and there is strong evidence to show that it has an effect on the growth of children.

Peter Whitehead: And carbon dioxide?

Frances Kelly: Well, in a way this is the least dangerous of the pollutants we've mentioned but in the longer term it may be the most damaging.

Peter Whitehead: Why?

Frances Kelly: There is clear evidence that the build-up of carbon dioxide in the atmosphere is the main cause of the Greenhouse Effect. This will have dreadful results like the melting of the polar ice caps and subsequent flooding of low-lying areas.

Peter Whitehead: So what you're saying is that the increased amounts of carbon dioxide in the atmosphere is making it warmer.

Frances Kelly: Yes, that's right and the results will be catastrophic.

Peter Whitehead: And what should we be doing about this?

Frances Kelly: Frankly, the government has got to impose far stricter controls on these emissions and bring in tough legislation to deal with the problem.

Peter Whitehead: Frances Kelly, thank you very much.

Frances Kelly: Thank you.

Peter Whitehead: After the news we hope to be talking to the Minister for the Environment, Patrick Hilliard ...

UNIT 8

PAGE 94 The news item

Newsreader: Police have stepped up their hunt for eight-year-old Neil Graham who's been missing since Friday when he left St. Mark's Primary School to walk home. Neil was wearing jeans, a dark blue pullover and a red anorak and was carrying a yellow satchel. The police have issued a description of a man they would like to interview. The man, who was seen in Castle Street getting into a yellow Renault 5 with a child answering Neil's description shortly before half past four on Friday, is described as being in his early forties, white, balding and of medium height and wearing a leather jacket, jeans and metal-framed spectacles. Police are appealing to anyone with information to come forward.

PAGE 95 Clive and Jenny discuss their weekend dates

Clive: Hi, Jenny.

Jenny: Hi.

Clive: How did it go, then?

Jenny: Pretty mixed, really.

Clive: Oh yeah.

Jenny: Yeah, he wasn't exactly the man of my dreams.

Clive: What happened then?

Jenny: It was pretty nerve-wracking, actually, waiting outside the station for him to turn up. Like being 14 all over again.

Clive: Yes, I know what you mean. Still, he didn't stand you up, did he?

Jenny: No, no. He turned up all right.

Clive: So what did he look like?

Jenny: Well, he had reddish hair, glasses — quite good-looking, I suppose, not very tall, about your height, in fact.

Clive: Charming!

Jenny: I didn't mean it like that but I guess I was expecting someone much sportier, someone who likes the outdoor life.

Clive: Well-dressed?

Jenny: Not particularly. Bit scruffy, really. Wore a leather jacket and a pullover.

Clive: Really?

Jenny: Yeah.

Clive: And what was he like?

Jenny: Not that exciting, I'm afraid.

Clive: Why not?

Jenny: Well, at first I thought he was OK but then we went off to a pub and all he could talk about was politics.

Clive: But you're into that, aren't you?

Jenny: Yeah, but not *all* the time. He went on and on. He said he had a great time but I couldn't get away fast enough.

Clive: Oh dear.

Jenny: He wants to see me again. Asked me if I wanted to go to a demo on Saturday.

Clive: You're kidding.

Jenny: No. I'm not going. Anyway, how about you?

Clive: Well, I have to admit that I almost chickened out.

Jenny: Typical.

Clive: Well, I didn't and I had a great time.

Jenny: Did you? Tell us all about it then.

Clive: We just went out to an Italian I know and had a nice meal and chatted away merrily. You know, we found out that we'd lived in the same street as kids.

Jenny: How amazing!

Clive: But we couldn't remember each other.

Jenny: Was she pretty?

Clive: Very. She was very chic — all in black, short black hair and not much make-up.

Jenny: She sounds a bit serious to me. Not really your type.

Clive: No, no, not at all. She had a great sense of humour. Funny, you don't expect that from someone who's an accountant.

Jenny: Going to see her again?

Clive: Yeah, she said to give her a call.

UNIT 9

PAGE 99 In the clothes shop

1 **Customer:** Yes, these jeans are a really good fit. I'll take 'em.
Shop assistant: And what about the dungarees?
Customer: The dungarees? I think I'll leave them. They don't really suit me. They make me look enormous.

2 **Customer:** Oh, these trousers are fine but they're a little too long in the leg.
Shop assistant: Well, they are a bit on the long side but we can always get them turned up for you.
Customer: I supose that costs extra.
Shop assistant: I'm afraid so, sir. They have to go to an outside tailor and the charge is £7.50.
Customer: £7.50! That's outrageous. I don't think I'll bother with them at all.
Shop assistant: And the shirt?
Customer: Oh yeah, I'll take that. You accept Visa, don't you?
Shop assistant: Yes.

3 **Customer:** What do you think, Carol?
Carol: Well, to tell you the truth, I don't think it goes with the top at all.
Customer: It does clash a bit but I think it'll be right with some of my other blouses. The only thing is it's a bit loose.
Carol: A bit loose! It could hardly be much tighter.
Customer: I think I'll take it but I'll leave the top. I can't afford both.

PAGE 108 The radio phone-in

Part A

Presenter: Our next caller is Rachel who is from South London. Go ahead, Rachel.
Rachel: Hello, Doctor Howard.
Dr Howard: Hello, Rachel. How can I help you?
Rachel: Well, you see it's about my son, Mark. He's almost 18 and he hasn't been able to find a job since he left school.
Dr Howard: When did he leave?
Rachel: It'll be a year in July.
Dr Howard: And what seems to be the problem?
Rachel: It's like this. Mark used to be such a nice, outgoing sort of boy but over the last few months he's changed quite a bit.
Dr Howard: So, can you describe what has happened?
Rachel: Well, after he was turned down for several jobs he got depressed and withdrawn which was bad enough, but now it's got much worse — he's become really moody and aggressive.
Dr Howard: Moody and aggressive?
Rachel: Yes, and he's started mixing with some boys I don't like very much. But to tell you the truth, I think he's started taking drugs.
Dr Howard: What makes you think that?
Rachel: Well, as I said, there are his change of moods. One minute he's very depressed and the next minute he becomes very excited — you know, he can't sit still. Another thing is stuff has disappeared from the house. Some of my jewelry has gone and some money and so has Mark's cassette player.
Dr Howard: Does he know you know about the cassette player?
Rachel: Yes, he does. He told me he had let a friend borrow it. I was really surprised because he's always been so keen on music. When I asked him about it a couple of days later, he told just to me mind my own business. Another thing is that he just doesn't look after himself any more or care what he looks like.

And I've noticed strange smells in the house too.
Dr Howard: May I ask you, Rachel, are you still married?
Rachel: Yes, I am but my husband spends a lot of time away. He's in the merchant navy, you see.

Part B

Rachel: Yes, I am but my husband spends a lot of time away. He's in the merchant navy, you see.
Dr Howard: From what you've said, the change in Mark has been quite dramatic and what I'd suggest is that you try and sit down with him and have a quiet chat about things. Approach him as a friend rather than as a mother. Try to get to the bottom of things and see how he feels. Something else which I would suggest is that you get in contact with one of his old teachers or your family doctor and ask them to have chat with Mark. Someone he respects and could have a chat with.
Rachel: And what if that doesn't work?
Dr Howard: Well, if you do feel he is taking drugs, then I should contact the police.
Rachel: Turn in my own son to the police!
Dr Howard: It may seem harsh but it's probably the best course of action in the long run.
Presenter: OK, thank you Rachel. I hope things sort themselves out for you and Mark. Our next caller is ...

UNIT 10

PAGE 119 The debate on vivisection

Presenter: Good morning everybody. I'm Joe Templer. It's eleven o'clock which means it's time for another edition of Crosstalk, the phone-in programme which looks at today's hot issues. The subject of today's discussion is whether vivisection — that's experimenting on live animals — is ever justified. Now if you want to take part in today's debate, the number to ring is 01 — if you're outside London — 833 3974. But before that, in the studio I have two guests to open the debate. They are Professor Anna Wright from Queen Margaret Hospital and Peter Savage of the Free the Animals Movement. Good morning to the both of you.
Anna Wright: Good morning.
Peter Savage: Good morning.
Presenter: OK then, if you'd like to put your point of view first, Professor Wright.
Anna Wright: Thank you. Now I must state categorically that for advances in medicine we count on being able to carry out experiments on animals. Without them, there would be no progress. We are unable to observe human beings in scientifically controlled conditions so unfortunately we have to rely on animals. Medicine has made enormous advances based on the results of vivisection. For example, our knowledge of the nervous system is largely due to vivisection. It has allowed us to find cures for many illnesses. Diptheria, smallpox and TB used to be killers in the old days but not any more. If you were bitten by a dog with rabies, you had very little chance of surviving. Now there is an antidote. Cancer recovery rates have greatly improved thanks to the work done on animals. And I'm afraid drugs have to be tested on animals prior to their release on the market to check for side effects. Nobody takes any pride in causing suffering and I can assure the listeners it is kept to an absolute minimum.

Presenter: Thank you very much, Professor Wright. Over to you, Peter.

Peter Savage: Thanks. I'd like to start by saying that I'm speaking on behalf of animals. On the issue of testing drugs on animals for side effects in human beings, as we know from the thalidomide case, it's very difficult to predict what the effect of a drug will be on human beings from tests done on animals. They just don't tell us the whole story. As for understanding the nervous system, I think most experts would agree that this could have been done equally well by careful observation and nothing more. Professor Wright points to the reduction in the number of deaths from diseases like diptheria, TB and smallpox. This is utter nonsense because these diseases were in decline already and they've been on the decline primarily because of improvements in hygiene, not animal experiments. No, the whole thing is rubbish. If we look at penicillin and aspirin, two of the most famous modern drugs, these drugs were found by accident! So much for medical research! And Professor Wright's argument completely ignores the moral dimension. The point is experiments on animals should be stopped because they are cruel and inhumane. Dogs are made to smoke cigarettes and rats and mice have shampoo and cosmetics squirted in their eyes to see what will happen. Dogs don't smoke and mice don't wash their hair. Very often these animals have suffered so much they have to be put down. Basically, we should take care of animals not take advantage of them.

Presenter: Thanks, Peter. OK then. So it's over to you, the listeners. Our first call ...

UNIT 11

PAGE 130 At the museum

Curator: Hello everybody. I'm glad you've been able to make it. It's a shame about the weather though, isn't it? Anyway, if you'd like to follow me into the first room, I'll tell you a little bit about some of the exhibits there.

Well, as you can see, there are a number of farming and domestic implements here which we have collected over the years. Of course, none of them are used any longer. In actual fact, we can sometimes have quite a job finding out just exactly what they were for! Now this first one I suppose you'd describe as a giant comb. And that's just what it is — not for human beings, though, but for wool. Once the wool has been sheared from the sheep, then it would have to be combed to make it ready for spinning. Now if you look over here, you can see something which looks just like a huge frying pan with a very long handle. We had an Italian visitor in here last year who thought it was for baking pizza in a deep oven but it's actually a warming pan. In the old days you'd pop it into your bed to make it nice and warm. You'd take some coals from the fire or a hot brick, then you'd put it into the copper pan and make sure the lid was tight. Then, as I say, pop it in the bed. This one is an original but I should warn you about some of the ones you may come across in antique shops. They're quite often reproductions. So don't be taken in.

Now, this next object is rather strange-looking. It is called a flail and, as you can see, it is a couple of poles of about equal length which are held together by a strap. Now this was used before the days of modern agricultural machinery to beat the corn to separate the wheat from the chaffe, the bits you didn't want. The men used to put the cut corn on the ground and

then they'd swing the flail and beat it until they had separated all the wheat out.

The last thing in this room I want to draw your attention to before we move on to our Roman collection is this evil-looking contraption in the corner. Now this is in fact a *man* trap. It just shows how much crueller the world was in the nineteenth century. Farm workers and their families often had very little to eat and so to supplement their meagre diet they would go onto the farm owner's land to hunt for rabbits and other game, poaching in other words. And the farm owners would set these traps to stop them from doing this. Not very pleasant. And if someone did get caught in a trap, then their leg would certainly have been broken. After that, it would be a short step from the courthouse onto one of those terrible prison ships bound for Australia.

Page 131 The picture by John Millais

Woman: This is a painting of a country scene. I think it was probably painted about a hundred years or so ago. Anyway, in the foreground there are two girls. They both look very poor. Their clothes are old and shabby, and there's tears and patches in them. They are sitting by the side of a field and, well I suppose they look as though they are having a rest. The elder of the two girls has got some sort of — oh, I think it's an old-fashioned accordion. She's young, quite pretty with red hair. She is sitting with her eyes half closed, most likely because of the sun. In the background there are fields with a few animals in them and some farm buildings on the top of a hill and the most beautiful rainbow in the sky. It must have been raining but the sky is quite dark and it looks as though it might rain again. The little girl is quite enchanted by the rainbow. She seems to be telling her friend, or perhaps it's her sister, to have a look too. The other girl doesn't appear to be that interested. Oh, wait a minute. She's got something around her neck. It says 'Pity the blind'. I see. I get it. The elder of the two girls is blind and the younger one is trying to tell her all about the rainbow. Quite sad really. The colours of the painting are marvellous. Just like you get after it's been raining. There's so much beauty all around but all the blind girl can feel is the warmth of the sun on her face. She can't even appreciate the butterfly which has settled on her. I suppose she must play the accordion and hope that people give her money. Yes, it's a lovely painting, it's lovely, although in general I'm not a fan of this kind of art. I prefer Impressionist pictures, people like Monet, Cezanne. I recently went to see a big exhibition ...

UNIT 12

PAGE 141 The traffic accident

Woman A: Have you heard the news?
Woman B: No.
Woman A: There's been an accident up near the school.
Woman B: Oh dear.
Woman A: Yes, Mark Brown, Jackie Brown's kid — you know who I mean, don't you?
Woman B: Yes, bit of a dreamer, always in a world of his own.
Woman A: That's right. Anyway, Mark's been knocked over by a car.
Woman B: Oh, is he badly hurt?
Woman A: Well, it could have been a lot worse. He's been taken to hospital with suspected concussion but no broken bones as

far as I know. I expect they'll keep him for a few days just to keep an eye on him.

Woman B: Well, how did it happen then.

Woman A: It seems that some fellow in a Jaguar ran him over as he was crossing the road outside the school.

Woman B: It's a terrible corner that one near the school. There's always such a lot of traffic. But wasn't there someone there to supervise the children crossing the road?

Woman A: Apparently not. It seems the lollipop lady was off sick and, to make matters worse, Jason's class teacher had let them out ten minutes early because he wasn't feeling well. Can you believe it?

Woman B: Well, that's very irresponsible.

Woman A: That's what I said.

Woman B: But what about Mark's mum? Wasn't she meant to be picking him up?

Woman A: In fact, it was his dad who was picking him up and he was late 'cause he'd been chatting with some of his mates.

Woman B: Typical!

Woman A: Isn't it just. Anyway, it's Mark's fault as much as anybody's.

Woman B: Why's that?

Woman A: Apparently, he just rushed across the road without looking to get to the ice cream van and around the corner comes this Jaguar and — bang! — Mark's in hopital.

Woman B: Was the driver going too fast?

Woman A: Yes, late for his appointment, I'm told.

Woman B: Do you think he'll have to go to court?

Woman A: Oh, I'm sure he will. He was being breathalized by a policeman when I arrived.

Woman B: Mind you. That sort always get off.

Woman A: Well, I'm not so sure it was his fault. Anyway, the lucky thing was there was a nurse walking past when it all happened and she was able to give Mark first aid treatment until the ambulance arrived. So that was a bit of luck, wasn't it?

UNIT 13

PAGE 144 The Chaffin Will affair

Storyteller: One of the most famous and extraordinary cases of contact with the dead was the so-called Chaffin Will affair. In 1921 a certain James Chaffin died leaving his entire fortune to his third son, Marshall, in a will which had been written a full 15 years earlier in 1905 and signed in front of witnesses. His wife and two other sons were virtually cut off without a penny. Marshall was not inclined to split up the inheritance he had come into any more fairly. Four years went by and then, strangely, James Chaffin's ghost started to appear before one of his other two sons. The apparition had on an old overcoat which Chaffin had often worn in life. On the ghost of Chaffin's second visit to his son, he told him that he would find a will in the overcoat pocket. The coat was actually in the possession of the third brother. Once it was found, they came across a note sewn in the lining of one of the pockets saying they should look in an old family bible. This bible was found in the keeping of Chaffin's widow and examined in front of independent witnesses. Sure enough, there in the bible they discovered a later version of the will, one which divided the property and money up evenly between the widow and the three sons. The will appeared to be genuine and Marshall was not prepared to challenge it in court.

PAGE 147 A discussion of reincarnation

Yolanda: What's that book you're reading, Juliet? You seem very engrossed in it.

Juliet: What? Oh sorry, yes, it's about reincarnation. Quite rivetting.

Malcolm: Reincarnation! Ah, you surely don't believe in all that.

Juliet: That's why I'm reading this book — I'm trying to make my mind up about it.

Yolanda: I'm absolutely positive there's something in it.

Malcolm: But how can we know one way or the other? I mean, there's no proof, is there?

Juliet: That's what I used to think but now I'm not so sure. There are some fascinating stories in this book, you know.

Malcolm: Oh yeah. Like what?

Juliet: Well, first of all, if we are reincarnated, this means that we must have been someone else in a previous life, right?

Yolanda: Right. Go on.

Juliet: You see, people investigating reincarnation came up with the idea that if you hypnotized someone, they might be able to go back in time and tell you about their previous lives. And one of …

Malcolm: What a load of rubbish! Do you believe this?

Yolanda: Come on, Malcolm. Let Juliet finish what she has to say.

Juliet: Thank you, Yolanda. Now, as I was saying, one of the people they hypnotized was someone called Jane Evans and she managed to recall something like six or seven lives. She'd been a Jewish girl who was murdered during the Middle Ages, a servant to one of Henry VIII's wives and a nun in a convent in the USA.

Malcolm: Blimey! She's been busy. I mean, come off it! She'd probably read some stories about these characters somewhere or other. I'm sure there's a logical explanation for all of this.

Juliet: Well, maybe you're right. She could have read something which entered her subconsciousness. That's certainly true in the case of one of her other lives. She claimed to be the servant to a French merchant. And all of the details she could remember of this past life were readily available in books. Strangely enough though, she forgot to mention the fact that the merchant was married and had five kids.

Malcolm: There you are. What did I tell you?

Juliet: Hold on a minute! Going back to the Jewish girl, what's incredible about this past life is that she could say exactly where the girl had been killed, under a church in a, in some kind of cellar. No sooner had she told this story than some archaeologists found it. Quite by chance — they were doing some other work on the church — when they came across it *and* they found some skeletons down there!

Malcolm: Skeletons! You'd surely expect to find skeletons under a church, or at least I would.

Yolanda: I'm afraid I agree with Malcom, Juliet. Were there any other cases?

Juliet: Well, there's another one that's very interesting. A housewife called Dolores was hypnotized and she took on the character of someone called Gretchen Gottlieb. Now she was murdered in Germany in a forest during the last century and what's interesting about this case is that, when she was hypnotized, Dolores spoke in German and yet she'd never learnt the language at school or anything. What's more, when she came out of hypnosis, she couldn't speak any German at all.

Yolanda: What was her German like?

Juliet: Well, not very good, I'm afraid. It was pretty incorrect and she avoided using verbs. Some of her answers didn't make sense and some of the time she hadn't understood questions she'd been asked.

Malcolm: So did this Gretchen actually exist?

Juliet: Well, they tried to verify the story but they couldn't confirm it either way. There weren't any records or anything like that.

Krishna: Do you think Dolores was trying to take the researchers in?

Yolanda: Well, according to the book, they were sure she was acting in good faith but, well, you never know.

Malcolm: In good faith! If you believe that, you'll believe anything.

UNIT 14

PAGE 158 Saying numbers

1 Phone numbers
A 0223 68991
B 010 33 1 4476 1085
2 Account numbers
A 87640328
B 925487234
3 Decimals
A 3.2
B 2.54
C 0.38
4 Fractions
A ¼
B ⅔
C ⅜
D ⁵⁄₁₆

5 Dates
A 11/11/1918
B 14/7/1789
C 1/3/1963
6 Amounts
A $6.92 cents
B £10.03p
7 Scores
A Lendl won the tennis match 6-0, 3-6, 6-1.
B Italy beat Holland 2-0.
8 Large numbers
A 23, 927, 421
B 9, 867, 364
C 989, 774

UNIT 15

PAGE 172 The future of the world's cities

Part 1

Interviewer: In Britain we are often told that people are leaving the big cities to live in the countryside but is this the case worldwide?

Expert: Not at all. If you look at the biggest cities in 1950, seven out of the top ten were in the developed countries the year 2000 the developing countries but by will have eight out of the top ten. New York, which in 1950 was number one with a population of around 12 million, will only be the sixth largest city in the world but with an extra two million.

Interviewer: And London?

Expert: London, which was number two, won't even be in the top ten. Its population in 1950, by the way, was about ten million.

Interviewer: And why is this happening? Why are people moving to the big cities from the country in developing countries?

Expert: The reasons are complex but many are moving to look for work. And the problems this creates are enormous. It's estimated that 26 million people will be living in Mexico City by the year 2000, with São Paulo in Brazil not far behind.

Interviewer: It's difficult to believe.

Expert: I know. Rio de Janeiro will have a population of a mere 13 million. Well, just imagine the kinds of difficulties this is going to cause in terms of health, transport and education!

Interviewer: What about the cities of Asia? Will they be experiencing a similar sort of growth?

Expert: In some cases, yes. Calcutta in India which was number ten in the league in 1950 is expected to be the fourth biggest city in the world with a population of 16 million — quadrupling its size in just 50 years. Bombay and Delhi too are expected to be in the top ten.

Interviewer: What about Japan?

Expert: Ah! Well, Tokyo was number three in 1950 and that's where it'll be at the beginning of the next century, although its population will have trebled to about 18 million. Looking at the other major cities in Asia, Shanghai and Seoul will be in the top ten as well but, perhaps surprisingly, not Bejing or Hong Kong.

Interviewer: Now, if we could turn our attention to home, what about the trend of people moving out of the cities ...

Part 2

Interviewer: Now if we could turn our attention to home, what about the trend of people moving out of the cities like London?

Expert: Ah! We should be a bit careful about saying people are moving out of London. Another way of looking at it is to say London itself is moving into the country.

Interviewer: How do you mean?

Expert: With improved transport and better living standards, people can actually afford to spread out far more than they did before and commute into town from greater distances. People can travel to work from distances that would have been inconceivable even 20 years ago.

Interviewer: All the same, isn't there a drift away from the capital?

Expert: Oh, certainly, but it shouldn't be exaggerated. Lots of people have got fed up with the dirt and the hassle and the higher levels of crime, and have moved to the country because it's more peaceful and less stressful. And it's true companies have moved out to escape high rents and office costs, particularly in the service industries like insurance.

Interviewer: Are there any specific things which has allowed this to happen?

Expert: One of the things which has given people more choice in where they live is the new technology. People can communicate with each other through computer networks from anywhere in the country and so work from home in the spare bedroom.

Interviewer: And how has business coped with this kind of change?

Expert: Well, to give you one example, a company selling office equipment took the brave step of closing down its London office and allowing its ex-employees, its sales people, to set up businesses on their own account from home but using the old company just as their supplier. What happened was that turnover increased dramatically, the new technology was crucial for fast and efficient ordering.

Interviewer: Finally, what about the impact of this trend on agriculture? Assuming that people are moving to the country, doesn't this mean that there is less land to farm?

Expert: Yes, indeed. And there's no doubt that we're losing fields for housing. But this doesn't matter too much as we have in recent times been overproducing and also yields from the land have increased with modern, scientific farming methods. So what's happening is that we are getting more from less.

We are grateful to the following for permission to reproduce copyright material:

The Automobile Association for extracts from *AA/Baedeker's New York*; Authors' agents for an adapted version of 'Cinderella Re-examined' by Maeve Binchy from *Rapunzel's Revenge — Fairytales for Feminists* pubd. Attic Press, Dublin and a slightly adapted extract from an article by Maeve Binchy from *Cosmopolitan* Magazine; the Author, Peter Everett for an adaptation of his article 'You'll Never be 16 Again — an illustrated history of the British Teenager' BBC Publications 1986; Authors' agents for article by Graham Greene in *The Independent* 21.9.87; Guerba Expeditions Ltd for a slightly adapted extract from 'West African Train Holiday' in *Guerba Expeditions 1987/8 Travel Brochure* pp11-12; Independent Television Publications Ltd for the article 'Letters of Love' by Doris Stokes in *Chat* magazine 24.1.87; News Group Newspapers Ltd for an adapted article from *The Sun* 12.12.85; Solo Syndication & Literary Agency Ltd for London Evening Standard & Mail on Sunday for adapted articles 'Blind Man who tried to rob Bank' from the *Evening Standard* 14.11.85 & 'A Life of Crime' from *Mail on Sunday*; the Author, Polly Toynbee for an adaptation of her article 'Jungle Warfare' in *The Guardian* 19.12.87.

We have unfortunately been unable to trace the copyright holders of the extracts in 'In the year 2000' article, and would appreciate any information which would enable us to do so.

We are grateful to the following for permission to reproduce copyright illustrative material:

Adams Picture Library for page 63; All-Sport (UK) Limited for page 161; Art Directors Photo Library for page 2 (bottom) and 3 (top and bottom right); Aspect Picture Library for page 56 and 166; George Ball for page 30 (top); Barnabys Picture Library for page 33 (right); Maeve Binchy for page 68 (bottom); Piers Bizony Photographer for page 57; The Bridgeman Art Library/Birmingham Museum for page 131 and The Bridgeman Art Library/Musée de Beaux Arts, Brussels for page 132; 'Family and Friends' by Anita Brookner, published by Jonathan Cape Limited for page 18 (middle right); J. Allan Cash Photo Library for page 55 (middle right), 57 and 129; 'The Far Side', cartoon by Gary Larson is reprinted by permission of Chronicle Features, San Francisco for page 33 (left); Colorific Photo Library Limited for page 120 (top); Greg Evans Photo Library for page 66 (top right); Format Photographers for page 97 (top); Fortean Picture Library for page 144; 'Foundation and Earth' by Isaac Asimov/copyright Chris Foss, published by Grafton Books for page 18 (left); Mark Gerson for pages 20 and 68 (top); Our thanks to Greenpeace for the use of their material on page 76; Susan Griggs Agency for pages 103 and 125 (top); 'Bygone Days' by Leonard De Vries, published by Paul Hamlyn Publishing Division for pages 48/49; Robert Harding Picture Library Limited for page 125 (bottom); Harlow Council for page 126 (middle bottom); 'Hollywood Husbands' by Jackie Collins, published by William Heinemann Limited for page 18 (middle left); The John Hillelson Agency Limited for page 51; The Hulton Picture Company for pages 61, 123 (left), 126 (top) and 153 (middle bottom); Hulton/Bettman for pages 97 (bottom) and 153 (bottom left); 'London Match' by Len Deighton, published by Century Hutchinson Publishing Group Limited for page 18 (right); The Hutchinson Library for page 3 (bottom left); The Image Bank for page 3 (top left); The Kobal Collection for page 72; Taken from 'In The Shadow of Man', by Jane van Lawick-Goodall, published by Collins Publishers/photo copyright Hugo van Lawick for page 113; London Features International Limited for page 145; Longman Photo Unit/Trevor Clifford Photographer for pages 12, 66, and 126 (bottom); John Mann for page 30 (bottom); The Mansell Collection Limited for page 153 (top left); Mary Evans Picture Library for page 153 (bottom right); National Museums and Art Galleries, Merseyside for page 153 (top right); New Internationalist Publications for page 83; Picturepoint Limited for pages 55 (top), 75 (middle right), 159 (middle left) and 160; Popperfoto for page 101 (left); The Press Association Limited for page 155; Private Eye for pages 19 and 106; Punch Publications Limited for pages 74, 115, 136, 141 and 152; The Reader's Digest Association Limited for page 36; Rex Features Limited for pages 22, 23, 35, 75 (left), 86 (top left, middle and right, bottom left and right), 87, 150 and 154 (right); John Shelley Illustrator for page 119; Spectrum Colour Library for pages 29 and 159 (top left); Frank Spooner Pictures for page 126 (middle top); Tony Stone Photo Library/London for pages 11, 55 (middle top), 55 (bottom), 75 (middle left and right), 127, 159 (top right) and 170; David Reed/Sunday Times Magazine 7/12/86 for page 116; Survival Games (UK) Limited for page 40; Syndication International Limited for page 86 (middle bottom); The Telegraph Colour Library for page 123 (right); From 'The Times Atlas of World History' © Times Books Limited for page 154 (left); Reproduced by permission of United Features Syndicate for page 162; Viewfinder Colour Photo Library for page 101 (right); Xinhua News Agency for page 8; Zefa Picture Library (UK) Limited for page 2 (top), 101 (middle), 120 (bottom), 124, 159 (bottom left and right).

We have been unable to trace the copyright holder of the photograph on page 134, and would be grateful for any information that would enable us to do so.

Our special thanks to Stansted Airport for allowing us to use their premises for the photograph on page 12.

Illustrated by Andrew Aloof, Susannah English, Norah Fitzwater, Terry Gabbey (A.F.A. Ltd), Hardlines, Jane Hughes, Frances Lloyd, Gillian Martin (Guitty Talberg), Ed McClaghlan, Andrew Oliver, George Parkin, Paul Rickwood, Michael Salter, Richard Shipsey, Brian Sweet (Young Artists), Shirley Tourret (B. L. Kearley Ltd), Joanna Troughton (B. L. Kearley Ltd) and Stephen Wright.

Cover illustration by Paul Wearing (Beint & Beint).

Cassette acknowledgements
We are indebted to the Author's agents for permission to reproduce an adapted version of 'Cinderella Re-examined' by Maeve Binchy from *Rapunzel's Revenge — Fairytales for Feminists* pubd. Attic Press, Dublin and a slightly adapted extract from an article by Maeve Binchy from *Cosmopolitan* Magazine.